Welcome

Welcome to the 2017 UK Warbird Directory – a publication dedicated to listing as many of the UK's ex-military aircraft as possible.

Great Britain has one of the world's most diverse ranges of flyable ex-military aircraft. From genuine century-old Great War fighters to Cold War era jets via the glamorous 1930s 'silver winged' biplanes and a growing fleet of veteran helicopters there really is something for everybody.

For many, the core interest will lie in the World War Two warriors – including the large piston-powered fighters and heavy bombers. UK-based enthusiasts (and overseas visitors to British events) can marvel at a world class range of flyable 1940s hardware that includes more than 30 Spitfires, ten UK registered Hurricanes (nine of which are based in Britain) and countless Mustangs, Curtiss Hawks and Grumman fighters. Fans of the big bombers are rewarded with examples of the B-17 and Lancaster as well as rarities such as the unique Bristol Blenheim I.

However, the warbird 'scene' in Britain is much more diverse than just the expensive heavy-metal hardware. Tucked away in hangars and workshops the length of the nation more 'attainable' aircraft such as Austers, Cubs, Tiger Moths, Chipmunks, Bulldogs and Gazelles carry the warbird label with pride.

What is a Warbird?

So what is a 'warbird'? The subject causes much debate and many will have strong views on the subject. For the purposes of this directory we have defined a warbird as a flyable ex-military aeroplane regardless of the colour scheme it now wears (thereby including ex-military Tiger Moths flying in civilian colours). The definition has also been stretched to feature civilian aeroplanes flying in military markings (such as a J-3 Cub painted to represent a L-4 Grasshopper).

For the sake of completeness we have also included replica military aeroplanes such as the Currie Wot SE.5a and Supermarine Spitfire Mk 26.

Perhaps the UK's first warbird was Sopwith Dove/Pup G-EBKY – acquired by Richard Shuttleworth in the mid 1930s and restored to military markings as a Pup. More than 80 years later that aeroplane is still flyable with the Shuttleworth Collection and the warbird industry in Britain has never been stronger.

Each time a newly restored historic aeroplane emerges from either a small workshop or a one of the country's warbird restoration businesses the nation's engineering reputation increases a notch. Restorers are both keeping alive century-old techniques and skills and also innovating in new technologies that will benefit the aviation industry as a whole.

How to use this Directory

This directory only includes flyable (or ground running) aeroplanes, aircraft under restoration to fly or those airframes stored pending possible future restoration to flying status. It does not include static airframes held in museums or private collections.

These pages are split into sections discussing specific eras or types of aircraft. Within those sections aircraft are listed alphabetically according to manufacturer and tables list the surviving aeroplanes. Each table includes columns listing: 1) Aircraft Model, 2) Owner, 3) Civil Registration, 4) Former Military Registration, 5) Military Markings Worn Today (if any) and 6) Aircraft Status. For the privacy of aircraft owners the exact location of machines has not been included.

It is worth noting that by its very nature this directory will almost immediately be out of date as aircraft are bought, sold, rebuilt or repainted. The information included here is as accurate as possible as of mid June 2017.

Dedication

This directory is dedicated to the uniquely keen band of owners, operators, collectors, restorers, engineers and pilots without whom the UK warbird scene would be much poorer. The majority of historic aircraft owners are enthusiasts themselves and whether you own a Spitfire or an Auster the nation salutes you for the time, effort and expenditure devoted to preserving and sharing your own piece(s) of history.

Stephen Bridgewater
Stamford – June 2017

The pilots of the Great War Display Team are among the most enthusiastic aviators and evangelical exponents of historic aviation. Their aircraft may 'only' be replicas but they are more than worthy of inclusion in this guide. Steve Bridgewater

CONTENTS

4	Great War Veterans	54	World War Two Heavies	117	Post War Trainers & Liaison Types
12	On Silver Wings	64	Big Piston Fighters of World War Two (& Beyond)	131	Rotary Wings
28	Word War Two Trainers & Liaison Types			136	Cold War Warriors

FRONT COVER: Elaine and Chris Fairfax's Spitfire VC EE602/G-IBSY is one of a large number of the type based with the Biggin Hill Heritage Hangar at the famous Battle of Britain airfield in Kent. John Dibbs/Plane Picture Company

Warbird Directory © Key Publishing 2017
Editor: Stephen Bridgewater **Proof Reading:** Jamie Ewan **Design and Layout** Paul Silk. **Group Editor:** Nigel Price
Publisher and Managing Director Adrian Cox. **Executive Chairman** Richard Cox. **Commercial Director** Ann Saundry.
Distribution Seymour Distribution Ltd +44 (0)20 7429 4000. **Printing** Warners (Midlands) PLC, The Maltings, Manor Lane, Bourne, Lincs PE10 9PH.
ISBN 978 1 910415 99 3 All images via the Key Publishing Archive unless stated

All rights reserved. Reproduction in whole or in part and in any form whatsoever is strictly prohibited without the prior permission of the Publisher. Whilst every care is taken with submissions, the Publisher cannot be held responsible for any loss or damage incurred. All items submitted for publication are subject to our terms and conditions which are regularly updated without prior notice and downloadable from www.keypublishing.com. We are unable to guarantee the bona fides of any of our advertisers. Readers are strongly recommended to take their own precautions before parting with any information or item of value, including, but not limited to, money, manuscripts, photographs or personal information in response to any advertisements within this publication.

Published by Key Publishing Ltd, PO Box 100, Stamford, Lincs PE19 1XQ.
Tel: +44 (0) 1780 755131. Fax: +44 (0) 1780 757261. Website: www.keypublishing.com

GREAT WAR VETERANS

With the centenary of the 1914-1918 Great War upon us interest has never been higher in aeroplanes of the era. In addition to a variety of original Great War fighters flying or under restoration in the UK in 2017 the country is also blessed with a large variety of replicas – from the semi-scale SE.5a 'lookalikes' to highly accurate renditions such as the BE.2s and Albatros created by The Vintage Aviator Ltd in New Zealand.

Airco DH.2

Geoffrey de Havilland's DH.2 first flew in July 1915 and was the first effectively armed British single-seat fighter which enabled Royal Flying Corps (RFC) pilots to counter the so-called 'Fokker Scourge.' No original DH.2s exist but a flyable replica is based in the UK. Early air combat over the Western Front indicated the need for a single-seat fighter with forward-firing armament. However, as no means of firing forward through the propeller of a tractor aeroplane was available to the British, de Havilland designed the DH.2 as a smaller, single-seat development of the earlier two-seat DH.1 pusher design. It was armed with a single .303in Lewis gun which could originally be re-positioned in flight.

▶ The UK's sole airworthy DH.2 replica is based at Wickenby, Lincolnshire and powered by a Kinner radial engine. Darren Harbar

| DH.2 (Replica) | Stephen Turley | G-BFVH | - | '5964' | Flyable |

Airco DH.9

Although underpowered the 1917-designed DH.9 flew as a bomber during the Great War and then continued in RAF service until 1920 operating in all corners of the British Empire. Aero Vintage's example was recovered from India in 2000 and is now rapidly reaching the stage when it should fly again.

| DH.9 | Aero Vintage Ltd | G-CDLI | E8894 | E8894 | Restoration |

Albatros

The Imperial German Air Service's Albatros D.V fighter was the final development of the Albatros family. Around 900 D.V and 1,612 D.VA aircraft were built between April 1917 and the end of the Great War.

▶ Just two original Albatros fighters have survived but in recent years The Vintage Aviator Ltd has created a small production run of highly authentic replicas, complete with remanufactured Mercedes engines. One such example is Oliver Wulff's ZK-TGY, which is operated by the WW1 Aviation Heritage Trust from the former Great War airfield at Stow Maries. Darren Harbar

| D.VA | Oliver Wulff | ZK-TGY | - | '87' | Restoration |

Avro 504

Used as a fighter, bomber and trainer from 1913 the Avro 504 served in various roles until the mid 1930s. By the end of the Great War 8,970 had been built and when production finally ended in 1932 more than 10,000 had been produced. A century later a handful of original examples remain flyable in Britain along with a very accurate replica.

504K	Shuttleworth Trust	G-ADEV	E3273	E3273	Flyable
504K	Thomas Harris	G-EBHB	E2977	E2977	Flyable
504K	Eric Verdon-Roe t/a British Aviation 100	G-EROE	-	-	Flyable
504L	Geoffrey New	G-EASD	-	-	Restoration

4 WARBIRD DIRECTORY

Jamie Ewan

Above left: The Shuttleworth Collection's rotary-powered Avro 504K E3273 was built in 1918 and later converted to radial engined 504N configuration while still in RAF service. It was later sold into civilian ownership as G-ADEV but in 1940 it was impressed into military service and towed gliders during radar experiments. After the war it was returned to civilian use and converted back to 504K specification by Avro apprentices for the 1956 film *Reach for the Sky* and then donated to Shuttleworth. It now wears the colours of a 77 Sqn night fighter based at East Lothian in late 1918. Steve Bridgewater

Above right: Avro 504K replica G-EROE belongs to Eric Verdon-Roe (grandson of designer Alliott Verdon Roe aka 'A V Roe') and was produced in Argentina in 2010 by Pur Sang Aero Historic. Originally registered LV-X430, it was imported to the UK in 2015 and flew again in May 2016. It is powered by a modern Australian-built 150hp Rotec radial engine.

Thomas Harris' little-seen Avro 504K G-EBHB is based at RAF Henlow, Bedfordshire. Darren Harbar

Bristol Fighter

The Bristol Fighter (or 'Brisfit' or 'Biff') was a British two-seat biplane fighter and reconnaissance aircraft dating from 1916 created as a replacement for the BE.2c. The type was popular and remained in RAF service until the 1930s. For many years the Shuttleworth Collection's F.2B was the only flying example in the UK – then The Fighter Collection and Historic Aircraft Collection had examples restored to fly. They have now been exported and D8096 is now the sole UK-based flyer once again.

The Shuttleworth Collection's F.2B D8096 was built in 1918 and while it saw no operational wartime service it did operate with 208 Sqn in Turkey in 1923. Its remains were acquired in 1936 by Capt C P B Ogilvie, who intended to restore it to flying condition but failed to complete the project. The project then passed to the Bristol Aeroplane Company, which restored it as G-AEPH and entrusted it to the collection. Today it flies in Great War markings along with its original serial umber. Steve Bridgewater

F.2B Fighter	Shuttleworth Trust	G-AEPH	D8096	D8096/D	Flyable

Bristol Monoplane

Created as a private venture in 1916, the Bristol M.1 Monoplane demonstrated impressive performance during official testing, reaching a speed of 111kts (40kts faster than the Fokker E.III) and climbing to 10,000ft in just over 8 minutes. However, the forward and downward view was criticised and the type was initially rejected. The reason given was that the landing speed was too high for small French airfields but it is more likely to do with the RFC's distrust of monoplane designs. Eventually an order for 125 examples was placed in August 1917,

Just one original Bristol M.1 exists but the Shuttleworth Collection commissioned the Northern Aircraft Workshops to create this highly authentic flying replica. The aircraft – which now wears the markings of 'C4918' based at Mesopotamia in 1918 – was delivered in 1997 and is powered by an original 110hp Le Rhône rotary engine. Steve Bridgewater

M.1C (Replica)	Shuttleworth Trust	G-BWJM	-	'C4918'	Flyable

Bristol Scout

The Scout was a single-seat rotary-engined biplane originally designed in 1914 as a racing aircraft. The type was later modified for war and operated as an armed reconnaissance aircraft. It was one of the first single-seaters to be used as a fighter.

▶ This highly accurate replica Scout C was built by David and Rick Bremner and Theo Willford as a tribute to the Bremner's grandfather - Flt Sub Lt FDH 'Bunny' Bremner. 'Bunny' flew the original Scout 1264 with the Royal Naval Air Service' 2 Wing in the Easter Mediterranean at the beginning of World War One. *Steve Bridgewater*

| Scout C (Replica) | Bristol Scout Group | G-FDHB | - | '1264' | Flyable |

Fokker D.VII

Considered by many to be the most capable of Great War fighters more than 3,300 D.VIIs were produced before the end of the conflict. The D.VII quickly proved itself to be a formidable aircraft and the 1918 Armistice specifically called for the surrender of all know examples – making it the only aircraft mentioned by type in the truce.

| D.VII (Replica) | Stephen Green | G-JUNO | - | - | Restoration |

Fokker DR.1

Perhaps the most famous and easily the most recognisable of all Great War fighters was the Fokker DR.1 Dreidecker ('Triplane'). Immortalised as the aircraft in which Manfred von Richthofen gained his last 19 victories, and in which he was killed on April 21, 1918, a large number of DR.1 replicas fly around the world – including four in the UK with a fifth close to completion.

Three of the UK's flyable triplanes gather together at Duxford – from left to right: Iron Maiden front-man Bruce Dickinson's G-CDXR, Paul & Sarah Ford's appropriately registered G-FOKK and Robert Fleming's Breighton-based G-BVGZ. *Steve Bridgewater*

DR.1 (Replica)	Robert Fleming	G-BVGZ	-	'152/17'	Flyable
DR.1 (Replica)	Bruce Dickinson	G-CDXR	-	'403/17'	Flyable
DR.1 (Replica)	Peter Bond	G-CFHY	-	'556/17'	Flyable
DR.1 (Replica)	Paul & Sarah Ford	G-FOKK	-	'477/17'	Flyable
DR.1 (Replica)	Peter Brueggemann	G-DREI	-	'425/17'	Restoration

Fokker Eindecker

Germany's Eindecker ('Monoplane') fighters were the first purpose-built German fighter aircraft and the first in the world to be fitted with a synchronisation gear, enabling the pilot to fire a machine gun through the arc of the propeller without striking the blades. The aircraft gave the Germans a degree of air superiority from July 1915 until early 1916 – the period known as the 'Fokker Scourge'. Just one original Eindecker survives (in the Science Museum in London) but a number of replicas are airworthy in the UK – mostly in the form of SSDR (single-seat de-regulated) microlights marketed by Grass Strip Aviation.

▶ Fokker Eindecker G-AVJO was built in 1965 by Doug Bianchi and has appeared in countless feature films over the years. It spent much of its career at Booker/Wycombe Air Park but is now based at Stow Maries.

E.III Eindecker (Replica)	Bianchi Aviation Film Services	G-AVJO	-	'422/15'	Flyable
E.III Eindecker (Replica)	Ian Brewster	G-CGJF	-	'E37/15'	Flyable
E.III Eindecker (Replica)	Stephen Duckworth	G-CHAW	-	'33/15'	Flyable
E.III Eindecker (Replica)	Russell Myles	G-FOKR	-	'422/15'	Flyable
E.III Eindecker (Replica)	Grass Strip Aviation Ltd	G-GSAL	-	'416/15'	Flyable
E.III Eindecker (Replica)	Michael Clark	G-UDET	-	'105/15'	Flyable

Junkers CL.1

The Junkers CL.I was a German ground-attack aircraft developed in Germany in 1917. Like the other Junkers designs of the period, the aircraft featured a metal framework that was skinned with corrugated duralumin sheets. Almost 50 examples were delivered before the Armistice and although none survive today two replicas fly at UK airshows.

▶ Rob Gauld-Galliers and the late John Day built the first CL.1 lookalike (G-BNPV) in 2002 by modifying a Bowers Fly Baby kitplane. A square tail fin was fitted, Spandau machine guns mounted in the cowling and 'dummy' tail gunner placed behind the single cockpit. The aircraft was painted in a lozenge paint scheme and proved such a success that Robb Metcalfe later asked for a second example (G-BUYU) to be converted for his own use. Although both aircraft now have new owners they form an integral part of the Great War Display Team. Steve Bridgewater

| CL.1 (Replica) | Andrew Berry | G-BNPV | - | '1801/18' | Flyable |
| CL.1 (Replica) | Richie Piper | G-BUYU | - | '1803/18' | Flyable |

Morane-Saulnier Type N

The French-designed Morane-Saulnier Type N was a French monoplane fighter aircraft dating from 1914. It entered service in April 1915 with the Aéronautique Militaire and later equipped four RFC squadrons. No original examples survive but an airworthy replica is currently located at Stow Maries.

| Type N (Replica) | Personal Plane Services | G-AWBU | - | 'MS824' | Stored |

Nieuport 11

The Nieuport Bébé, was a single seat sesquiplane (one wing much smaller than the other) fighter aircraft designed in France. It entered service in 1916 and effectively ended the 'Fokker Scourge'. A microlight replica is under construction in Bedfordshire.

| Type 11 (Replica) | Roger Peirse | G-CILI | - | 'A126' | Restoration |

Nieuport 17/23

The Nieuport 17 was a slightly larger development of the earlier Nieuport 11, with a larger 130hp Le Rhône rotary engine that gave it an excellent rate of climb and outstanding manoeuvrability. Just a single original example survives (in Belgium) but the type is very popular with homebuilders around the world – with one such example based in the UK.

▶ Nieuport 17 replica G-BWMJ was built by Rob Gauld-Galliers and John Day over a five-year period in the 1990s. In 2016 Rob sold the aeroplane to John Gillbert and it is now based at Stow Maries.

| Scout 17/23 (Replica) | John Gilbert | G-BWMJ | - | 'N1977' | Flyable |

Royal Aircraft Factory BE.2

The B.E.2 was a two-seat biplane in service with the RFC from 1912 until 1919. Around 3,500 were built and although they were initially used as front-line reconnaissance aircraft and light bombers; variants of the type were also used as night fighters and trainers. Although originals survive in museums just one flies (in New Zealand) – however three replicas are now registered in the UK.

BE.2c (Replica)	Matthew Boddington & Stephen Slater	G-AWYI	-	'687'	Flyable
BE.2e-1 (Replica)	Oliver Wulff	G-CJZO	-	'A2943'	Flyable
BE.2e-1 (Replica)	The Vintage Aviator Ltd	G-CJZP	-	'A2767'	Flyable

Left: The 'Biggles Biplane' is a replica BE.2c based on the airframe of a Tiger Moth. Built by Charles Boddington in 1969 for the abandoned film project *Biggles Sweeps the Skies* G-AWYI was later shipped to the USA and crashed in 1977. In 2004 the wreck was located in Wisconsin and acquired by Matt Boddington (Charles' son) and returned to the UK for restoration. It flew again in May 2011. Steve Bridgewater **Right:** The Vintage Aviator Ltd in New Zealand has also built several airworthy BE.2 reproductions including c and f models. Two of the BE.2c airframes are currently in the UK on loan to the WW1 Aviation Heritage Trust. Darren Harbar

Royal Aircraft Factory SE.5a

The British SE.5 was one of the fastest aircraft of the war, while also being both stable and manoeuvrable. However, although it flew in November 1916 problems with its Hispano-Suiza engine meant that there was a shortage of the new fighters until well into 1918. SE.5as remained in RAF service for some time following the Armistice and a number were also adopted by civilian operators for sky-writing. The type is phenomenally popular with homebuilders with a myriad of plans and kits (of varying scales and level of accuracy) available to those wanting to build themselves a Great War fighter.

This Shuttleworth Collection's original SE.5a was built by Wolseley Motors and issued to 84 Sqn in France in November 1918. It was in action on November 10, piloted by Maj C E M Pickthorn MC, the squadron commander, when he successfully destroyed a Fokker D.VII in Belgium. Post war the aircraft was bought, with others, by Major J C Savage for his sky-writing business and, registered G-EBIA, was used from 1924 to 1928. In 1955 it was recovered from storage in the roof of the Armstrong Whitworth flight shed at Coventry Airport and restored for the Shuttleworth Collection, flying again in August 1959. It is now powered by a 200hp Wolseley Viper engine and is displayed in its original 84 Sqn colours and markings. Steve Bridgewater

Left: A total of 50 SE.5as were rebuilt in 1922-23 by the Eberhardt Steel Products Co for use by the US Army Air Service as SE.5e advanced and combat trainers. One example of the SE.5e survives in the UK today and recently flew again following restoration by Richard Grace's Air Leasing. Formerly owned by the Hon Patrick Lindsay G-BLXT now wears its original USAAS markings as 22-296. Darren Harbar **Right:** Nine SE.5a replicas were airworthy in the UK in the summer of 2017 – a number of which are regular participants in Great War Display Team formations at airshows. Steve Bridgewater

SE.5a	Shuttleworth Trust	G-EBIA	F904	F904	Flyable
SE.5e	Chartered to Richard Grace	G-BLXT	22-296	22-296	Flyable
SE.5a	Westh Flyg AB (Sweden)	G-ECAE	A2-25	-	Restoration
SE.5a	Hawker Restorations	-	C8996	-	Restoration
SE.5a (Replica)	David Linney	G-BDWJ	-	'F8010'/Z	Flyable
SE.5a (Replica)	David Silsbury & Brendan Proctor	G-BFWD	-	'C3009/B'	Flyable
SE.5a (Replica)	Neil Geddes	G-BKER	-	'F5447'/N	Flyable
SE.5a (Replica)	David Blaxland	G-BMDB	-	'F235'/B	Flyable
SE.5a (Replica)	Michael Waldron	G-BUOD	-	'B595'/W	Flyable
SE.5a (Replica)	Victor Lockwood	G-CCBN	-	'80105' US Air Service	Flyable
SE.5a (Replica)	Clinton Morris	G-CCXG	-	'C5430'/V	Flyable
SE.5a (Replica)	David Porter	G-INNY	-	'F5459'/Y	Flyable
SE.5a (Replica)	G-SEVA Trust	G-SEVA	-	'F141'/G	Flyable
SE.5a (Replica)	Oliver Wulff	N125QB	-	'D3540'	Restoration
SE.5a (Replica)	Sywell SE5 Group	G-AVOU	-		Restoration
SE.5a (Replica)	Roy Palmer	G-ERFC	-	'C1096'	Restoration
SE.5a (Replica)	Airpark Flight Centre Ltd	G-BUWE	-	'C9533'	Stored
SE.5a (Replica)	John Seed	G-PFAP	-	'C1904/Z'	Stored

Sopwith Camel

The Camel was introduced on the Western Front in 1917 as a successor to the earlier Sopwith Pup. Though proving difficult to handle, it provided for a high level of manoeuvrability to an experienced pilot. In total, Camel pilots have been credited with the shooting down of 1,294 enemy aircraft, more than any other Allied fighter of the conflict.

▶ Shuttleworth's Camel replica is the third and final aircraft built by Northern Aeroplane Workshops (NAW) for the collection. Building of the Camel started in 1995 and the airframe moved to Old Warden in 2013 for completion. On May 18, 2017 the aircraft – which wears the markings of 'D1851' - performed its maiden flight in the hands of chief pilot 'Dodge' Bailey. Darren Harbar

Camel (Replica)	Personal Plane Services	G-BPOB	-	'N6377'	Flyable
Camel (Replica)	Shuttleworth Trust	G-BZSC	-	'D1851'	Flyable
Camel (Replica)	Colin Law & Philip Hoeft	G-SOPC	-	-	Restoration

Sopwith Dove

After the end of the Great War ten Sopwith Pup airframes were converted to two-seat configuration for the civilian market. Branded as the Dove they also had slightly swept wings to maintain the original centre of gravity despite having an extra person aboard.

▶ This faithful replica of a Dove was built by Skysport Engineering in the 1990s and is now based at Old Warden. The 80hp La Rhône rotary powered aircraft carries the registration originally allocated to a Dove that was sold abroad in May 1919. Steve Bridgewater

Dove (Replica)	Andrew Wood	G-EAGA	-	-	Flyable

Sopwith Pup

Perhaps the most iconic British fighter of the Great War period the Pup first flew in February 1916 and more than 1,700 were built for the RFC and Royal Naval Air Service. The Pup was eventually outclassed by newer German fighters, but it was not completely replaced on the Western Front until the end of 1917. Today two 'original' Pups fly in the UK with a third undergoing restoration to fly and a replica currently in storage.

Pup	Shuttleworth Trust	G-EBKY	3004/14	'9917'	Flyable
Pup	Roy Palmer	G-ELRT	N6161	N6161	Flyable
Pup	Kelvyne Baker	G-EAVX	B1807	-	Restoration
Pup (Replica)	Mark Goddard	G-BZND	-	'N5199'	Stored

Left:: Although listed (and registered) as a Pup the Shuttleworth Collection's G-EBKY was actually built as a two-seat Dove in 1919. Richard Shuttleworth found it in the mid-30s being flown from a field at Kempston, west of Bedford, by Geoff Chamberlain. The aircraft had no Certificate of Airworthiness and so the owner was not interested in a legal sale so a deal was done to swap the Dove for an Avro 504K. By being what the collection refers to as "economical with the truth" he sorted out the paperwork and set about restoring the Dove to Pup configuration. It has been based at Old warden ever since and in 2004 it was repainted to represent '9917', a Beardmore built aircraft which was fitted with Le Prieur Rockets when it served for a time on HMS *Manxman*, a seaplane carrier. Steve Bridgewater **Right:** Pup N6161 was built at Kingston on Thames and delivered to France on January 25, 1917. On February 1, while being flown by George Elliott on his first operational mission, the Pup was forced down near Bruges by two Rumpler floatplanes. The aircraft was captured intact and flown by the Germans for evaluation purposes. Some original items were later retained by a museum and over the last few years these have been combined with other original Sopwith items to reconstruct N6161. The work was done by Retrotec and, registered G-ELRT, the aircraft flew again on October17, 2016. Steve Bridgewater

Sopwith Snipe

The Snipe came into RAF squadron service just a few weeks before the end of the Great War, in late 1918. It was not particularly fast, but its excellent climb and manoeuvrability meant it was selected as the standard postwar single-seat RAF fighter and the last examples were not retired until 1926.

▶ Although only two original Snipes remain a number of very accurate replicas have been produced in New Zealand by The Vintage Aviator Ltd – complete with 'new-build' 230hp Bentley rotary engines. One such example is marked as 'F2367' and based in the UK with the WW1 Aviation Heritage Trust. In the summer of 2017 it was in the process of transferring onto the UK register as G-CKBB. Steve Bridgewater

Snipe	The Vintage Aviator Ltd	G-CKBB	-	'F2367'	Flyable

Sopwith Triplane

The Triplane began as a private venture by the Sopwith Aviation Company. The fuselage and empennage closely mirrored those of the earlier Pup, but chief engineer Herbert Smith gave the new aircraft three narrow-chord wings to provide the pilot with an improved field of view. Ailerons were fitted to all three wings. It was the first military triplane to see operational service (beating the Fokker DR.1 by almost 9 months). Two original examples survive (one in London and one in Moscow) but two replicas fly at UK airshows.

▶ Shuttleworth's Sopwith Triplane was built entirely by volunteer members of Northern Aeroplane Workshops to original plans and delivered to Old Warden in June 1990. On seeing the quality and accuracy of the workmanship Sir Thomas Sopwith declared it to be a late production aircraft rather than a replica! Power comes from an original 130hp Clerget rotary engine. It now represents N6290/*Dixie II* of 8 Naval Squadron. Steve Bridgewater

Inset: Triplane G-BWRA began life in 1979 as a two-seat replica built by John Penny and registered G-PENY. It was later much modified, fitted with a Warner Scarab radial engine and finished to represent N500 – the prototype Sopwith Triplane. Steve Bridgewater

Triplane (Replica)	Shuttleworth Trust	G-BOCK	-	'N6290'	Flyable
Triplane (Replica)	John Brander	G-BWRA	-	'N500'	Flyable

10 | WARBIRD DIRECTORY

AVIATION SPECIALS

ESSENTIAL READING FROM KEY PUBLISHING

RAF BATTLE OF BRITAIN MEMORIAL FLIGHT
Spectacularly celebrates the Flight's activities and achievements.
£5.99 inc FREE P&P*

VALOUR IN THE AIR
A comprehensive salute to some of the greatest pilots ever take to the skies.
£6.99 inc FREE P&P*

SPITFIRE 80
Tribute to Britain's greatest fighter and possibly the best known combat aircraft in the world.
£5.99 inc FREE P&P*

VULCAN
A tribute to the most challenging and complex return-to-flight project ever.
£3.99 inc FREE P&P*

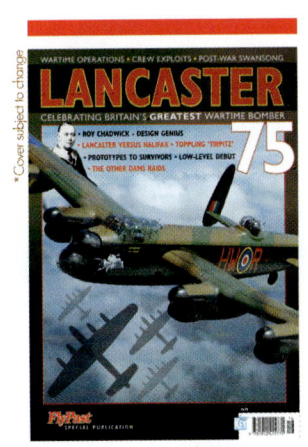

LANCASTER 75
Pays tribute to all who built, maintained and flew Lancasters, past and present.
£5.99 inc FREE P&P*

SCALE MODELLING MOSQUITO
Celebrates with five full model builds, type histories, kit/decal/accessory listings and exclusive scale drawings.
£5.99 inc FREE P&P*

GULF WAR
A must-have for those seeking to understand the conflict that changed the shape of warfare.
£3.99 inc FREE P&P*

RAF OFFICIAL ANNUAL REVIEW 2017
Behind the scenes insight into the aircraft, equipment and people of one of the world's premier air forces.
£5.99 inc FREE P&P*

AVIATION SPECIALS
ESSENTIAL reading from the teams behind your FAVOURITE magazines

HOW TO ORDER

OR

PHONE
UK: 01780 480404
ROW: (+44)1780 480404

*Prices correct at time of going to press. Free 2nd class P&P on all UK & BFPO orders. Overseas charges apply. Postage charges vary depending on total order value.

FREE Aviation Specials App 
Simply download to purchase digital versions of your favourite aviation specials in one handy place! Once you have the app, you will be able to download new, out of print or archive specials for less than the cover price!

IN APP ISSUES £3.99

562/17

ON SILVER WINGS

Preserved examples of the RAF's silver-winged biplanes of the 1930s have seen a resurgence in recent years. This chapter of the directory lists inter-war military types as well as 1930s civilian aircraft that were impressed into military service at the outbreak of World War Two. For the sake of 'neatness' post-war examples of pre-war aeroplanes (such as the Anson) are also included in this section.

Avro Anson

The 'Faithful Annie' was designed in the mid-1930s as a development of the Avro 652 airliner in response to an Air Ministry request for tenders for a maritime reconnaissance aircraft. An initial order for 174 aircraft was placed in July 1935 and by the time World War Two erupted in 1939 the type was in use as a multi-engined trainer as well as the anti-submarine and transport roles. The Anson continued to be used in the training role after the conflict, remaining in RAF service until 1968. Of the 8,138 examples built just three remain flyable – two of which are in the UK. Both of these are post war examples, one being a purely civil Avro 19 variant.

Anson C.21	Glenn James	G-VROE	WD413	WD413	Flyable
Anson C.19	BAE Systems (Operations) Ltd	G-AHKX	-	-	Flyable
Anson C.19	Private Owner	-	TX226	-	Stored
Anson C.19	Private Owner	-	TX235	-	Stored

Avro Tutor

The Avro 621 Tutor was developed as a two-seat training aeroplane for the inter-war RAF. More than 600 of the Armstrong Siddeley Mongoose powered biplanes were built from 1929 onwards but today just one example survives.

The Shuttleworth Collection's Tutor K3215 served with the Central Flying School (CFS) at Cranwell until 1946. A year later it was registered G-AHSA as part of the Darlington & District Aero Club fleet. It was later owned by Wing Commander Heywood at Burnaston, Derby and suffered crankshaft failure when taking part in the film *Reach for the Sky*. It was then bought by the Shuttleworth Collection and the Mongoose engine was rebuilt by Armstrong Siddeley at Coventry from the best parts of three non-working units. The aircraft is now painted in CFS Aerobatic team colours to represent 'K3241'.

Steve Bridgewater

| Tutor | Shuttleworth Trust | G-AHSA | K3215 | 'K3241' | Flyable |

BA Swallow

The BA Swallow first flew in 1933 and was, effectively, a license-built version of the German Klemm L.25. A total of 135 were built and a number were impressed into the military at the outbreak of World War Two. Just 22 survived the war and only two of these remain on the UK register today.

▶ Swallow II G-AFGE first flew on April 4, 1938 and was delivered to Sir DH Caine & TH Clayton in Hanworth. On August 1, 1940 'GE was impressed into the RAF as BK894 and did not return to its civil registration until May 1946.
Steve Bridgewater

| Swallow II | Charlie & Anna Huke | G-AFGE | BK894 (Impressed) | - | Flyable |
| Swallow II | South Wales Swallow Group | G-AFGD | BK897 (Impressed) | - | Stored |

12 WARBIRD DIRECTORY

Beechcraft Staggerwing

In the late 1920s Walter H Beech and designer Ted Wells joined forces on a project to produce a large, powerful, and fast cabin biplane specifically for the business executive. The Beechcraft Model 17, popularly known as the 'Staggerwing' because its top wing was (unusually) behind the lower wing, flew in November 1932. During World War Two a number of Staggerwings were impressed into military service as fast transports and others were built new as 'Travellers' for the USAAC and US Navy – the USAAC calling them the YC-43 Traveler and the Navy dubbing them the GB-2 Traveler. The RAF and Royal Navy also operated them as the Traveller I (with two 'Ls') through the Lend-Lease arrangement.

D.17 Staggerwing/GB-2 Traveler	Private Owner	N9405H	BuNo 33004	-	Flyable
D.17 Staggerwing/Traveller I	Patina Ltd/The Fighter Collection	G-BRVE	BuNo 32784/FT475	-	Restoration
D.17 Staggerwing/Traveller I	Private Owner	N18V	44-67761/FT507	'DR628'	Stored

Left: The Fighter Collection's G-BRVE flew with the Royal Navy as FT475 and then returned to the USN as BuNo 32784. It subsequently became N11193V before being re-imported to the UK in 1990 by Pink Floyd guitarist Dave Gilmour. He sold it to Peter Teichman who in turn sold it to TFC in 2005. The aircraft was undergoing deep maintenance/restoration during the summer of 2017. *Steve Bridgewater* **Right:** Staggerwing N18V is a genuine ex-RAF example (FT507) but wears the markings of 'DR628', a Staggerwing attached to 24 Sqn at RAF Hendon and flown by Prince Barnard of the Netherlands while he was in exile during the war years.

de Havilland DH.60 Moth

The DH.60 was the first of the Moth family of light aircraft manufactured by de Havilland. The first flew in 1925 and although the military DH.60T variant was promoted to them the RAF was initially not keen. However, by 1931 it had acquired 124 DH.60M Moths for use by the Central Flying School and at the outbreak of war numerous other Moths were impressed into military service. Other examples served with air arms around the globe and six ex-military DH.60s are thought to be in the UK in the summer of 2017.

DH.60G Gipsy Moth	Personal Plane Services	G-ABDA	DG583 (Impressed)	-	Flyable
DH.60G Gipsy Moth	Ben Cox	G-ABJJ	BK842 (Impressed)	-	Flyable
DH.60G Gipsy Moth	Paul Groves	G-AAYT	DR606 (Impressed)	-	Restoration
DH.60G Gipsy Moth	English Family	G-AAZG	30-94 (Spanish AF)	-	Restoration
DH.60G Gipsy Moth	Mike Vaisey	G-ABSD	A7-96 (RAAF)	-	Restoration
DH.60G II Moth Major	Paul & Tracey Groves	G-BVNG	30-81 (Spanish AF)	-	Stored

de Havilland DH.80A Puss Moth

The Puss Moth was a three-seat high-wing monoplane built between 1929 and 1933. It was one of the highest-performance private aircraft of its era making it a favourite with air racers and at the start of World War Two a number were impressed into service as high-speed communications aircraft.

▶ Puss Moth G-AAZP was built in 1930 and sold to Egypt in June 1932 as SU-AAC. It returned to the UK in 1936 and was impressed into RAF service as HL537 on September 27, 1941. It re-joined the civil register in November 1946 and now flies in a glorious pre-war blue scheme. *Steve Bridgewater*

DH.80A Puss Moth	Robert Williams	G-AAZP	HL537 (Impressed)	-	Flyable
DH.80A Puss Moth	Paul & Andrew Wood	G-AEOA	ES921 (Impressed)	-	Stored

de Havilland DH.84 Dragon

Following the commercial success of its single-engined Fox Moth de Havilland received an order from Hillman Airways for a larger twin-engined version to be built. The prototype first flew at Stag Lane Aerodrome on November 12, 1932 and could carry six passengers with their baggage from London to Paris with ease. In 1934 British production switched to the more powerful Dragon Rapide (see page 56) but several Dragons were impressed into RAF service during the war. Furthermore, during World War Two, the DH.84 was put back into production in Australia as a navigational trainer for the Royal Australian Air Force. Two DH.84s fly in the UK in 2017 – both with military ties.

▶ Torquil Norman's Dragon was built by de Havilland Australia and served the RAAF as A34-59. It was later registered as VH-AQU and VH-DCX before being imported to the UK and restored by Cliff Lovel as G-ECAN. Steve Bridgewater

| DH.84 Dragon | George Cormack | G-ACET | AW171 (Impressed) | - | Flyable |
| DH.84 Dragon | Norman Aircraft Trust | G-ECAN | A34-59 (RAAF) | - | Flyable |

de Havilland DH.85 Leopard Moth

The Leopard Moth was a successor to the Puss Moth and while it was similar in configuration to the earlier aircraft the tubular steel fuselage framework was replaced with an all-plywood structure to reduce weight and increase range and performance. Of the 133 built some 44 were impressed into military service in Britain, mostly as communications aircraft. Only a few managed to survive six years of hard usage but four currently grace the UK register – one of which recently flew again following restoration.

▶ Peter Vacher's newly restored DH.85 was built at G-ACMA in March 1934 and delivered to National Benzole Ltd. In August 1940 it was impressed into the RAF as BD148. Post-war it passed through various owners until Peter Vacher acquired it in 2009 and set about a complete restoration to immaculate condition. Steve Bridgewater

DH.85 Leopard Moth	Peter Vacher	G-ACMA	BD148 (Impressed)	-	Flyable
DH.85 Leopard Moth	Mark Miller	G-ACGS	AX858 (Impressed)	-	Restoration
DH.85 Leopard Moth	Martin & Kathryn Slack	G-ACMN	X9381 (Impressed)	-	Restoration
DH.85 Leopard Moth	David & Valerie Stiles	G-ACLL	AX165 (Impressed)	-	Stored

de Havilland DH.87 Hornet Moth

The Hornet Moth had an enclosed cabin for two occupants and was designed in 1934 as a potential replacement for de Havilland's Tiger Moth trainer. Although there was no interest from the RAF the aircraft was put into production for private buyers and during the war many of the 84 British registered Hornet Moths were impressed into military service.

Hornet Moth G-ADND was built in August 1935 for Fairey Aviation in Hayes but was impressed as W9385 on February 22, 1940. The aircraft passed through various owners after the war, including the Shuttleworth Collection - which repainted it into its impressed markings as a tribute to the unsung work undertaken by the hundreds of requisitioned aircraft between 1939 and 1945. Today G-ADND is based at Oaksey Park with David & Sylvia Weston and retains its camouflage and RAF markings. Steve Bridgewater

DH.87B Hornet Moth	Christopher & Susan Winch	G-ADKC	X9445 (Impressed)	-	Flyable
DH.87B Hornet Moth	Stephen Barratt & Andrew Herbert	G-ADKK	W6749 (Impressed)	-	Flyable
DH.87B Hornet Moth	Peter & Jean Johnson	G-ADKL	W5750 (Impressed)	-	Flyable
DH.87B Hornet Moth	John Miller	G-ADKM	W5751 (Impressed)	-	Flyable
DH.87B Hornet Moth	Totalsude Ltd (Netherlands)	G-ADLY	W9388 (Impressed)	-	Flyable
DH.87B Hornet Moth	David & Sylvia Weston	G-ADND	W9385 (Impressed)	-	Flyable
DH.87B Hornet Moth	G-ADNE Group	G-ADNE	X9325 (Impressed)	-	Flyable
DH.87B Hornet Moth	Mark Millar	G-AELO	AW118 (Impressed)	-	Flyable
DH.87B Hornet Moth	Ben Cox	G-AESE	W5775 (Impressed)	-	Flyable
DH.87B Hornet Moth	Shipping & Airlines Ltd	G-AHBL	P6787 (Impressed)	-	Flyable
DH.87B Hornet Moth	Paul & Elisabeth Gliddon	G-AHBM	P6785 (Impressed)	-	Flyable
DH.87B Hornet Moth	Private Owner	ZS-APD	1550 SAAF (Impressed)	-	Restoration
DH.87B Hornet Moth	Private Owner	ZS-ROY	1591 SAAF (Impressed)	-	Restoration

de Havilland DH.88 Comet

Although most famous as an air racing aeroplane the DH.88 Comet was also evaluated by the RAF. It made several flights in 1935 before being written off in a heavy landing and sold.

▶ After the 1934 MacRobertson Air Race G-ACSS was shipped back to Britain and later bought by the Air Ministry. Given the military serial K5085 and painted silver with RAF markings it was flown to Martlesham Heath for evaluation. It made several flights before being written off in a heavy landing and sold for scrap. It was subsequently sold on, rebuilt and fitted with Gypsy Six series II engines and a castoring tailwheel before taking part in further air races. G-ACSS was requisitioned for the RAF once again in 1943 but soon passed on to de Havilland. The Shuttleworth Collection at Old Warden acquired it in 1965 and it was returned to flying condition in 1987. Steve Bridgewater

DH.88 Comet	Shuttleworth Trust	G-ACSS	K5084	-	Flyable

de Havilland DH.94 Moth Minor

The Moth Minor was designed as a low-wing monoplane to replace the biplane Moth series, and was intended to give similar performance with less power. Nearly 100 examples had been built by the outbreak of World War Two and production then shifted to Australia. A number of privately owned DH.94s in the United Kingdom were commandeered for use by the RAF and Fleet Air Arm and one example was also used by the United States Army Air Corps.

DH.94 Moth Minor	John Jennings	G-AFNI	W7972 (Impressed)	-	Stored
DH.94 Moth Minor	Karen Cantwell	G-AFOB	X5117 (Impressed)	-	Stored
DH.94 Moth Minor	The Moth Minor Group	G-AFPN	X9297 (Impressed)	-	Flyable

Desoutter I

Created as a light transport aircraft the Desoutter I dates from 1930 and owes its existence to an order by National Flying Services for 19 examples - all painted black and bright orange. NFS based them at various British flying clubs where they were used for instruction, pleasure flights and taxi flights. Today just two examples remain airworthy, one of which is in the UK.

▶ The Shuttlworth Collection's Desoutter I was built in 1931 as an air taxi for National Flying Services. It was entered in the King's Cup Air Races in 1933 and 1934 and the following year it was acquired by Richard Shuttleworth. It flew in camouflage during early World War Two and then fell into disrepair following Richard's death in 1940. The aircraft passed through various hands until returning to Old Warden in the late 1970s. It flew again after restoration in January 1998 and wears its original NFS livery. Steve Bridgewater

Desoutter I	Shuttleworth Trust	G-AAPZ	-	-	Flyable

WARBIRD DIRECTORY | 15

Fairey Swordfish

The venerable 'Stringbag' torpedo bomber was designed in the early 1930s and although it was already considered obsolescent at the outbreak of World War Two in 1939 it remained in frontline service throughout the entirety of the conflict. The Royal Navy Historic Flight has three Swordfishes – one is airworthy, another currently under restoration and a third now in storage following the cancellation of plans to return it to flight.

Swordfish II	RN Historic Flight	-	W5856	W5856/4A	Flyable
Swordfish II	RN Historic Flight	-	LS326	LS326/L2	Restoration
Swordfish III	RN Historic Flight	-	NF389	NF389	Stored

◀ W5856 is the oldest surviving Swordfish in the world. She first flew on October 21, 1941 and served with Royal Navy's Mediterranean Fleet for a year before transferring to the Royal Canadian Navy in 1944. Passing through the hands of at least two civilian operators after disposal, she was purchased by Sir William Roberts to join his Strathallan Collection in Scotland and arrived in crates in August 1977 – the airframe being badly corroded condition. In 1990 the aircraft was bought by British Aerospace and restored to flying condition for the RNHF by 1993. W5856 was grounded with corrosion in her wing spars in 2003 and her future looked uncertain. However with great generosity BAE Systems stepped in and constructed a new set of wings which were delivered to the RNHF in 2012. W5856 was finally restored to full flying condition and saved for the nation by a major grant from the Peter Harrison Heritage Foundation. The aircraft re-joined the display circuit in 2015 and is now painted in the markings of an 820 NAS aircraft from HMS *Ark Royal*, which participated in the sinking of the German battleship *Bismark* in May 1941.
Steve Bridgewater

◀ When first restored in the 1990s W5856 wore the pre-war colours of 810 NAS embarked on HMS *Ark Royal*. The horizontal stripes on the fin denote the Commanding Officer's aircraft, and the blue and red fuselage stripes are the colours for *Ark Royal* with the letter code 'A' being for the ship, '2' for the second squadron and 'A' for the first aircraft of that squadron. The long yellow fuselage strip identified 810 as Yellow Squadron in the summer air exercises held in

Fostner Wickner Wicko

The Wicko was a 1930s British two-seat cabin monoplane built by the Foster Wikner Aircraft Company at Southampton Airport. At the start of the Second World War production ceased and the eight GM.1s so far completed were impressed into the military. One joined the Royal New Zealand Air Force and the other seven were used by the RAF and named the Warferry. A single example remains today.

Wicko GM.1	John Dible	G-AFJB	DR613 (Impressed)	-	Flyable

Gloster Gamecock

The Gamecock was a development of the Grebe and first flew in February 1925. It differed from the Grebe primarily by way of its Bristol Jupiter engine, which replaced the unreliable Armstrong Siddeley Jaguar. Retro Track & Air's Gamecock project was acquired from the Finnish Air Force having been operational in the Winter War with the Soviet forces. It is the only privately owned example capable of being returned to flight and is described as being "two years from completion."

Gamecock	Retro Track & Air	G-CGYF	GA-43 (Finnish AF)	-	Restoration

Gloster Gladiator

The Gladiator was the RAF's last biplane fighter and although it was soon rendered obsolete by newer monoplane designs the type acquitted itself well in combat during the early days of World War Two. Two examples remain flyable – both in the UK.

▶ Gladiator N5903 was delivered in 1939 and briefly served with 141 Sqn at Grangemouth before being allocated to the Air Ministry Development Pool as a flight trials platform in December 1939. The aircraft was then stored throughout the war years and in 1950 it was acquired by Air Service Training for ground instructional use at Ansty, near Leicester. It was eventually acquired (along with L8032) by Viv Bellamy who combined the two airframes and returned L8032 to flyable condition. In 1960 N5903 was presented to the Shuttleworth Collection, who in turn loaned it to the Fleet Air Arm Museum in 1971. In 1994 it was sold to The Fighter Collection and following an epic restoration the aircraft flew again – now as G-GLAD and wearing 72 Sqn markings – on July 10, 2008.

Steve Bridgewater

Hawker Audax

The Audax was an army co-operation variant of the Hawker Hart family. It was very similar to the Hart although it had some significant modifications, including a hook to pick up messages. The first Audax flew in late 1931 and over 700 Audaxes were produced. The sole survivor is 1937-built K5600 which served with 226 Army Co-Operation Squadron but was with 10 School of Technical Training in Liverpool by 1940. The remains were recovered from a Cheshire scrap yard and it is slowly being rebuilt to fly again.

| Audax | Aero Vintage Ltd | G-BVVI | K5600 | - | Restoration |

Hawker Demon

The Demon was a fighter variant of the Hart light bomber selected by the Air Ministry as an interim fighter until higher-performance fighters could be bought in larger numbers. The Demon's first flight was on February 10, 1933 and 305 were ultimately built.

| Demon | Demon Displays Ltd | G-BTVE | K8023 | K8023 | Flyable |

Left: Hawker Demon K8203 was taken on charge by the RAF on October 27, 1937 and initially assigned to 64 Sqn at RAF Church Fenton, whose livery now adorns the aircraft. It was struck off charge in September 1940 but used as a training aid by Air Cadet units until 1943. The rear fuselage ended up in the RAF Museum's storage facility at RAF Cardington until it was acquired by AeroVintage Ltd. Demon Displays Ltd purchased it in 1991 and restoration began at SkySport Engineering Ltd. The aircraft flew again on June 23, 2009 as G-BTVE and is now based at the Shuttleworth Collection. *Steve Bridgewater*

Right: The restoration of Demon K8023 was undertaken by SkySport Engineering Ltd and parts were sourced from around the globe, including Kestrel V engines acquired in Australia. The project has been awarded the Historic Aircraft Association's ConRod Trophy in recognition of an 'outstanding contribution to the preservation and safe operation of historic aircraft' and the 2010 Freddie March 'Spirit of Aviation' Trophy at the annual concours d'elegance. *Steve Bridgewater*

WARBIRD DIRECTORY | 17

In Focus: Fairey Swordfish LS326

Since 1987 LS326 has worn her original wartime colour scheme for North Atlantic convoys with 'L' Flight of 836 Squadron. Following extensive work by BAE Systems at Brough to her wings, LS326 flew again on July 1, 2008 for the first time in nine years and by that time she had been adopted by the City of Liverpool, the name she proudly wears on her port side.

LS326 was the first Swordfish operated by the Royal Navy Historic Flight (RNHF). Built by Blackburn Aircraft (as a 'Blackfish') at Sherburn-in-Elmet in 1943 she went on to fly as part of 'L' Flight of 836 NAS on board the MAC ship *Rapana*, on North Atlantic Convoy duties.

Following her active service she was used for training and communications duties at various station until 1947 when she was acquired by Fairey Aviation and displayed at various RAeS Garden party displays. The following year she was sent to White Waltham for storage and remained there until Sir Richard Fairey gave orders for the aircraft to be rebuilt. The restoration was completed in October 1955 and she was rolled out in a 'Fairey' Blue and silver scheme complete with the civil registration G-AJVH.

In 1959 LS326 was repainted for a starring role in the film *Sink the Bismarck!* and a year later she was presented to the Royal Navy by the Westland Aircraft Company and has been flown ever since.

LS326 is currently undergoing an engine rebuild and while she is 'grounded' the RNHF team is taking the opportunity to conduct other non-essential work so that the aircraft is in top condition when it returns to flight.

For many years LS326 retained her *Sink the Bismarck!* film colour scheme and carried a dummy torpedo beneath the fuselage.

In 1984, D-Day invasion stripes were also added to LS326 for the 40th Anniversary celebrations which saw the aircraft overfly the beaches of Normandy in the scheme.

▲ Following her initial rebuild by Fairey Aviation in the 1950s LS326 was repainted into the Fairey 'house' colours of blue and silver. She is seen here at an RAeS Garden Party at White Waltham.

▶ During the 1980s the RNHF fielded a fleet of Swordfish, two Hawker Sea Furies (TF956 seen here), Fairey Firefly (WB271 illustrated) and a Hawker Sea Hawk.

WARBIRD DIRECTORY | 19

IN FOCUS

Gloster Gladiator I L8032/G-AMRK

Since 2007 G-AMRK has appeared in the 73 Sqn markings of 'K7985', the aircraft flown by the World War Two Ace 'Cobber' Kain at the 1937 Hendon Air Pageant. *Steve Bridgewater*

Gladiator L8032 was the last production Gladiator I built. It was delivered in 1938 and spent most of the war in storage. In 1944 the aircraft (along with N5903 – now G-GLAD) was earmarked for meteorological survey work and returned to Gloster at Hucclecote for conversion. However, the work did not happen as more modern types became available and the two Gladiators were placed in storage again.

In 1948 the two Gladiators were bought by Glosters and two years later they were delivered to Air Service Training for use as instructional airframes at Hamble (L8032) and Ansty (N5903). The aircraft eventually passed to Viv Bellamy who scavenged parts from N5903 to return L8032 to the skies as G-AMRK.

In 1953 Glosters re-purchased the aeroplane and returned it to full military specification – complete with 72 Sqn markings, albeit carrying the incorrect serial 'K8032'. When Gloster Aircraft closed the Gladiator was presented to Shuttleworth Collection in November 1960. Today it is one of the most popular aeroplanes in the collection and also appears at airshows away from its normal base at Old Warden, Bedfordshire.

20 | WARBIRD DIRECTORY

Above and below: In 1996 the Gladiator was restored and recovered, emerging in the markings of the Royal Norwegian Air Force for filming. It carried the serial '423' on one side and '427' on the other so as to represent two different aircraft in the film.

▲ To mark the 50th anniversary of the Battle of Britain in 1990 G-AMRK was repainted into a camouflage scheme, depicting a Gladiator operated by 247 Sqn in defence of Portsmouth during the battle.

◄ When it was presented to the Shuttleworth Collection in 1960 G-AMRK flew in 72 Sqn markings complete with the incorrect serial 'K8032.' This was later corrected to L8032.

WARBIRD DIRECTORY | 21

Hawker Fury

The agile Fury first flew on March 25, 1931 and was the first interceptor in RAF service capable of more than 200mph (174kts). Considered by many to be the epitome of a glamorous silver winged inter-war biplanes the type has long been popular with homebuilders but enthusiasts had to wait until 2012 before a genuine Fury (K5674) took to the skies. The Cambridge Bomber & Fighter Society at Little Gransden is also building a highly accurate replica using a number of original parts.

Fury I	Historic Aircraft Collection Ltd	G-CBZP	K5674	K5674	Flyable
Fury I	Cambridge Bomber & Fighter Society	-	-	'K1928'	Restoration
Isaacs Fury II (Replica)	Roger Redknap	G-ASCM	-	'K2050'	Flyable
Isaacs Fury II (Replica)	James Norris	G-AYJY	-	'K2065'	Flyable
Isaacs Fury II (Replica)	Stephen Vince	G-BBVO	-	'K5682/6'	Flyable
Isaacs Fury II (Replica)	Charles Styles	G-BEER	-	'K2075'	Flyable
Isaacs Fury II (Replica)	Jonathan Marten-Hale	G-BWWN	-	'K8303/D'	Flyable
Isaacs Fury II (Replica)	Simon Johnston	G-BZNW	-	'K2048'	Flyable
Isaacs Fury II (Replica)	Michael Bond	G-RODI	-	'K3731'	Flyable
Isaacs Fury II (Replica)	Lawrence Wells	G-BKZM	-	'K2060'	Stored
Isaacs Fury II (Replica)	Ian Harrison	G-BMEU	-	'S1615'	Stored
Isaacs Fury II (Replica)	Nicholas Stone	G-BZAS	-	'K5673'	Stored
Isaacs Fury II (Replica)	Guy Smith	G-CCKV	-	'K7271'	Stored
Isaacs Fury II (Replica)	Cathy Silk & David Phillips	G-PFAR	-	'K2059'	Stored

Left: Fury I K5674 was delivered to the RAF in November 1935 and joined 43 Sqn at RAF Tangmere the following June. In August 1940 the aircraft was sold to the South African Air Force and on March 31, 1941 it crashed after the pilot ran out of fuel. The wreckage was scrapped but in 1994 Guy Black's Historic Aircraft Collection (HAC) acquired the remnants following a tip-off by from the RAF Museum. Restoration was undertaken by Retrotec (the restoration arm of Aero Vintage and HAC) and on July 30, 2012 K5674 (now G-CBZP) returned to the skies from Goodwood. It is now based at Duxford and wears its original 43 Sqn markings. Steve Bridgewater **Right:** The Isaacs Fury was designed by John Isaacs as a seven-tenths scale replica of the Hawker Fury. The prototype (G-ACSM – illustrated) first flew on August 30, 1963 with a 65hp Walter Mikron III piston engine in the nose. This was later changed to a 125hp Lycoming O-290 and it is thought some 18 airframes have so far been completed – seven of which are flyable in the UK in 2017.

Hawker Hart

The Hart was designed in response to a 1926 Air Ministry requirement for a two-seat, high-performance, all-metal light day-bomber. The type was also exported widely and a former Swedish Air Force Bristol Mercury-powered example is being renovated by Hawker Restorations for Swedish collector Joakim Westh.

Hart B.4A	Westh Flyg AB (Sweden)	G-CIAJ	726	'726'	Restoration

Hawker Hind

The Hind was an improved version of the Hawker Hart bomber with the new Kestrel V powerplant. The prototype flew in September 1934 and 528 were built for the RAF and export operators. The Afghan Air Force acquired 20 aircraft in 1938, the final example retiring in 1957. Four of these aircraft were donated to Canada and the UK by the Afghan president in 1970 and a further batch of six Afghan Hinds were recovered from a scrapyard behind the Kabul Military training area in 2006 – the current status of these is currently unclear.

◀ The Shuttleworth Collection's Hind was one of a batch of eight aircraft delivered new to the Afghan Air Force in 1938 (along with 12 ex-RAF airframes) and carries the makers number 41.H.8. 1902. Little is known of its career but it is thought to have been in service until 1956. In 1968 two Hinds were donated to Canada and two to the UK – with one going to the RAF Museum and a second to the Shuttleworth Collection. The RAF Museum example was collected by C-130 Hercules, but the Shuttleworth example was collected by road – thanks to Ford who donated the use of a lorry for the 6,000 mile journey. The aircraft arrived in 1971 and it flew again – as G-AENP – on August 17, 1981. Today the aircraft wears the markings of 'K5414' of 15 Sqn. Steve Bridgewater

Hind (Afghan)	Shuttleworth Trust	G-AENP	'1902'	'K5414/XV'	Flyable
Hind	Private Owner	-	K6636	-	Stored
Hind (Afghan)	Aero Vintage Ltd	G-CBLK	L7181	-	Stored
Hind (Afghan)	Private Owner	-	K5409	-	Stored
Hind (Afghan)	Private Owner	-	K5462	-	Stored
Hind (Afghan)	Private Owner	-	K5554	-	Stored
Hind (Afghan)	Private Owner	-	K6618	-	Stored
Hind (Afghan)	Private Owner	-	K6833	-	Stored
Hind (Afghan)	Private Owner	-	L7191	-	Stored

◀ Following its initial ten year restoration G-AENP was initially painted in Afghan colours.

▶ Hind L7181 was built in 1937 and served with 211 Sqn until being sold to Afghanistan in 1939. In 1970 it was donated to the Canadian government and gifted to the Canada Aviation Museum collection. In 1995 the airframe was acquired by Aero Vintage and shipped to the UK for eventual restoration to airworthy condition as G-CBLK.
Steve Bridgewater

Hawker Nimrod

The Nimrod was the navalised version of the Fury and built in two main variants – one each of which now flies in the UK. The Nimrod never fired its guns in anger but served with both the Home and Mediterranean Fleets until May 1939.

| Nimrod I | Patina Ltd/The Fighter Collection | G-BWWK | S1581 | S1581 | Flyable |
| Nimrod II | Historic Aircraft Collection Ltd | G-BURZ | K3661 | K3661 | Flyable |

Left: The Fighter Collection's Nimrod I (S1581) was the third production aircraft built and was subsequently delivered to 408 Fighter flight (later 803 NAS) as '573' embarked upon HMS *Glorious*. The aircraft remained aboard *Glorious* until she was written off in early 1938. The substantial remains were recovered from a scrapyard in West London in the early 1970s and donated to the RAF Museum but in the early 1980s they were passed to Viv Bellamy to act as a pattern for his Fury replica (now based in the USA). In 1994 the remains were purchased by Aero Vintage who set about restoring the Nimrod to fly as G-BWWK. The first flight took place in July 2000 and the aircraft joined TFC in 2004. She carries her original 803 NAS markings. Steve Bridgewater **Right:** The Historic Aircraft Collection's Nimrod II (K3661) was completed on September 5, 1934 and eventually joined 802 Flight in the Mediterranean with the side code number '562'. In 1972 the complete but corroded aircraft was discovered on a rubbish dump in Ashford, Kent and donated to the RAF Museum. The fuselage was later sold to Mike Cookman, who in turn sold it to Aero Vintage in August 1991 and later that year the organisation was able to acquire the wings from the RAF Museum. Restoration commenced in 1992, helped by the fortuitous discovery of a large number of Nimrod drawings in Denmark, and the aircraft flew again on November 16, 2006. Steve Bridgewater

Hawker Tomtit

The Tomtit was designed to meet a 1927 Air Ministry specification for a metal framed two-seat trainer to replace the Avro 504 in RAF service. Only 35 were built and just one example remains extant in 2017.

▶ K1786 was the last Tomtit to be built and is the sole surviving example of its type. During World War Two it was flown as a 'hack' by Alex Henshaw and after the war it was sold to Neville Duke, who displayed it regularly until he sold it to Hawker Aircraft in 1951. They presented it to the Shuttleworth Collection in 1956 and it returned to Hawker-Siddeley at Dunsfold in 1967 to be restored to its original service livery. Steve Bridgewater

Tomtit	Shuttleworth Trust	G-AFTA	K1786	K1786	Flyable

Miles Whitney Straight

The Whitney Straight was designed by F.G. Miles as the result of collaboration with Grand Prix motor racing driver Whitney Straight. At the outbreak of World War Two the Air Ministry impressed 23 Whitney Straights into military service, for use as communications aircraft.

▶ Miles Whitney Straight G-AERV was built in 1936 for a private owner in Heston, London but was impressed into the RAF as EM999 in June 7, 1941. Steve Bridgewater

M11 Whitney Straight	Peter Bishop	G-AERV	EM999 (Impressed)	-	Flyable

Miles Monarch

The Monarch was the last civil type produced by Phillips and Powis before the war. It was a development of the Whitney Straight but had an enlarged fuselage allowing provision for a third seat. Eleven aircraft were built between 1938 and 1939, six of these to British customers and five of those were impressed into the RAF at the start of the war.

| M17 Monarch | Bob Mitchell | G-AFRZ | W6463 (Impressed) | - | Stored |

Miles Falcon

The Falcon was designed in 1934 and while structurally similar to the earlier Miles M.2F Hawk Major family it had side-by-side seating for two behind the pilot in a glazed cockpit. At the outbreak of the war ten were impressed into service by the RAF, Royal Navy, RAAF and the Swedish Air Force.

▶ Peter Holloway's Falcon was sold to Sweden in 1936 as SE-AFN and used as an air taxi until it was impressed into the Swedish Air Force in 1940 as Fv7001. In 1944 it was returned to its former owner but in 1961 it was flown to the UK for Doug Bianchi's Personal Plane Services. In 1964 Edward Eves acquired the aircraft (in exchange for a vintage Alfa Romeo sports car) and it was restored it to airworthiness and flown to victory in the 1979 Kings Cup Air Race. In 1989 it was sold to Tim Moore's SkySport Engineering and restored to pristine condition. Peter Holloway acquired it in 2001 and it has lived at Old Warden ever since. Steve Bridgewater

| M3 Falcon | Peter Holloway | G-AEEG | Fv7001 SwAF (Impressed) | Flyable |

Morane-Saulnier MS.315

The Morane-Saulnier MS.315 was designed in 1932 as a parasol-winged trainer for the French Air Force powered by a 135hp Salmson radial engine. A production run of 346 aircraft followed the four prototypes (including 33 built after World War Two). In the 1960s around 40 were converted to MS.317 standard with 200hp Continental W670-K engines.

Antony Whitehead's recently restored MS.317 is based at Manchester Barton airfield and wears the markings of the French Aéronavale. Steve Bridgewater

| MS.315 | Ronald Cooper/Steven Swallow | G-BZNK | 354 French AF | 354 French AF | Flyable |
| MS.317 | Antony Whitehead | G-MOSA | 351 French AF | 351 French Navy/HY22 | Flyable |

WARBIRD DIRECTORY | 25

Percival Q.6 Petrel

The Percival Q.6 was a 1930s communications aircraft built by Percival Aircraft Limited at Luton. Although designed as a civil transport seven examples were acquired by the RAF as the Petrel and others were impressed into military service at the start of the war.

▶ G-AFFD was the first production Q.6 and was delivered to Sir Philip Sassoon in March 1938. It was later impressed into RAF service as X9407 and is now being restored to airworthy condition by the G-AFFD Restoration Group/Fordaire Aviation for new owners Finest Hour Warbirds. It will ultimately be based at Bicester airfield and available for pleasure flying. Darren Harbar

Q.6 Petrel	G-AFFD Restoration Group	G-AFFD	X9407 'Impressed'	X9047	Restoration

Percival Vega Gull

The Vega Gull was a development of Percival's earlier 'D-Series' Gull and differed in having a fourth seat, dual controls and flaps. The prototype first flew from Gravesend in November 1935 and 90 were ultimately made by the time production ended in July 1939. Of those, 15 were ordered by the Air Ministry and a further 21 were impressed into service at the start of the war – one of which survives today.

Vega Gull	David Hulme	G-AEZJ	X9339 (Impressed)	-	Flyable

Ryan SCW

The Ryan SCW was a low-wing monoplane, designed to be an up-market version of the Ryan S-T trainer. Production aircraft were fitted with a 145hp Warner Super Scarab radial engine but only 12 were built. One example was impressed into service with the USAAF and designated the L-10.

▶ Stephen Carter's Australian-based Ryan SCW VH-SCW is currently touring the UK and attending various events. The aircraft was built in 1937 but in 1941 it was impressed into the USAAF as 42-107412. Today it wears a stylish civilian scheme with a highly polished fuselage. Steve Bridgewater

Ryan SCW	Stephen Carter	VH-SCW	42-107412 (Impressed)	-	Flyable

Supermarine Walrus

The Walrus was designed by R J Mitchell as a single-engined amphibious biplane reconnaissance aircraft and first flew in 1933. Intended for use as a fleet spotter to be catapult launched from cruisers or battleships, the Walrus was later employed in a variety of other roles, most notably as a rescue aircraft for downed aircrew.

▶ When it finally takes to the skies G-RNLI will be the only airworthy example of the Walrus. Restoration was begun by Dick Melton in the 1980s and it has since passed through various owners before arriving with James Lyle's Walrus Aviation Ltd. The aircraft is now at Audley End with Vintage Fabrics Ltd where it is being worked on once again. Tim Badham

Walrus I	Walrus Aviation Ltd	G-RNLI	W2718	-	Restoration

FlyPast

Your favourite magazine is also available digitally.
DOWNLOAD THE APP NOW FOR FREE.

INCLUDING BONUS VIDEO AND PHOTO CONTENT

FREE APP with sample issue
IN APP ISSUES £3.99

SUBSCRIBE & SAVE
Monthly £2.99
6 issues £19.99
12 issues £34.99

SEARCH: FlyPast

Read on your: iPhone & iPad · Android · PC & Mac · kindle fire · Blackberry · Windows 10

ALSO AVAILABLE FOR DOWNLOAD

SEARCH BRITAIN AT WAR
FREE APP with sample issue
IN APP ISSUES £3.99

SEARCH AEROPLANE
FREE APP with sample issue
IN APP ISSUES £3.99

NEW Aviation Specials App FREE DOWNLOAD

IN APP ISSUES £3.99

Simply download to purchase digital versions of your favourite aviation specials in one handy place! Once you have the app, you will be able to download new, out of print or archive specials for less than the cover price!

How it Works.

Simply download the FlyPast app and receive your sample issue completely free. Once you have the app, you will be able to download new or back issues (from September 2010 onwards) for less than newsstand price or, alternatively, subscribe to save even more!

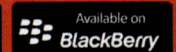

Don't forget to register for your Pocketmags account. This will protect your purchase in the event of a damaged or lost device. It will also allow you to view your purchases on multiple platforms.

Available on: iTunes · App Store · Google play · BlackBerry · kindle fire · PC, Mac & Windows 10

Available on PC, Mac, Blackberry, Windows 10 and kindle fire from **pocketmags.com**

Requirements for app: registered iTunes account on Apple iPhone, iPad or iPod Touch. Internet connection required for initial download.
Published by Key Publishing Ltd. The entire contents of these titles are © copyright 2017. All rights reserved. App prices subject to change. Prices correct at time of going to press. 560/17

WORLD WAR TWO TRAINERS & LIAISON AIRCRAFT

Often the most affordable and attainable of warbirds to own the training and liaison types remain the most numerically popular of all ex-military aircraft flying in the UK today. For the sake of 'filing' some post-war aircraft (most notably Austers and Piper Super Cubs) are grouped with their World War Two brethren in this section.

Aeronca

The Aeronautical Corporation of America (Aeronca) was a large-scale manufacturer of light aircraft from 1928 to 1951. A number of those were militarised for USAAC and USAAF forces, and examples of the L-16 Grasshopper and O-58 Defender grace the UK civil register. Examples of the post-war Aeronca 7AC Champion and 11AC Chief also operate in World War Two-esque colour schemes.

7AC Champion	7AC Ltd	G-BPGK	-	USAAF	Flyable
11AC Chief	Robert Willcox	G-BJEV	-	'897/E USN'	Stored
11AC Chief	Peter Green	G-BRXL	-	'42-78044'	Flyable
L-16A Grasshopper	David Crompton	G-BFAF	47-0797	7797 USAAC	Stored
O-58 Defender	Reg McComish	G-BRHP	43-1923	31923 USAAF	Flyable
O-58 Defender	Alexander Kutz (Germany)	G-BRPR	43-1952	31952 USAAF	Stored

1956-built Aeronca 7AC G-BPGK is a regular attendee at fly-in events wearing a pseudo World War Two scheme.
Steve Bridgewater

Reg McCormish's 1942 Aeronca O-58 Defender G-BRHP is currently the only example of the type flying outside the USA.
Steve Bridgewater

Auster

Perhaps the Army Air Corps' most famous fixed wing aeroplane of all time, the Auster was supplied in a myriad of versions. The company began in 1938 by making light observation aircraft designed by the Taylorcraft Aircraft Corporation of America and 1,604 Taylorcraft Austers were built during World War Two – the majority used in the Air Observation Post (AOP) role. Post war variants ranged from the AOP.6 (and dual control T.7 version) built by Beagle to the advanced AOP.9 and the sole AOP.11. For ease of filing both post-war and wartime 'Austers' of all types are listed together in this section, as are a pair of original Taylorcraft DCO-65s currently in storage.

Taylorcraft Auster Plus D	Simon Griggs	G-AHCR	LB352	-	Flyable
Taylorcraft Auster Plus D	Peter Cole	G-AHGZ	LB367	LB367	Flyable
Taylorcraft Auster Plus D	Jennifer Pothecary	G-AHXE	HH982	'LB312'	Flyable
Taylorcraft Auster Plus D	Nigel Dickinson	G-AHUG	LB282	-	Restoration
Taylorcraft Auster Plus D	Kingsley Owen	G-AHGW	LB375	LB375	Stored
Taylorcraft Auster Plus D	Adrian Hall-Carpenter	G-AHSD	LB323	LB323	Stored
Taylorcraft DCO-65	Brian Robe	G-BWLJ	42-35870	42-35870 USAAF/129	Stored
Taylorcraft DCO-65	Selby Potts	G-BRIY	42-58678	42-58678 USAAF/Y	Stored
Taylorcraft Auster 4	Barbara Farries	G-AJXV	NJ695	NJ695	Flyable
Taylorcraft Auster 4	Mike Tango Group	G-ANHS	MT197	MT197	Flyable
Taylorcraft Auster 4	X-Ray Yankee Group	G-AJXY	MT243	MT243	Stored
Taylorcraft Auster 5	James Gibson	G-AIKE	NJ728	NJ728	Flyable
Taylorcraft Auster 5	Auster RT486 Flying Group	G-AJGJ	RT486	RT486	Flyable

Type	Owner	Registration	Serial	Markings	Status
Taylorcraft Auster 5	Robin Helliar-Symons/Katherine Williams/Simon Wyndham-Williams	G-AJXC	TJ343	TJ343	Flyable
Taylorcraft Auster 5	Stephen Farrant	G-AKSY	TJ534	TJ534	Flyable
Taylorcraft Auster 5	Martin Nicholson	G-AKXP	NJ633	NJ633	Flyable
Taylorcraft Auster 5	Brian Vigor	G-ALBJ	TW501	TW501	Flyable
Taylorcraft Auster 5	Maurice Hammond	G-AMVD	-	TJ652'	Flyable
Taylorcraft Auster 5	Roy Ingram	G-ANIE	TW467	TW467	Flyable
Taylorcraft Auster 5	Connor Petty	G-ANRP	TW439	TW439	Flyable
Taylorcraft Auster 5	Jerome Mostyn	G-APAF	-	'TW511'	Flyable
Taylorcraft Auster 5	Paul Tyler	G-ALXZ	NJ689	NJ689	Flyable
Taylorcraft Auster 5	Gavin Rundle	G-ANIJ	TJ672	TJ672/TS-D	Restoration
Taylorcraft Auster 5	Michael Hayes	G-AKWS	RT610	RT610	Stored
Taylorcraft Auster 5	Ronald & Jennifer Cooper	G-AKPI	NJ703	'TJ207'	Stored
Taylorcraft Auster 5J1	Stephen Alexander	G-AJIH	-	'TJ518'	Flyable
Taylorcraft Auster III	John Powell-Tuck	G-AHLK	NJ889	NJ889	Flyable
Taylorcraft Auster III	Richard Webber	G-AREI	MT438	MT438	Flyable
Taylorcraft Auster III	Iestyn Leek	G-BUDL	NX534	NX534	Flyable
Taylorcraft Auster J1N	Warwick Bayman	G-AJDY	-	'MT182'	Flyable
Taylorcraft Auster J1N	Annic Marketing	G-BLPG	-	'16693' (RCAF)	Flyable
Taylorcraft Auster J5G	Arthur Boon & Christopher Towell	G-ARKG	-	'A11-301' (RAN)	Flyable
Auster D5 Husky	David Baker	G-ANHX	TW519	TW519/ROA-V	Flyable
Auster D5 Husky	Daryl Hill	G-AOCR	NJ673	NJ673	Flyable
Auster D.5 Husky	Windmill Aviation	G-AWSW	XW635	XW635	Flyable
Auster AOP.6 (Terrier)	Marcus Wills	G-ARNO	VX113	VX113/36	Flyable
Auster AOP.6 (Terrier)	Terence Dann	G-ARUI	VF571	-	Flyable
Auster AOP.6 (Terrier)	Trevor Bailey	G-ASAJ	WE569	WE569	Flyable
Auster AOP.6 (Terrier)	G-ASCH Group	G-ASCH	VF565	-	Flyable
Auster AOP.6 (Terrier)	Folland Aircraft Ltd	G-ASMZ	VF516	VF516	Flyable
Auster AOP.6 (Terrier)	Geoffrey Delmege	G-ASOI	WJ404	WJ404	Flyable
Auster AOP.6 (Terrier)	GASOM.ORG	G-ASOM	VF505	-	Flyable
Auster AOP.6 (Terrier)	Robert & Douglas McDonald	G-ASYG	VX927	VX927	Flyable
Auster AOP.6 (Terrier)	David Ockleton	G-ASZE	VF552	-	Flyable
Auster AOP.6 (Terrier)	Richard Webber	G-ASZX	WJ368	WJ368	Flyable
Auster AOP.6 (Terrier)	Trevor Jarvis	G-ATBU	VF611	-	Flyable
Auster AOP.6 (Terrier)	Susan Saggers	G-ATDN	TW641	TW641	Flyable
Auster AOP.6 (Terrier)	Kevin Hale	G-BNGE	TW536	TW536/TS-V	Flyable
Auster AOP.6 (Terrier)	Joseph Irwin	G-ATHU	WE539	-	Flyable
Auster AOP.6 (Terrier)	Terry Lee	G-AYDX	VX121	-	Flyable
Auster AOP.6 (Terrier)	David Capon	G-NTVE	VX924	-	Flyable
Auster AOP.6 (Terrier)	Gemini Flying Group	G-ARLP	VX123	-	Stored
Auster AOP.6 (Terrier)	Michael Palfreman	G-ARLR	VW996	-	Stored
Auster AOP.6 (Terrier)	Andrew Hodgkinson	G-ASAX	TW533	-	Stored
Auster AOP.6 (Terrier)	James Swallow	G-ASDK	VF631	-	Stored
Auster AOP.6 (Terrier)	Roger Burgun	G-AVYK	WJ357	-	Stored
Auster AOP.6A (Terrier)	Roger Brookhouse	G-ARHM	VF557	VF557/H	Flyable
Auster AOP.6A (Terrier)	Michael Jordon	G-ARIH	TW591	TW591/N	Flyable
Auster AOP.6A (Terrier)	John Mackie	G-ARRX	VF512	VF512/PF-M	Flyable
Auster AOP.6A (Terrier)	Stuart & Sharon Allen	G-ARXU	VF526	VF526/T	Flyable
Auster AOP.9	CW Tomkins Ltd	G-AVHT	WZ711	WZ711	Flyable
Auster AOP.9	Auster Nine Group	G-AZBU	XR246	XR246	Flyable
Auster AOP.9	Richard Webber	G-BDFH	XR240	XR240	Flyable
Auster AOP.9	Kilo Tango Group	G-BGKT	XN441	XN441	Flyable
Auster AOP.9	Ian Churm & Jeffrey Hanson	G-BJXR	XR267	XR267	Flyable
Auster AOP.9	Jeffrey Houlgrave	G-BKVK	WZ662	WZ662	Flyable
Auster AOP.9	Annic Aviation	G-BURR	WZ706	WZ706	Flyable
Auster AOP.9	Michael Bichan & Charles Wheeldon	G-CEHR	XP241	XP241	Flyable
Auster AOP.9	Historic Aircraft Flight Trust/ Army Air Corps	G-CICR	XR244	XR244	Flyable
Auster AOP.9	Andrew Thomas	G-BXON	WZ729	WZ729	Restoration
Auster AOP.9	Robert Warner	G-CIUX	WZ679	WZ679	Restoration
Auster AOP.9	Gary Siddall	G-AVXY	XK417	XK417	Stored
Auster AOP.9	Richard Webber	G-AXRR	XR241	XR241	Stored
Auster AOP.9	Clive Edwards	G-AXWA	XN437	XN437	Stored
Auster AOP.9	Terrane Auster Group	G-BGTC	XP282	XP282	Stored
Auster AOP.9	Historic Aircraft Flight Trust/ Army Air Corps	G-BUCI	XP242	XP242	Stored
Auster AOP.11	Robert Warner	G-ASCC	XP254	XP254	Flyable
Taylorcraft DF-65	Brian Robe	G-BWLJ	-	42-35870 USAAF/129	Stored
Taylorcraft DF-65	Selby Potts	G-BRIY	-	42-58678 USAAF/Y	Stored

Left: Jennifer Pothecary's Auster Plus D G-AHXE began life as HH982 but now wears the markings of 'LB312'. **Right:** Maurice Hammond's Auster 5 is actually a civilian aeroplane with no military history, but it has been painted to represent 'TJ652' complete with D-Day stripes. It is seen here being flown by Maurice's daughter Leah. *Steve Bridgewater*

Left: Auster III G-AREI flies in South East Asia Command markings and carries its original MT438 serial. **Right:** Trevor Bailey's Auster AOP.6 G-ASAJ began life as WE569 and retains its original Army Air Corps markings. *Steve Bridgewater*

Left: One of the most colourful Austers flying today is Windmill Aviation's D.5 Husky G-AWSW/XW635. **Right:** The 1955 Auster AOP.9 replaced the earlier AOP.6 and had a larger wing and a more powerful engine. The wing and tail were also metal-skinned and the fin and rudder assembly were more angular with a noticeable dorsal fillet. It had much improved take-off and landing performance and could operate from ploughed fields and muddy surfaces using low pressure tyres. XP241 now flies as G-CEHR following restoration. *Both Steve Bridgewater*

Left: The single AOP.11 was converted from AOP.9 XP254 in 1961. It shed the 173hp Blackburn Cirrus Bombardier four-cylinder inverted inline piston engine in favour of a 260hp Continental IO-470 six-cylinder horizontally opposed engine. No orders were forthcoming and in 1971 it was sold into private hands. Today it is owned by Robert Warner and flown as G-ASCC. *Steve Bridgewater* **Right:** Auster J1N G-BLPG currently flies in an RCAF scheme although it never flew with the Canadians (or any other military air arm).

30 | WARBIRD DIRECTORY

Beechcraft Expeditor

Developed from the pre-war Beech 18 civilian transport the Beechcraft C-45 Expeditor saw extensive service with air arms around the globe during World War Two. More than 4,500 saw military service, primarily as pilot, bombing, navigation and gunnery trainers.

C-45 Expeditor	Anthony Houghton	G-BKGL	1564 RCAF	'1164/64'	Flyable
C-45 Expeditor	Bristol Airways	G-BKGM	2324 RCAF	-	Flyable
C-45 Expeditor/D18S	Beech Restorations	G-BKRN	1500 RCAF	-	Restoration

Owned for many years by The Aircraft Restoration Company and Tim Darrah G-BKGL has recently been sold to Anthony Houghton. Steve Bridgewater

A familiar sight with the Harvard Display Team in the 1980s, with whom it operated in SEAC markings, the former Anthony Hutton C-45 G-BKGM now flies in a stylish civilian scheme with Bristol Airways. Steve Bridgewater

Boeing Stearman

The Boeing Model 75 Steraman was the primary trainer for the USAAF (PT-17) and US Navy (N2S) during World War Two. More than 10,500 were built and hundreds of examples remain airworthy today – including a large number in the UK where they are used for private flying, pleasure flying and airshow appearances.

Left: G-AWLO was built as 75-5563 and has previously been registered VP-KRR and 5Y-KRR. It was imported in to the UK in 1968 by Maurice Fewcott and ten years later was sold to Doug Arnold's Warbirds of Great Britain collection. In 1986 it was passed to Nigel Pickard and has been based at Little Gransden ever since. **Right:** After its military service the Stearman that would become G-BAVO was despatched to Israel where it became 4X-AIH in 1980. Seven years later it was imported to the UK as G-BAVO by Keenair Services. In 1989 it was sold to Anthony Hodgson and it then passed through various owners before it was acquired by actor Martin Shaw in 2001. Between 2011 and 2017 it was owned by Rory McCarthy but was recently acquired by Thomas Gibert.

Stearman 41-7976 was taken on charge by the USAAF in 1941 and the aircraft served until the end of the war when it became N49291. In 1967 it was involved in a ground-loop that resulted in substantial damage and in 1987 the wreck was imported into the UK by AJD Engineering and registered G-BNIW. In 1997 it was registered to Richard Goold and has been based at Nottingham East Midlands Airport ever since.

Steve Bridgewater

Robert Horne's Golden Apple Trust is perhaps best known for operating F-86 Sabre G-SABR for many years but it has also operated Stearman G-RJAH since 1990. The aircraft was taken on charge by the USAAF in 1943 as 42-15852 and later joined the Royal Canadian Air Force as FJ991. Post war it flew as N75957 before it was imported to the UK.

WARBIRD DIRECTORY | 31

Stearman	James Mann	G-AROY	42-16612	-	Flyable
Stearman	Nigel Pickard	G-AWLO	42-109351	-	Flyable
Stearman	Anthony Poulsom	G-AZLE	BuNo 43449	102 USN	Flyable
Stearman	Thomas Gilbert	G-BAVO	-	26 USAAC	Flyable
Stearman	Vic Norman	G-BIXN	41-8689	'FJ777 RCAF'	Flyable
Stearman	Richard Goold	G-BNIW	41-7967	-	Flyable
Stearman	Robert McDonald	G-BRUJ	42-16136	205 USN/6136	Flyable
Stearman	Leslie Scattergood	G-BSDS	38-0470	118 USAAC	Flyable
Stearman	David Jack	G-BSWC	42-17397	112 USAAC	Flyable
Stearman	TG Aviation Ltd	G-BTFG	BuNo 30010	441 USN	Flyable
Stearman	Skymax (Aviation) Ltd	G-CCXA	BuNo 37869	669 USAAC	Flyable
Stearman	Christopher Walker	G-CCXB	BuNo 38233	699 USAAC	Flyable
Stearman	Mike dentith	G-CGPY	BuNo 61181	671 USN/VN2S-5	Flyable
Stearman	Richard King (Portugal)	G-CIJN	BuNo 61042	317 USAAC	Flyable
Stearman	Skymax (Aviation) Ltd	G-CIOC	BuNo 55724	-	Flyable
Stearman	Retro Track & Air	G-CIPE	42-17152	-	Restoration
Stearman	Richard Leigh	G-CJIN	42-16663	-	Restoration
Stearman	Thomas Gilbert	G-CJYK	BuNo 4304	-	Restoration
Stearman	Thomas Harris	G-EDMK	42-17313	-	Restoration
Stearman	Stearman G-IIIG Group	G-IIIG	42-16191	309 USAAC	Flyable
Stearman	AeroSuperBatics Ltd	G-IIIY	BuNo 30054	-	Flyable
Stearman	Astor Anstalt (Liechtenstein)	G-ILLE	42-16865	379 USAAC	Flyable
Stearman	David Jones	G-ISDN	BuNo 03486	'14 USAAC'	Flyable
Stearman	G-KAYD Flying Group	G-KAYD	42-16338	31 USAAC	Restoration
Stearman	Rob Davies	G-NZSS	BuNo 43517	227 USN/43517	Flyable
Stearman	Peter Smith	G-OBEE	BuNo 3397	174 USN/3397	Flyable
Stearman	Mach Eight 3 Ltd	G-PTBA	37-0089	466 USAAC/3789	Flyable
Stearman	Robert Horne	G-RJAH	42-15852/FK991	44 USAAC	Flyable
Stearman	Eastern Stearman	N10053	BuNo 55749	286 USN	Flyable
Stearman	Eastern Stearman	N1325M	BuNo 43390	-	Stored
Stearman	Tranzair Inc	N1364V	BuNo 43578	578 USAAC	Flyable
Stearman	Private Owner	N1544M	BuNo 38438	-	Restoration
Stearman	Eastern Stearman	N1731B	42-17553	716 USAAC	Flyable
Stearman	Black Barn Aviation	N38940	41-8263	822 USAAC	Flyable
Stearman	Eastern Stearman	N3922B	42-17642	805 USAAC	Flyable
Stearman	Vintage Aeroplane Collection	N43YP	42-17855	443 USAAC	Flyable
Stearman	Private Owner	N4596N	42-17782	'US Mail'	Flyable
Stearman	Hardwick Warbirds	N4712V	42-16931	104 USAAC	Flyable
Stearman	Merkel Air Inc Operated by AeroSuperBatics Ltd	N5057V	42-17435	-	Flyable
Stearman	Eastern Stearman	N5345N	42-17555	718 USAAC	Flyable
Stearman	3G Classic Aviation Inc	N56200	BuNo 38192	-	Flyable
Stearman	Eastern Stearman	N60320	41-0823	164 USAAC	Flyable
Stearman	Aviator Flying Museum	N62658	42-16107	107 USAAC	Flyable
Stearman	Ian Stockwell	N63590	BuNo 07539	143 USN	Flyable
Stearman	Eastern Stearman	N65200	42-15628/FJ767	-	Flyable
Stearman	Private Owner	N65565	BuNo 7859	-	Restoration
Stearman	Private Owner	N66576	41-8559	-	Restoration
Stearman	Eastern Stearman	N68427	BuNo 55771	427 USN	Flyable
Stearman	Merkel Air Inc/AeroSuperBatics Ltd	N707TJ	BuNo 3173	-	Flyable
Stearman	Merkel Air Inc/AeroSuperBatics Ltd	N74189	41-0957	-	Flyable
Stearman	Eastern Stearman	N74650	BuNo 7874	586 USAAC	Flyable
Stearman	Private Owner	N74677	BuNo 38254	131 USAAC	Flyable
Stearman	Private Owner	N75TQ	BuNo 3403	180 USN	Flyable
Stearman	Operated by AeroSuperBatics Ltd	SE-BOG	BuNo 7524	-	Flyable
Stearman	Private Owner	XB-RIY	BuNo 07671	-	Stored

Bücker Bü 131 Jungmann

German-born Carl Bücker moved to Sweden after the Great War where he became managing director of Svenska Aero AB. He later returned to Germany with Swedish designer Anders Andersson and formed Bücker Flugzeugbau in 1932. Their first aeroplane was the Bü 131 Jungmann (Young Man) which served as a primary trainer with the Luftwaffe. Although ex-Luftwaffe examples are a rarity these days Spanish (CASA) and Swiss-built Bücker examples were sold off by their governments in the 1970s and many found their way onto the UK civil register where they are prized as very capable aerobatic mounts.

Left: This Spanish built CASA 1-131E Jungmann served the Spanish AF as E3B-504 before being imported into the UK by Spencer Flack in 1976 as G-BEDA. **Right:** Despite its ageing looks G-BSAJ was not actually built for the Spanish AF until 1954. It flew with the Ejercito de Aire as E3B-209 and in 1990 was sold to Richard Parker, who registered it G-BSAJ. In 1991 it was acquired by Pete Kynsey and it is a familiar sight at British airshows flown by either Pete himself or Anna Walker. Both Steve Bridgewater

Type	Owner	Reg	Serial	Previous ID	Status
Bü 131B Jungmann (Replica)	Christopher Maher	G-EMJA	-	-	Flyable
Bü 131B Jungmann (Aero C-104)	Artemis Aviation Group LLC	N131LE	-	-	Flyable
CASA 1-131-E3B Jungmann	Pete Kynsey	G-BSAJ	E3B-209	-	Flyable
CASA 1-131-E3B Jungmann	Robert Fleming	G-TAFF	E3B-114	-	Flyable
CASA 1-131E Jungmann	Alpha 57 Group	G-BECT	E3B-338	'A-57' (Swiss AF)	Flyable
CASA 1-131E Jungmann	Lynne Atkin	G-BEDA	E3B-504	-	Flyable
CASA 1-131E Jungmann	G-BJAL Group	G-BJAL	E3B-114	-	Flyable
CASA 1-131E Jungmann	Edward Parkin	G-BPTS	E3B-153	E3B-153 (Spanish AF)	Flyable
CASA 1-131E Jungmann	Michael Warden (Switzerland)	G-BSLH	E3B-622	-	Flyable
CASA 1-131E Jungmann	Cirrus Aircraft UK Ltd	G-BTDT	E3B-505	-	Flyable
CASA 1-131E Jungmann	Richard & Michael Pickin	G-BTDZ	E3B-524	-	Flyable
CASA 1-131E Jungmann	Roy Crossland	G-BUCC	E3B-109	BU+CC (Luftwaffe)	Flyable
CASA 1-131E Jungmann	Miklos Voest (Netherlands)	G-BUOR	E3B-508	-	Flyable
CASA 1-131E Jungmann	Wilhelmina Van Egmond (Netherlands)	G-BUVN	E3B-487	BI005 (RNLAF)	Flyable
CASA 1-131E Jungmann	Bucker Group (ROI)	G-BVPD	E3B-482	-	Flyable
CASA 1-131E Jungmann	John Hopkins	G-BWHP	E3B-513	S4-A07 (Luftwaffe)	Flyable
CASA 1-131E Jungmann	Roy Crosland	G-BYIJ	E3B-514	-	Flyable
CASA 1-131E Jungmann	Robert Cumming	G-BZJV	E3B-367	NM+AA (Luftwaffe)	Flyable
CASA 1-131E Jungmann	Peter Gaskell	G-CDJU	E3B-379	CX+HI (Luftwaffe)	Flyable
CASA 1-131E Jungmann	Roland Loder	G-CDLC	E3B-494	E3B-494 (Spanish AF)	Flyable
CASA 1-131E Jungmann	Peter Cunniff	G-CDRU	E3B-530	-	Flyable
CASA 1-131E Jungmann	Gavin Hunter & Tim Rayner	G-CGTX	E3B-599	E3B-599 (Spanish AF)	Flyable
CASA 1-131E Jungmann	John Sykes	G-CHII	E3B-174	-	Flyable
CASA 1-131E Jungmann	Edward Howard	G-EHBJ	E3B-550	-	Flyable
CASA 1-131E Jungmann	Peter Scandrett	G-JGMN	E3B-407	-	Flyable
CASA 1-131E Jungmann	John & Jennefer Whicher	G-JWJW	E3B-419	-	Flyable
CASA 1-131E Jungmann	Geoffrey Lynch	G-WJCM	E3B-449	-	Flyable
Bü 131B Jungmann	Private Owner	N102L	A77 Swiss AF	-	Restoration
CASA 1-131-E3B Jungmann	Hugh Taylor	G-BHSL	E3B-236	-	Restoration
CASA 1-131-E3B Jungmann	Brian Charters	G-JMNN	E3B-335	-	Restoration
CASA 1-131E Jungmann	Jungmann Flying Group	G-BUCK	E3B-322	-	Restoration
CASA 1-131E Jungmann	Robert Fleming	G-CIUE	E3B-471	'A-44' (Swiss AF)	Restoration
CASA 1-131E Jungmann	Ian Underwood	G-EHDS	E3B-131	-	Restoration
CASA 1-131E Jungmann	Chris Rampton	G-BECW	E3B-423	'A-10' (Swiss AF)	Stored
CASA 1-131E Jungmann	Annabelle Burroughes	G-BHPL	E3B-350	E3B-350 (Spanish AF)	Stored
CASA 1-131E Jungmann	Desmon Watt	G-BIRI	E3B-113	-	Stored
CASA 1-131E Jungmann	James Haslam	G-BPDM	E3B-369	E3B-369 (Spanish AF)	Stored
CASA 1-131E Jungmann	Cyrille & Jan-Willem Labeij	G-BPVW	E3B-559	-	Stored
CASA 1-131E Jungmann	John Sykes	G-JUNG	E3B-143	E3B-143 (Spanish AF)	Stored
CASA 1-131E Jungmann	Shuttleworth Trust	G-RETA	E3B-305	CD+EG (Luftwaffe)	Stored
CASA 1-131E Jungmann	Christopher Willoughby	G-WIBS	E3B-401	-	Stored

◀ CASA-built Jungmann G-BTDT began life as E3B-505 in 1957 and in 1991 it was sold to Trevor Reed. In 2014 it was sold to Cirrus Aircraft UK Ltd and now flies in an immaculate cream scheme. Steve Bridgewater

▶ Such is the demand for Jungmanns that G-EMJA was built up from spare parts in 1995 – thus increasing the total production number, even though it is technically registered as a 'replica'. Steve Bridgewater

WARBIRD DIRECTORY | 33

IN FOCUS ▶ Boeing N2S Stearman G-IIIY/BuNo 30054

The first sponsor's logo to appear on N54922 was that of Yugo Cars. The aeroplane is seen here in 1988 with Helen Tempest atop the wing and Vic Norman at the controls.

Built by Boeing as an N2S-4 Stearman, BuNo 30054 was delivered to the US Navy in 1944. At the end of World War Two it was placed into storage and it would be 1977 before it finally entered the civilian world. Registered as N54922 it was converted to crop dusting configuration with 450hp Pratt & Whitney R-985 Wasp Junior engine and it was used as a working aeroplane until it arrived in the UK in 1987. Vic Norman's AeroSuperBatics converted the aeroplane with a wing-walking rig and it was the first of many Stearmans to be operated by the company. In October 2015 the aircraft was finally placed on the UK civil register as G-IIIY and continues to operate from AeroSuperBatics base at Rendcomb.

34 | WARBIRD DIRECTORY

From 1989 sponsorship changed to Cadbury's Crunchie and N54922 was one of a pair of Stearmans repainted into new markings to form the Crunchie Flying Circus. The scheme changed a number of times over the coming years.

Above left: From the mid-1990s N54922 and her teammates were repainted into the markings of yet another sponsor – Utterly Butterly spread.

Above right: From 2007, cosmetics company Guinot sponsored the AeroSuperBatics team and although N54922 rarely displayed in Guinot colours – normally being used for corporate work on behalf of the sponsor instead – it is seen here leading a formation at the 2008 Flying Legends Airshow at Duxford.

◄ In 2015 N54922 was re-registered as G-IIIY and gained a flamboyant flying circus style colour scheme.
Emily Guilding/AeroSuperBatics Ltd

Bücker Bü 133 Jungmeister

The Bü 133 Jungmeister (Young Master) was a single-seat advanced trainer development of the two-seat Jungmann. It was first flown in 1935 by Luise Hoffmann (the first female works pilot in Germany) and proved to be a very capable aerobatic aeroplane. The radial-powered Bü 133C chalked up many victories in international aerobatic competitions during the 1930s and the type remained competitive well into the 1960s. More than 50 were manufactured under licence by Dornier for the Swiss Air Force (which kept it in service until 1968) and a similar number were built for the Spanish Air Force by CASA as the CASA 1-133. The UK survivors come from those sources.

Bü 133C Jungmeister	Personal Plane Services	G-BVGP	U-95	U-95 (Swiss AF)	Flyable
CASA 133C Jungmeister	Stephen Stead	G-BUTX	ES.1-4	-	Flyable
CASA 1-133 Jungmeister	Robert Cumming	G-CIJV	ES-1-16	'LG+01' (Luftwaffe)	Flyable
Bü 133C Jungmeister	James McEntee	G-BUKK	U-80	U-80 (Swiss AF)	Restoration
Bü 133C Jungmeister	Trevor Reeve & Matthew Pettit	G-PTDP	TBC	-	Restoration
CASA 1-133 Jungmeister	Brian Charters	G-MEIS	ES-1-36	-	Restoration
CASA 1-133 Jungmeister	Anthony Smith	G-RPAX	ES-1-31	-	Restoration

Left: Former Spanish AF Jungmeister G-BUTX is now owned by Stephen Stead (who also owns Spitfire XVI TE184) and is based at Biggin Hill. **Right:** Although it wears Luftwaffe markings as LG+01 Jungmeister G-CIJV is actually an ex-Spanish AF example. It is seen here in formation with ex-Spanish Jungmann G-CDJU, which is marked as CX+HI despite really being E.3B-37. Both Steve Bridgewater

Bücker Bü 181 Bestmann

The Bücker Bü 181 was named Bestmann after a German maritime term designating a member of the deck crew on coastal vessels. The prototype made its maiden flight in February 1939 with Bücker Chief Pilot Arthur Benitz at the controls. After flight testing by the Reichsluftfahrtministerium (RLM) the Bü 181 was nominated to be the standard primary trainer for the Luftwaffe and the first of 3,400 was built in 1940. The type was also licence built in Czechoslovakia by Zlin as the Z.281 and in Sweden as the Sk.25. In turn the Zlin was built under licence in Egypt in the 1950s as the Heliopolis Gomhouria (meaning 'Republic').

The most famous flying Bestmann in the UK is Will Greenwood's G-TPWX, an aircraft that began life as an Egyptian built Gomhouria and passed through the ownership of Glenn Lacey and Peter Holloway before being acquired by Will in 2011.

Steve Bridgewater

Bü 181 Bestmann (Kader Gomhouria 181)	Anthony Brier	G-CGEV	-	'CG+EV' (Luftwaffe)	Flyable
Bü 181 Bestmann (Kader Gomhouria 181)	Will Greenwood	G-TPWX	-	'TP+WX' (Luftwaffe)	Flyable
Bü 181 Bestmann	Antony Whitehead	G-CIEZ	-	-	Restoration
Bü 181 Bestmann	William & Graeme Snadden	G-CBKB	-	-	Restoration

Culver Cadet

In 1940 the Cadet was selected by the USAAC as a radio-controlled target that could also be flown as a manned aircraft when needed. More than 600 were built before the end of the war and several survive today as private aeroplanes. The UK-based example has not flown since it was involved in a landing accident in 2010 but remains on the civil register.

Cadet	John Gregson	G-CDET	c/n 129	Restoration

de Havilland DH.82 Tiger Moth

First flown in October 1931 the Tiger Moth was operated by the RAF and many other air arms as a primary trainer. It was also used for maritime surveillance, defensive anti-invasion preparations and some were even outfitted to function as armed light bombers. The type remained in RAF service until it was replaced by the Chipmunk during the early 1950s – at which point many of the military surplus aircraft entered civil hands. Today more than 120 UK registered 'Tiggies' remain airworthy alone. Those listed here include aircraft built for the military and civilian aircraft impressed into RAF use during the war.

Type	Owner	Registration	Serial	Markings	Status
DH.82A Tiger Moth	Ronald & Jennider Cooper	G-ACDJ	BB729 (Impressed)	-	Stored
DH.82A Tiger Moth	Jonathan Turnbull	G-ACDA	BB724 (Impressed)	-	Flyable
DH.82A Tiger Moth	The Tiger Club (1990) Ltd	G-ACDC	BB726 (Impressed)	-	Flyable
DH.82A Tiger Moth	Doublecube Aviation Ltd	G-ACDI	BB742 (Impressed)	-	Flyable
DH.82A Tiger Moth	Michael Bonnick	G-ACMD	33-2 (Spanish AF)	-	Flyable
DH.82A Tiger Moth	Finest Hour Warbirds Ltd	G-ADGT	BB697 (Impressed)	BB697	Flyable
DH.82A Tiger Moth	Mikel van der Straaten & Martinus van Dijk (Netherlands)	G-ADGV	BB694 (Impressed)	-	Flyable
DH.82A Tiger Moth	Stuart Beaty	G-ADIA	BB747 (Impressed)	-	Flyable
DH.82A Tiger Moth	Jonathan Preston	G-ADJJ	BB819 (Impressed)	-	Flyable
DH.82A Tiger Moth	David Wall	G-ADNZ	DE673	DE673	Flyable
DH.82A Tiger Moth	Paul & Sarah Ford	G-ADPC	BB852 (Impressed)	-	Flyable
DH.82A Tiger Moth	Kevin Crumplin	G-ADWJ	BB803 (Impressed)	BB803	Flyable
DH.82A Tiger Moth	DH Heritage Flights Ltd	G-ADXT	BB860 (Impressed)	-	Flyable
DH.82A Tiger Moth	Malcolm Paul	G-AFGZ	BB759 (Impressed)	-	Flyable
DH.82A Tiger Moth	Paul Harvey	G-AFWI	BB814 (Impressed)	-	Flyable
DH.82A Tiger Moth	Norman Aircraft Trust	G-AGEG	R4769	-	Flyable
DH.82A Tiger Moth	G-AGHY Group	G-AGHY	N9181	-	Flyable
DH.82A Tiger Moth	Sheila Firth	G-AGYU	DE208	DE208	Flyable
DH.82A Tiger Moth	Tiger Associates Ltd	G-AHAN	PG644	-	Flyable
DH.82A Tiger Moth	CFG Flying Ltd	G-AHIZ	PG624	-	Flyable
DH.82A Tiger Moth	Martin Waring	G-AHLT	N9128	-	Flyable
DH.82A Tiger Moth	Jeffrey Milsom	G-AHOO	EM967	-	Flyable
DH.82A Tiger Moth	Nicholas Wareing	G-AHPZ	T7280	-	Flyable
DH.82A Tiger Moth	Eaglescott Tiger Moth Group	G-AHUF	NL750	'T7997'	Flyable
DH.82A Tiger Moth	Andrew Gordon	G-AHUV	N6593	-	Flyable
DH.82A Tiger Moth	Andrew Barton	G-AHVU	T6313	T6313	Flyable
DH.82A Tiger Moth	Margaret Arter	G-AHVV	EM929	-	Flyable
DH.82A Tiger Moth	Keith Pogmore & Terence Dann	G-AIDS	T6055	-	Flyable
DH.82A Tiger Moth	David Green	G-AIXJ	DE426	-	Flyable
DH.82A Tiger Moth	Flying Wires (Netherlands)	G-AJHS	N6866	-	Flyable
DH.82A Tiger Moth	Ron Gammons	G-AJVE	DE943	-	Flyable
DH.82A Tiger Moth	Francis Curry	G-ALIW	R5006	-	Flyable
DH.82A Tiger Moth	Sarah Ford	G-ALNA	T6774	-	Flyable
DH.82A Tiger Moth	Tiger Moth Experience Ltd	G-ALUC	R5219	-	Flyable
DH.82A Tiger Moth	James Norris	G-ALWS	N9328	N9328/69	Flyable
DH.82A Tiger Moth	David Findon	G-ALWW	NL923	-	Flyable
DH.82A Tiger Moth	Mark Masters	G-AMCK	T6193	-	Flyable
DH.82A Tiger Moth	Anthony West	G-AMHF	R5144	-	Flyable
DH.82A Tiger Moth	Ian Perry	G-AMNN	NM137	-	Flyable
DH.82A Tiger Moth	Hamish Monro	G-AMTF	T7842	T7842	Flyable
DH.82A Tiger Moth	Edward Scurr	G-AMTV	N6545	-	Flyable
DH.82A Tiger Moth	Clive Edwards & Elizabeth Higgins	G-ANCS	R4907	-	Flyable
DH.82A Tiger Moth	Nicholas Stagg	G-ANDM	N6642	-	Flyable
DH.82A Tiger Moth	Anthony Diver	G-ANDP	R4950	-	Flyable
DH.82A Tiger Moth	Graham Wells	G-ANEH	N6797	N6797	Flyable
DH.82A Tiger Moth	Totalsure Ltd (Netherlands)	G-ANEL	N9238	-	Flyable
DH.82A Tiger Moth	Peter Benest	G-ANEM	R5052	-	Flyable
DH.82A Tiger Moth	G-ANEN Group	G-ANEN	DE410	-	Flyable
DH.82A Tiger Moth	Kevin Crumplin	G-ANEW	NM138	NM138/41	Flyable
DH.82A Tiger Moth	Christoper Bland	G-ANEZ	T7849	-	Flyable
DH.82A Tiger Moth	Geoffrey Graham	G-ANFI	DE623	DE623	Flyable
DH.82A Tiger Moth	Felthorpe Tiger Group Ltd	G-ANFL	T6169	-	Flyable
DH.82A Tiger Moth	Reading Flying Group	G-ANFM	T5888	-	Flyable
DH.82A Tiger Moth	Richard Santus (Czech Republic)	G-ANFP	N5903	N5903/39	Flyable
DH.82A Tiger Moth	Thomas Jackson	G-ANHK	N9372	-	Flyable
DH.82A Tiger Moth	David Lewis	G-ANJD	T6226	-	Flyable
DH.82A Tiger Moth	Shuttleworth Trust	G-ANKT	T6818	'K2585'	Flyable
DH.82A Tiger Moth	G-ANKZ Tiger Moth Group	G-ANKZ	N6466	N6466	Flyable
DH.82A Tiger Moth	Kenneth Peters	G-ANLD	EM773	-	Flyable
DH.82A Tiger Moth	Paul Gliddon	G-ANLS	DF113	-	Flyable
DH.82A Tiger Moth	Keith Perkins/Aero Legends	G-ANMO	K4259	K4259/71	Flyable
DH.82A Tiger Moth	Andrew & Mark Baxter	G-ANMY	DE470	DE470/16	Flyable
DH.82A Tiger Moth	Doublecube Aviation LLP	G-ANNG	DE524	-	Flyable
DH.82A Tiger Moth	Clive, Oliver & Mark Ponsford	G-ANNI	T6953	T6953	Flyable
DH.82A Tiger Moth	John Kaye	G-ANNK	T7290	T7290	Flyable
DH.82A Tiger Moth	Penelope Watson	G-ANOD	T6121	-	Flyable

Type	Owner	Registration	Serial	Markings	Status
DH.82A Tiger Moth	Nicholas Parkhouse	G-ANOH	EM838	-	Flyable
DH.82A Tiger Moth	William Pitts	G-ANOM	NL6837	-	Flyable
DH.82A Tiger Moth	Mark Kelly	G-ANON	T7909	T7909	Flyable
DH.82A Tiger Moth	Christopher Cyster	G-ANRF	T5850	-	Flyable
DH.82A Tiger Moth	Spectrum Leisure Ltd	G-ANRM	DF112	DF112	Flyable
DH.82A Tiger Moth	Douglas Aviation	G-ANSM	R5014	-	Flyable
DH.82A Tiger Moth	G-ANTE Flyers Ltd	G-ANTE	T6562	-	Flyable
DH.82A Tiger Moth	Trevor Butcher	G-ANZZ	DE974	DE974	Flyable
DH.82A Tiger Moth	David Ross Flying Group	G-AOBX	T7187	-	Flyable
DH.82A Tiger Moth	Richard Harrowven	G-AODT	R5250	-	Flyable
DH.82A Tiger Moth	CFG Flying Ltd	G-AOEI	N6946	-	Flyable
DH.82A Tiger Moth	Rupert Clark	G-AOGR	XL714	XL714	Flyable
DH.82A Tiger Moth	Stephen Turley	G-AOHY	N6537	N6537	Flyable
DH.82A Tiger Moth	Roger Brookhouse	G-AOIM	T7109	T7109	Flyable
DH.82A Tiger Moth	Robert Moore & Briony Floodgate	G-AOIS	R5172	R5172/FIJE	Flyable
DH.82A Tiger Moth	JJ Flying Group	G-AOJJ	DF128	DF128/RCO-U	Flyable
DH.82A Tiger Moth	Peter Green	G-AOJK	R4896	-	Flyable
DH.82A Tiger Moth	Mark Blois-Brooke	G-AOZH	NM129	'K2572'	Flyable
DH.82A Tiger Moth	Philip Shotbolt	G-APAL	N6847	N6847	Flyable
DH.82A Tiger Moth	Myth Group	G-APAM	N6580	-	Flyable
DH.82A Tiger Moth	Howard Maguire	G-APAO	R4922	R4922	Flyable
DH.82A Tiger Moth	Tiger Leasing Ltd	G-APAP	R5136	R5136	Flyable
DH.82A Tiger Moth	Laurence Rice	G-APCC	PG640	-	Flyable
DH.82A Tiger Moth	Colin Hamilton	G-APFU	EM879	-	Flyable
DH.82A Tiger Moth	Klaus Stewering (Germany)	G-APIH	R5086	-	Flyable
DH.82A Tiger Moth	Mike Vaisey	G-APLU	T6825	-	Flyable
DH.82A Tiger Moth	Foley Farm Flying Group	G-APMX	DE715	-	Flyable
DH.82A Tiger Moth	David Porter	G-ARAZ	R4959	R4949/59	Flyable
DH.82A Tiger Moth	Alex Hastings & Alex Mustard	G-AREH	DE241	-	Flyable
DH.82A Tiger Moth	Fiona Clacherty	G-ARTL	T7281	T7281	Flyable
DH.82A Tiger Moth	Richard Menage	G-ASPV	T7794	T7794	Flyable
DH.82A Tiger Moth	Cathy Silk	G-AVPJ	NL879	-	Flyable
DH.82A Tiger Moth	Duxford Consulting Ltd	G-AXAN	EM720	EM720	Flyable
DH.82A Tiger Moth	G-AXBW Ltd	G-AXBW	T5879	T5879/RUC-W	Flyable
DH.82A Tiger Moth	Fly Tiger Moth Ltd	G-AXXV	DE992	DE992	Flyable
DH.82A Tiger Moth	Edward & George Woods	G-AYDI	DF174	-	Flyable
DH.82A Tiger Moth	Richard King	G-AZGZ	NM181	NM181	Flyable
DH.82A Tiger Moth	Stuart McKay	G-AZZZ	NL864	-	Flyable
DH.82A Tiger Moth	Boultbee Vintage LLP	G-BAFG	EM778	-	Flyable
DH.82A Tiger Moth	Henry Labouchere	G-BEWN	A17-529 (RAAF)	-	Flyable
DH.82A Tiger Moth	Stephen Towers	G-BHUM	DE457	-	Flyable
DH.82A Tiger Moth	Keith Knight	G-BJAP	-	'K2587'	Flyable
DH.82A Tiger Moth	John Smith & Jeffrey Hodgson	G-BPAJ	T7807	-	Flyable
DH.82A Tiger Moth	A17-48 Group	G-BPHR	A17-48 (RAAF)	A17-48	Flyable
DH.82A Tiger Moth	Nicola Mackaness	G-BWVT	A17-604 (RAAF)	-	Flyable
DH.82A Tiger Moth	Donald Sargant	G-BYLB	T5595	-	Flyable
DH.82A Tiger Moth	Tiger Leasing Company Ltd	G-BYTN	N6720	N6720/VX	Flyable
DH.82A Tiger Moth	Stephen Deane	G-CFII	HU-726 (Indian AF)	-	Flyable
DH.82A Tiger Moth	Mark Johnson	G-DHZF	N9192	N9192/RCO-N	Flyable
DH.82A Tiger Moth	Nicholas Wilson	G-ECDS	NL904	-	Flyable
DH.82A Tiger Moth	The GEMSY Group	G-EMSY	T7356	-	Flyable
DH.82A Tiger Moth	Willem Gerdes	G-ERDS	T6741	-	Flyable
DH.82A Tiger Moth	Paul Szluha	G-MOTH	DE306	'K2567'	Flyable
DH.82A Tiger Moth	Stephen Philpott & Christine Stopher	G-OOSY	DE971	DE971	Flyable
DH.82A Tiger Moth	Derek Leatherhead	G-TIGA	T7120	-	Flyable
DH.82A Tiger Moth	Southern Aircraft Consultancy Inc	N3549	PG645	'N3549'	Flyable
DH.82A Tiger Moth	David Shew	G-ALBD	T7748	-	Restoration
DH.82A Tiger Moth	Thomas Kinnaird	G-ALJL	T6311	-	Restoration
DH.82A Tiger Moth	David Shew	G-ALND	N9191	-	Restoration
DH.82A Tiger Moth	Jan Cooper	G-AMCM	DE249	-	Restoration
DH.82A Tiger Moth	David Shew	G-ANBZ	DE680	-	Restoration
DH.82A Tiger Moth	Keith Perkins/Aero Legends	G-ANDE	EM726	EM726/FY	Restoration
DH.82A Tiger Moth	Andrew Barton	G-ANHI	R5120	-	Restoration
DH.82A Tiger Moth	Andrew Hodgkinson	G-ANJA	N9389	N9389	Restoration
DH.82A Tiger Moth	Howard Haines	G-ANJK	T6066	-	Restoration
DH.82A Tiger Moth	Halfpenny Green Tiger Group	G-ANKK	T5854	T5854	Restoration
DH.82A Tiger Moth	Andrew Hodgkinson	G-AOBJ	DE970	-	Restoration
DH.82A Tiger Moth	David Shew	G-AOFR	NL913	-	Restoration
DH.82A Tiger Moth	Matthew Boddington	G-APVT	K4254	-	Restoration
DH.82A Tiger Moth	Brian Mills	G-AZDY	PG650	-	Restoration
DH.82A Tiger Moth	Howard Haines	G-BWIK	NL985	-	Restoration
DH.82A Tiger Moth	Kevin Crumplin	G-BWMK	T8191	T8191	Restoration
DH.82C Tiger Moth	Anthony Palmer	G-FCTK	5084 (RCAF)	5085 (RCAF)	Restoration
DH.82A Tiger Moth	Percy, Andrew & Peter Borsberry	G-AGNJ	SAAF 2366	-	Stored
DH.82A Tiger Moth	Trevor Butcher	G-AGPK	PG657	PG657	Stored
DH.82A Tiger Moth	Malcolm Jordan	G-AGZZ	A17-503 (RAAF)	-	Stored

DH.82A Tiger Moth	Peter & Jean Johnson	G-AIRK	N9241	-	Stored
DH.82A Tiger Moth	John Barker	G-AJTW	N6965	-	Stored
DH.82A Tiger Moth	Glen & John Eagles	G-AKXS	T7105	-	Stored
DH.82A Tiger Moth	John Eagles	G-AMBB	T6801	-	Stored
DH.82A Tiger Moth	Mike Vaisey & Stuart McKay	G-AMTK	N6709	-	Stored
DH.82A Tiger Moth	David Shew	G-AMVS	R4852	-	Stored
DH.82A Tiger Moth	Eric Lison (Belgium)	G-ANCX	T7229	-	Stored
DH.82A Tiger Moth	Jennifer Cooper	G-ANKV	T7792	-	Stored
DH.82A Tiger Moth	Ronald Packman	G-ANOO	DE401	-	Stored
DH.82A Tiger Moth	Trevor Butcher	G-ANPE	T7397	-	Stored
DH.82A Tiger Moth	Andrew Hodgkinson	G-ANPK	L6936	-	Stored
DH.82A Tiger Moth	Roger Brookhouse	G-AOAA	DF159	-	Stored
DH.82A Tiger Moth	Paul Nutley	G-AOBH	T7997	'NL750'	Stored
DH.82A Tiger Moth	G-AODR Group	G-AODR	NL779	-	Stored
DH.82A Tiger Moth	Paul & Sarah Ford	G-AOES	T6056	-	Stored
DH.82A Tiger Moth	Techair London Ltd	G-AOET	DE720	-	Stored
DH.82A Tiger Moth	William Taylor	G-AOGI	DF186	-	Stored
DH.82A Tiger Moth	Simon Darch	G-AOXN	EM727	-	Stored
DH.82A Tiger Moth	Christoper Zeal	G-APBI	EM903	-	Stored
DH.82A Tiger Moth	The Tiger Club (1990) Ltd	G-ASKP	N6588	-	Stored
DH.82A Tiger Moth	Roger Barham	G-BBRB	DF198	-	Stored
DH.82A Tiger Moth	Peter Harrison & Martin Gambrell	G-BFHH	DF197	-	Stored
DH.82A Tiger Moth	Roger Brookhouse	G-BHLT	T6697	-	Stored
DH.82A Tiger Moth	Tog Group	G-BTOG	NM192	-	Stored
DH.82A Tiger Moth	Stichting Vroege Vogels (Netherlands)	G-BWMS	R4771	-	Stored
DH.82A Tiger Moth	Daniele Dal Bon (Italy)	G-CDJO	A17-492 (RAAF)	-	Stored

Left: Tiger Moth G-ACDA was the prototype Gipsy Major powered DH82A Tiger Moth and joined the de Havilland School of Flying in 1933. It was impressed into the RAF as BB724 in 1940 and then returned to 'Civie Street' in 1945. Today it is owned by Jonathan Turnbull and based at RAF Henlow. **Right:** G-ADGT is one of the earliest surviving Tiger Moths and was first registered to Brooklands Aviation in May 1935. It was used to train RAF pilots throughout the 1930s but in 1940 it was impressed into the RAF itself and became BB697. Post War, G-ADGT was converted for use as a crop sprayer in Sudan and Norfolk until 1967. After a period of storage G-ADGT was restored for the Tiger Club but was purchased by Finest Hour Warbirds during 2014 and is now based at Bicester. *Both Steve Bridgewater*

Thruxton Jackaroo

A total of 19 ex-RAF Tiger Moths were converted into Thruxton Jackaroo between 1957 and 1960. The aircraft was designed as a general purpose biplane with an enclosed cabin and featured a widened fuselage to accommodate four occupants. Today two remain flyable in the UK with two others in store.

▶ Dennis and Tricia Neville's Jackaroo began life as Tiger Moth T7798 and is now based at RAF Henlow. It performs regularly with Captain Neville's Flying Circus.

Thruxton Jackaroo (DH.82A Mod)	Dennis & Tricia Neville	G-ANZT	T7798	Flyable
Thruxton Jackaroo (DH.82A Mod)	Keith Perkins/Aero Legends	G-AOIR	R4972	Flyable
Thruxton Jackaroo (DH.82A Mod)	Arthur Christian	G-AOEX	NM175	Stored
Thruxton Jackaroo (DH.82A Mod)	Arthur Perry	G-APAJ	T5616	Stored

de Havilland DH.82B Queen Bee

The Queen Bee was an unmanned radio-controlled target drone that used Tiger Moth wings and (for economy) a wooden fuselage based on that of the DH.60 Moth.   A total of 405 were built but just one remains flyable in 2017.

The Bee Keepers Group's Queen Bee is based at RAF Henlow and flies regularly throughout the year. It wears authentic Queen Bee colour complete with red high visibility wing tip markings. Steve Bridgewater

| DH.82B Queen Bee | The Bee Keepers Group | G-BLUZ | LF858 | LF858 | Flyable |

Fairchild Argus

The four-seat Fairchild Model 24 was a civilian light transport aircraft that found favour with the USAAC in the late 1930s as the UC-61.   The US Navy operated the type as the GK-1 and the RAF purchased it as the Argus. The majority of the 525 Warner Scarab powered examples built were delivered to the RAF under Lend Lease as the Argus I and used by the Air Transport Auxiliary as crew ferries. An additional 306 Ranger-powered Argus IIIs were also used by the ATA.

▶ **Richard Ellingworth's Argus III G-RGUS has recently been repainted into its original RAF ATA markings as KK527. It is based at Spanhoe Lodge, Northamptonshire.**
Steve Bridgewater

Argus III	Harry Mackintosh	G-BCBH	43-1501/HB737	HB737	Flyable
Argus III	Richard Ellingworth	G-RGUS	44-83184/KK527	KK527	Flyable
Argus III	Remko Sijben	G-AJPI	43-14887/HB614	314887 USAAF	Stored
Argus III	Francis Cox	G-BCBL	43-15025/HB751	HB751	Stored

Fairchild Cornell

The PT-19 served as a trainer with the USAAF and RCAF during World War Two and was used as an introductory 'pre-solo' trainer for introducing new pilots to flying before passing them on to the more agile Stearman. Two Ranger-powered PT-19s are currently flyable in the UK and a radial engined PT-23 remains in storage.

▶ **PT-19 N33870 is based at Tibenham, Norfolk and operates in a typical USAAF World War Two-era scheme.**
Steve Bridgewater

PT-19 Cornell II	CRNL Aviation Ltd	G-CRNL	FH768	'FJ662'	Flyable
PT-19 Cornell II	Aerospace Trust Management Inc	N33870	40-0237	'02538' USAAC	Flyable
PT-23	Flying Heritage Inc	N49272	42-49413	'23'	Stored

Fieseler Fi 156 Storch

The Fieseler Fi 156 Storch (Stork) was a small German liaison aircraft with incredible Short Take Off & Landing (STOL) capabilities. Although Peter Holloways's genuine example has now been sold overseas two potentially airworthy representations of the breed remain in the UK – one a French-built Morane-Saulnier MS.505 Criquet (a licence built Storch) which is currently being restored and one a semi-scale Slepcev Storch replica.

| Slepcev Storch (Replica) | Peter Clegg | G-BZOB | - | '6G+ED' | Flyable |
| MS.505 Criquet | Aero Vintage Ltd | G-BPHZ | 53 French AF | 'DM+BK' | Restoration |

40 | WARBIRD DIRECTORY

Focke-Wulf Fw 189 Uhu

The Fw 189 Uhu ('Eagle Owl') was a German twin-engine, twin-boom, three-seat tactical reconnaissance and army cooperation aircraft. It first flew in 1938 and 864 had been produced by the end of the war. Just one example survives, in the possession of Seattle, Washington-based Flying Heritage & Armour Collection. The aircraft is believed to be undergoing restoration to flying condition in the UK.

| Fw 189A-1 | Flying Heritage & Armour Collection | N189FW | WrkNr 112100 | Restoration |

Miles Magister

The 'Maggie' was a two-seat monoplane basic trainer built for the RAF and Royal Navy. Based on Miles' civilian Hawk Major and Hawk Trainer it was to be the first monoplane designed specifically as a trainer for the RAF. After the war many Magisters were converted for civilian uses and re-designated as the Hawk Trainer III, however today just four of the 1,303 Magisters built remain flyable – all of which are in the UK.

Magister (Hawk Trainer 3)	Francesco Baldanza	G-AHUJ	R1914	R1914	Flyable
Magister	Shuttleworth Trust	G-AJRS	P6382	P6382/C	Flyable
Magister (Hawk Trainer 3)	Robert Fleming	G-AKAT	T9738	T9738	Flyable
Magister (Hawk Trainer 3)	Magister PF Syndicate	G-AKPF	N3788	N3788	Flyable
Magister (Hawk Trainer 3)	Daniel Hunt	G-AIUA	T9768	T9768	Stored

Left: Magister R1914 was built in 1940 and for many years was stored with the Strathallan Collection in Scotland as G-AHUJ. In 2014 it was put up for auction and acquired by Francesco Baldanza who has had it lovingly restored and bases it at Breighton, Yorkshire. Tim Badham **Right:** The Shuttleworth Collection's Magister was built in 1939 and entered service with the RAF as P6382. However, when it was acquired in 1971 it bore the bogus civil registration 'G-AJDR'. The logbook revealed an earlier change of fuselage to that of P6382 which had never borne a civil registration so it has now been registered G-AJRS. It was restored to flying condition by Shuttleworth apprentices using components from three other examples and is now a regular flyer. Steve Bridgewater

Miles Messenger

The Messenger was designed to meet a British Army requirement for a robust, slow speed, low maintenance air observation post and liaison aircraft. Although no ex-military examples still grace UK skies a civilian example wears the markings of 'RG333', the aircraft used by Field Marshal Montgomery to fly over the D-Day beaches in June 1944.

| Messenger | Paul Beaver | G-AIEK | - | 'RG333' | Flyable |

Naval Aircraft Factory N3N

The N3N was a tandem two-seat, open cockpit, primary training biplane used by the US Navy from 1935. Production ended in January 1942 but the type remained in use through the rest of World War Two and the N3N was the last biplane in US military service when the final example was retired in 1961. Post-war, many surviving aircraft were sold onto the US civil aircraft market and one has migrated to the UK.

| Naval Aircraft Factory | N3N-3 | James Birnie | G-ONAF | 4406 4406/US Navy 12 | Flyable |

Messerschmitt Bf 108 Taifun

Designed as a high speed touring aeroplane in 1934 the Taifun (Typhoon) was adopted by the Luftwaffe as a VIP transport and liaison aircraft. Genuine German-built examples are rare these days but French licence built Nord 1002 Pingouin (Pengiun) aircraft are more common – often painted to represent the Bf 109 at airshows.

Anthony Fetherston imported Nord 1002 F-BVGX into the UK in 1965 and registered it as G-ATBG before selling it to Lindsey Walton in 1968. Lindsey painted it in Luftwaffe markings and it has been an almost constant attraction on the UK airshow scene for the last 49 years. Fitted with a smoke system the aircraft can perhaps justifiably claim to be the "most shot down" aircraft in history. Steve Bridgewater

Bf 108 (Nord 1002 Pingouin II)	Robert Fray	G-ASTG	-	'BG+KM'	Flyable
Bf 108 (Nord 1002 Pingouin II)	Ardmore Aviation Services Ltd	G-ATBG	-	'NJ+C11'	Flyable
Bf 108 (Nord 1002 Pingouin II)	108 Flying Group	G-ETME	-	'14'	Flyable
Bf 108 (Nord 1002 Pingouin II)	Simon O'Connell	G-OTME	-	-	Restoration

North American NA-64 Yale

The North American NA-64 closely resembles the later T-6 Texan/Harvard but the most noticeable difference is the fixed non-retractable undercarriage. The French ordered the type for the Armée de l'Air (200 examples) and Aéronavale (30 examples) and 111 had been delivered before France surrendered to the Germans. The remaining 119 were bought up by the British Purchasing Commission and transferred to the RCAF for the British Commonwealth Air Training Plan. The Canadians named the type the Yale and it served until 1946 when all the surviving examples were sold. Around 15 are currently in airworthy condition, including one in the UK.

▶ Rob van Dijk's Yale is the only example flying outside of North America. It served the RCAF as 3349 and has been restored into its original markings. Steve Bridgewater

NA-64 Yale	Rob van Dijk	G-BYNF	64-2171/3349	3349 RCAF	Flyable

North American T-6 Harvard/Texan/SNJ

The T-6 advanced trainer was used to teach pilots from the USAAF, US Navy, RAF and other air forces of the British Commonwealth during World War Two and went on to serve with almost every air force in the world. A total of 15,495 T-6s (of all variants) were built and hundreds remain airworthy in 2017.

Left: G-AZBN was built as an AT-16 by Noorduyn in 1943 and issued to the USAAF as 43-13132. It then joined the RAF as FT391 and the Netherlands East Indies Air Force as B-97. In the civilian world it flew as PH-HON before joining the Old Flying Machine Company at Duxford in 1990. A year later it was sold to Swaygate Ltd, which has operated it ever since. Steve Bridgewater Right: Although now Polish-owned Harvard IIB G-BBHK is still registered in the UK. It was built as 42-12540 but carries the markings of RCAF Harvard 'FH153'.

Type	Owner	Registration	Serial	Markings	Status
AT-6C	Colin Edwards	G-BICE	41-33275	'41-33275/CE'	Flyable
AT-6C	Century Aviation Ltd	G-TSIX	41-33262	'111836/JZ-6 US Navy'	Flyable
AT-6D	Peter Meyrick	G-BGOR	41-33908	'14863'	Flyable
AT-6D	Maurice Hammond	G-ELMH	42-84555	42-84555/EP-H	Flyable
AT-6D	Orion Enterprises Ltd	G-KAMY	42-85068	'8084/USAF'	Flyable
AT-6D	David Nock	G-TDJN	44-81506	'313048'	Flyable
AT-6D	Karl-Friedemann Grimminger	G-TXAN	41-33888	'51970/USN Glenview/*Finnish Fantasy*	Flyable
Harvard IIB	Swaygate Ltd	G-AZBN	43-13132	FT391	Flyable
Harvard IIB	Goodwood Road Racing Company Ltd	G-AZSC	43-13064	'43/SC' USAF	Flyable
Harvard IIB	Marcin Kubrak (Poland)	G-BBHK	42-12540	'FH153/58 RCAF'	Flyable
Harvard IIB	Black Star Aviation Ltd	G-BDAM	42-12479	'FE992'	Flyable
Harvard IIB	Patina Ltd/The Fighter Collection	G-BTXI	42-0892	'FE695/94'	Flyable
Harvard IIB	James Brown	G-CIUW	42-0708	'FE511'	Flyable
Harvard IIB	Propshop Ltd	G-CORS	KF183	KF183	Flyable
Harvard IIB	Biggin Hill Heritage Hangar	G-CTKL	3064	'FE788'	Flyable
Harvard IV	Aircraft Spares & Materials Ltd	G-BGPB	53-4619	1747/Portuguese AF/*Taz*	Flyable
Harvard IV	G-BJST Group	G-BJST	51-17110	'AJ841/*Wacky Wabbit*'	Flyable
Harvard IV	Anthony St John	G-BSBG	52-8562	28562/TA-562	Flyable
Harvard IV	Alexander Stendel (Germany)	G-BUKY	52-8543	52-8543/US Navy 66	Flyable
Harvard IV	Cirrus Aircraft UK Ltd	G-CJWE	20306	'481273/CALIF ANG'	Flyable
Harvard IV	Malcolm Paul	G-RAIX	51-17227	'KF584/RAI-X'	Flyable
Harvard IV	Rob Davies	G-TVIJ	52-8521	28521/TA-521	Flyable
SNJ-5	The Warplane Flying Company Ltd	G-CHIA	42-85501	'85061/US Navy 7F-061'	Flyable
SNJ-5	DH Heritage Flights	G-DHHF	42-85897	'72-JF/USMC'	Flyable
SNJ-7C	David Gilmour	G-BRVG	42-85895	VS-932/27 US Navy	Flyable
T-6G	Chris Bellhouse	G-BGHU	51-15042	115042/TA-042/*Carly*	Flyable
T-6G	First Air Ltd	G-BKRA	51-15227	51-15227	Flyable
T-6G	Keith Perkins/Aero Legends	G-DDMV	49-3209	49-3209/CALIF ANG	Flyable
T-6G	Boultbee Vintage LLP	G-TEXN	49-3072	3072/72 US Navy	Flyable
T-6G	Private Owner	N726KM	7726 SAAF	7726 SAAF	Flyable
AT-6D	Classic Flying Machine Collection Ltd	G-CCOY	41-33857	'FT323'	Restoration
AT-6D	Texan Restorations	G-TOMC	51-14700	-	Restoration
Harvard IIB	Steve Wilch	G-CPPM	3091	3091/AF-091 RCAF	Restoration
Harvard IV	Robert Warner & Michael Edwards	G-CHYN	1765 Portuguese AF	'BF+070'	Restoration
Harvard IV	Phil Earthey (France)	G-HRVD	53-4629	-	Restoration
T-6G	Anthony Murphy	G-BRBC	51-14470	-	Restoration
Harvard IIB	Ronald Cooper/Steven Swallow	G-BZHL	43-12859	'FT118'	Stored

Built as a Harvard IIB in 1943 G-AZSC flew with the USAAF as 43-13064, the RAF as FT323 and the Royal Netherlands Air Force as B-19. It then became PH-SKK before coming to the UK in 1972 as G-AZSC. In 1984 it was sold to pop star Gary Numan's Machine Music Ltd and was painted as a Japanese 'Zero' fighter for airshow work. In 2005 the aircraft passed to the Goodwood Road Racing Company, which has painted it in an all-over gloss black scheme.
Nigel Price

Left: Chris Bellhouse's T-6G G-BGHU was built in 1951 as 51-15042 and then delivered to the French AF as 115042. It later joined the Portuguese Aviação Naval Portuguesa as FAP1707 but was sold to the UK as G-BGHU in 1981. Chris has owned the aeroplane since 1986 and it flies as TA-042 and carries the name *Carly*. **Right:** Peter Meyrick's AT-6D G-BGOR began life as 41-33908. It flies as '14863' and is now based at Sleap airfield on the Welsh border.

Left: Taz is one of the most recognisable Harvard's in the UK. Registered to Aircraft Spares & Materials Ltd and operated by the Aircraft Restoration Company/Propshop Ltd the aircraft has previously served with the Luftwaffe as AA+050 and BF+050 as well as the Portuguese Aviação Naval Portuguesa as FAP1747, whose markings she wears today. **Right:** *Whacky Wabbit* is a familiar site at Duxford carrying out pleasure flying duties with Classic Wings. The aircraft is now painted as 'AJ841' to represent an RAF Desert Air Force Harvard that flew in the Middle East during World War Two providing currency and conversion training for pilots going on to fly the Hurricane and Spitfire in North Africa. In reality this is a Harvard built in Canada and sent to the Italian Air Force (as MM53795) as part of the Mutual Assistance Program. Both Steve Bridgewater

Left: The Fighter Collection's Harvard was built for the Canadian Air Force in 1942 and allocated the RAF serial FE695 as part of the Empire Air Training Scheme. FE695 was struck off charge by the RCAF in June 1947 and following refurbishment was transferred to the Swedish Air Force as Fv16105. In March 1972 she was retired and given to a Technical School as an instructional airframe but joined TFC in 1991. FE695 flew again in May 1996 and wears the colours she wore during the latter war years in Canada. Steve Bridgewater **Right:** G-BUKY now resides in Germany but is maintained on the UK civil register. It was built in 1952 as 52-8543 and then transferred to the Luftwaffe as AA+063 (later BF+063) before joining the Forca Aerea Portuguesa as FAP 1766. In 1992 it arrived in the UK as G-BUKY and passed through various owners before departing to Germany in 2016. Steve Bridgewater

Left: North American SNJ-5 G-CHIA is now operated by the Warplane Flying Company Ltd and carries its original markings as 85061/US Navy 7F-061 from the ime it was assigned to NAS Oakland. **Right:** Robert Warner & Michael Edwards Harvard IV G-CHYN is approaching the end of its restoration and has now been adorned with authentic Luftwaffe markings to represent 'BF+070'. The aircraft served the Forca Aviação Naval Portuguesa as FAP 1765. Tim Badham

44 | WARBIRD DIRECTORY

Left: James Brown recently acquired Harvard IIB 42-708 from Sweden where it had been flying as SE-BII since it was retired by the Swedish Air Force. The aircraft has now been registered as G-CIUW and repainted into the FE511 codes it wore when in use in Canada during World War Two. *Darren Harbar* **Right:** Cirrus Aircraft UK Ltd's Harvard IV G-CJWE (former RCAF 20306) has just emerged from a complete renovation by Air Leasing in the very shiny markings of a California ANG T-6. *Darren Harbar*

Left: Steve Wilch's ex-RCAF Harvard IIB G-CPPM is making progress towards the day it will fly again from Bruntingthorpe. It is now marked in its original scheme as RCAF 3091/AF-091. *Alan Longstaff* **Right:** Aero Legends' T-6G G-DDMV wears its original 49-3209 California ANG markings and is based at Headcorn. Following USAF service this 1949-built T-6 was sold to the Haitian AF as 3209 FAHa. It was imported into the UK in 1989 by the late Paul Morgan. *Steve Bridgewater*

Left: Maurice Hammond's G-ELMH was built as 42-84555 for the USAAF and joined the RAF as EZ341. It then served the Aviação Naval Portuguesa as FAP 1662 before arriving in the UK in 1992 to be based at Maurice's airstrip at Hardwick, Norfolk. **Right:** G-KAMY was imported into the UK in 1988 by the Old Flying Machine Company as LN-AMY. It had been built for the USAAF as 42-85068. It is now operated by Orion Enterprises from North Weald and Yeovilton. *Steve Bridgewater*

Left: Malcolm Paul's Harvard IV G-RAIX was built as 51-17227 and flew with the Aeronautica Militare Italiana as MM53846. It was imported into the UK in 1981 by Robs Lamplough and was then operated by Guy Black and Anthony Hutton. It now flies as 'KF584/RAI-X'. **Right:** David Nock's AT-6D joined the USAAF in 1944 as 44-81506. In 2009 it was restored and registered N7231C but in 2011 it was sold to the UK.

WARBIRD DIRECTORY | 45

Left: Boultbee Vintage LLP's T-6G Texan G-TEXN was built in 1949 for the USAF (as 49-3072) and after retirement became N2807G. Following a crash it was shipped to the UK and rebuilt as G-BHTH in 1980 but it crashed again in 1995. Following another restoration it emerged as G-TEXN in 2005 wearing US Navy markings. *Steve Bridgewater*
Right: The so-called 'Texan Tomcat' (G-TOMC) belongs to Texan Restorations and is being returned to the skies at Bruntingthorpe by the team at Beech Restorations. This is a 1942-built ex-USAF AT-6D (42-44514) that was later refurbished as 51-14700 for the French Armée de l'air. *Alan Longstaff*

Above left: Century Aviation Ltd's aptly registered AT-6C G-TSIX flew with the USAF as 41-32262, the RAF as EX289, the South African Air Force as SAAF 7183 and Brazil's Forças Aéreas da Armada as FAB 1535 but now flies in pseudo US Navy markings as '111836/JZ-6.'
Above right: Rob Davies' Harvard IV G-TVIJ was operated by the Luftwaffe as AA+652 and Força Aérea Portuguesa as FAP 1730. It was then registered G-BSBE before joining Rob's collection in 1993. *Steve Bridgewater*
◄ German-based AT-6D G-TXAN is still registered in the UK. The aircraft was formerly based in Wales with Anthony Hodgson as G-JUDI and earlier still flew with the South African Air Force as SAAF 7439 and the Força Aérea Portuguesa as FAP 1502. It is now painted as US Navy BuNo 51970 attached to USN Glenview and carries *Finnish Fantasy* nose art.

Percival Proctor

The Proctor was a British radio trainer and communications aircraft developed from the pre-war civilian Vega Gull. More than 1,100 were built in different variants and three remain flyable in the UK today.

Proctor III	John Moore	G-ALJF	Z7252		Flyable
Proctor IV	Nigel Cottrell	G-ANXR	RM221	RM221	Flyable
Proctor V	Air Atlantique Ltd	G-AKIU	AE129	AE129	Flyable
Proctor III	Michael Biddulph	G-AKEX	LZ791		Restoration
Proctor III	Mike Biddulph, John & Derek Tregilgas	G-ANPP	HM354		Restoration
Proctor IV	John Tregilgas	G-ANVY	H772		Restoration
Proctor IV	Private Owner	-	RM169	RM169	Restoration
Proctor IV	Private Owner	-	NP294	NP294	Restoration
Proctor V	Derek Tregilgas	G-AHTE	AE58		Restoration
Proctor IIA	Dr Ian Dalziel	G-AOGE	BV651		Stored

Left: G-ALJF is the only Proctor III left flying. It served during World War Two as Z7252 but today wears a smart civilian scheme. **Right:** Proctor IV RM221 was built for the RAF in 1945 and after retirement became G-ANXR. In 1955 the aircraft joined Folland Aircraft as a 'hack' and was retained until 1961. For many years G-ANXR was based at Biggin Hill but in recent time it has relocated to Headcorn.

Piper J-3 Cub/L-4 Grasshopper

When the Piper J-3 Cub first flew in 1938 it was originally intended as a trainer and private aircraft. However, its performance meant it was well suited a variety of military uses such as reconnaissance, liaison and ground control, and it was produced in large numbers during World War Two as the L-4 Grasshopper. Today a large number of L-4s are still airworthy, along with many J-3s masquerading as Grasshoppers. For the sake filing post-war Piper L-18/L-21 Super Cubs have been grouped together with their wartime ancestors in this guide.

Type	Owner	Reg	Serial	Markings	Status
J-3C Cub	Andrew Blackford	G-BCXJ	44-80752	480752 USAAF/39-E	Flyable
J-3C Cub	Giles Caunter	G-BPUR	-	'379994 USAAC'/52-J	Flyable
J-3C Cub	Paul Latham	G-BSFD	-	'16037 USAAF'	Flyable
L-4 Grasshopper	Adrian Pearce	G-AHIP	44-79826	'479712 USAAF/8-R	Flyable
L-4 Grasshopper	CubFly	G-AISX	43-30372	330372 USAAF	Flyable
L-4 Grasshopper	Donald Jarvis	G-AJES	43-30485	330485 USAAF/44-C	Flyable
L-4 Grasshopper	Jerome Stevens (France)	G-AKAZ	42-36375	42-36375 USAAF/57-G	Flyable
L-4 Grasshopper	Richard Horner	G-AKIB	44-80015	480015 USAAF/44-M	Flyable
L-4 Grasshopper	Adrian Acres	G-AXGP	44-80248	3681 USAAC	Flyable
L-4 Grasshopper	Christopher Rees	G-BAET	43-30314	-	Flyable
L-4 Grasshopper	Shipping & Airlines Ltd	G-BBLH	43-1145	31145 USAAF/26-G	Flyable
L-4 Grasshopper	Carl Marklew-Brown	G-BCOB	43-29405	329405 USAAF/23-A	Flyable
L-4 Grasshopper	Cubby Cub Group	G-BDCD	44-80133	480133 USAAF/44-B	Flyable
L-4 Grasshopper	Knight Flying Group	G-BDHK	42-38400	'329417 USAAF'	Flyable
L-4 Grasshopper	CN Cub Group	G-BECN	44-80480	480480 USAAF/44-E	Flyable
L-4 Grasshopper	Martin Shaw	G-BFBY	43-29707	329707 USAAF/44-S	Flyable
L-4 Grasshopper	Benjamin Nicholson	G-BFDL	45-4537	454537 USAAF/04-J	Flyable
L-4 Grasshopper	Michael Pettit & Paul Shenton	G-BFZB	44-80723	480723 USAAF/E5-J	Flyable
L-4 Grasshopper	Philip Whiteman	G-BGPD	44-79744	479744 USAAF/49-M	Flyable
L-4 Grasshopper	Anthony Higgins	G-BGSJ	42-36657	236657 USAAF/72-D	Flyable
L-4 Grasshopper	L4 Group	G-BHPK	42-38410	238410 USAAF/44-A	Flyable
L-4 Grasshopper	Frederick Rogers	G-BHXY	-	'44-79609 USAAF/PR'	Flyable
L-4 Grasshopper	G-BILI Flying Group	G-BILI	45-4467	454467 USAAF/44-J	Flyable
L-4 Grasshopper	Thomas Harris	G-BKHG	44-79766	479766 USAAF/63-D	Flyable
L-4 Grasshopper	Peter Monk	G-BMKC	43-29854	329854 USAAF/44-R	Flyable
L-4 Grasshopper	Anthony Bendkowski	G-BOXJ	44-79897	479897 USAAF/JD	Flyable
L-4 Grasshopper	James McTaggart	G-BWEZ	43-6021	436021 USAAF	Flyable
L-4 Grasshopper	Richard Cummings	G-CGIY	43-30244	330244 USAAF/46-C	Flyable
L-4 Grasshopper	Giuseppe & Helen Picarella	G-FINT	45-0583	3583 USAAC/44-D	Flyable
L-4 Grasshopper	Essex L4 Group	G-FRAN	44-80321	480321 USAAF/44-H	Flyable
L-4 Grasshopper	Denham Grasshopper Flying Group	G-HEWI	44-80270	-	Flyable
L-4 Grasshopper	Maurice Kirk	G-KURK	43-30236	-	Flyable
L-4 Grasshopper	Una Allman	G-LIVH	43-30238	330238 USAAF/24-A	Flyable
L-4 Grasshopper	Robin Roberts	G-RRSR	44-80606	'480173 USAAF'/57-H	Flyable
L-4 Grasshopper	International Air Services Inc	N61787	45-4884	54884 USAAF/57-K	Flyable
L-4 Grasshopper	Zebedee Flying Group	G-OCUB	45-4475	-	Flyable
L-4 Grasshopper	Private Owner	N46779	43-29282	329282 USAAF	Flyable
L-18 Super Cub	Delta Foxtrot Flying Group	G-BIYR	54-2441	R-151 (RNLAF)	Flyable
L-18 Super Cub	Aeroclub du Bassin d'Arachon (France)	G-BLLN	96+23 Luftwaffe	-	Flyable
L-18 Super Cub	Alejandro Pilato	G-CUBJ	52-2436	18-5395/CDG French AF	Flyable
L-18 Super Cub	JG Jones Haulage	G-LION	52-2457	R-167 (RNLAF)	Flyable
L-18 Super Cub	Suzanne Gaveston	G-ROVE	54-2446	R-156 (RNLAF)	Flyable
L-18C Super Cub	Anthony Houghton & John Tempest	G-AYPM	51-15373	115373 US Army/A-373	Flyable
L-18C Super Cub	John Nugent	G-BIZV	52-2401	'18-2001 US Army'	Flyable
L-18C Super Cub	Geoffrey Cline	G-FUZZ	51-15319	'51-15319 USAF'/A-319	Flyable

WARBIRD DIRECTORY | 47

Left: Donald Jarvis' L-4 Grasshopper G-AJES was built in 1943 and carries its original markings as 43-30485/44C.
Right: Adrian Acres' 1942-built L-4 Grasshopper G-AXGP performs a spirited display at Duxford's Flying Legends Airshow. The aircraft was built as 43-681 and is thought to have been assigned to the 67th Fighter Wing of the 20th FG at Kingscliffe as a 'hack'. It suffered an accident at Kingscliffe in January 1944 and was was struck off charge as 'damaged beyond repair.' Both Steve Bridgewater.

L-18C Super Cub	Robert Lough	G-OSPS	51-15555	51-15555 USAF'	Flyable
L-18C Super Cub	David & Alison Owen	G-OTAN	R-155 RNLAF	54-2445 USAF'/A-445	Flyable
L-18C Super Cub	Private Owner	N123SA	51-15372	'15372 USAF'	Flyable
L-18C Super Cub	Private Owner	N7238X	18-1629 French AF	'USAF'	Flyable
L-21 Super Cub	Spectrum Leisure Ltd	G-BIMM	54-2468	-	Flyable
L-21 Super Cub	Kathryn Burnham	G-BKJB	R-204 Belgian AF	-	Flyable
L-21 Super Cub	Cubair Flight Training Ltd	G-BMKB	R-127 Belgian AF	D-Day scheme	Flyable
L-21A Super Cub	Michael Medland	G-BKVM	51-15684	115684 US Army/849	Flyable
PA-18 Super Cub	Private Owner	EC-AIJ	18-2479 French AF	-	Flyable
PA-18 Super Cub	Private Owner	N45507	18-8566/024 IDF	-	Flyable
PA-18 Super Cub	Private Owner	N662KK	18-8209023/112 IDF	-	Flyable
L-4 Grasshopper	Kenneth Wood & Forrest Watson	G-AISS	44-79781	479781 USAAF	Restoration
L-4 Grasshopper	Graham Earl	G-BCPH	43-29934	329934 USAAF/72-B	Stored
L-4 Grasshopper	Paul King	G-BGXA	43-29471	329471 USAAF/44-F	Stored
L-4 Grasshopper	Thomas Kattinger	G-BHVV	43-1430	31430 USAAF	Stored
L-4 Grasshopper	Private Owner	F-BMHM	44-79611	-	Stored
L-18 Super Cub	Thomas van Erck	G-BLMI	52-2466	R-55 (RNLAF)	Stored
L-18C Super Cub	Glen Molloy	G-BJTP	51-15302	115302 USMC	Stored
L-21B Super Cub	Private Owner	-	MM54-2372	-	Stored

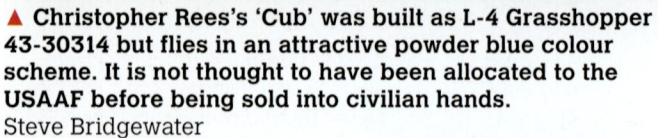

▲ Christopher Rees's 'Cub' was built as L-4 Grasshopper 43-30314 but flies in an attractive powder blue colour scheme. It is not thought to have been allocated to the USAAF before being sold into civilian hands.
Steve Bridgewater

Above right: Robin Roberts' L-4 Grasshopper G-RRSR was built as 44-80609 but is painted to represent 44-80173/57-H *Special Delivery* – an aircraft flown by Robin's father Bill in the Mediterranean Theatre of Operations as well as France and Belgium in 1943/44. As part of his duties Bill was the staff pilot for Major General Matthew Ridgway whilst in North Africa. Steve Bridgewater

▶ The West Sussex-based Cubby Cub Group operate former USAAF L-4 Grasshopper 44-80133 as G-BDCD. It wears its original markings as 44-B. Steve Bridgewater

48 | WARBIRD DIRECTORY

▲ Anthony Houghton and John Tempest's L-18C Super Cub G-AYPM was built as 51-15373 and then served the French Armee de l Air 18-1373. It was later sold into civilian hands and was owned in the 1980s by Dudley Pattison, who used it as the inspiration for the radio controlled Cub he designed for his Flair Models business. Today the aircraft wears a US Army scheme. Steve Bridgewater

▶ G-BLMI is one of a number of former Royal Netherlands Air Force Super Cubs operating on the UK register. It is configured as a glider tug.
Steve Bridgewater

Polikarpov Po-2

The Polikarpov Po-2 *Mule* was designed in 1927 as an uncomplicated training aircraft. It also proved suitable for ground attack, reconnaissance, psychological warfare and liaison missions and up to 30,000 are thought to have been made before production ended in the late 1950s. Today a handful are left flying, including one example in the UK.

Steve Bridgewater.

The Shuttleworth Collection's Po-2 was built in 1944 in the Soviet Union and although little is known of its operational history it was one of 30 given to the Yugoslavian Air Force in 1946. By 1952 it had been transferred to the Yugoslav Air Club where it was used for glider towing and parachute training as YU-CLJ. In 1961 it transferred to Slovenia and in 1979 it was donated to the Yugoslav National Museum. The museum sold it to Jim Pearce in 1990, who brought it to the UK and registered it as G-BSSY before selling it on to a collector in Seattle, USA. Its travels then took it to New Zealand in 2000 but four years later it was purchased for the Shuttleworth Collection and following complete restoration the aircraft flew for the first time on January 10, 2011.

| Po-2 | Shuttleworth Trust | G-BSSY | 94 | '28' | Flyable |

Reid and Sigrist R.S.4

The R.S.3 was a British twin-engined, three-seat advanced trainer developed during Second World War Two. The aircraft was a follow on from the company's R.S.1 Snargasher twin-engined advanced trainer but neither type received orders from the Air Ministry. The RS.3 was eventually rebuilt as the R.S.4 Bobsleigh (an experimental aircraft with the pilot in a prone position to try to minimise the effects of 'G') and it remained airworthy as a photo survey aircraft until 1973 when it was placed on display at the Snibston Discovery Park in Leicester. The aircraft was sold to a private owner in 2016 and is now being restored to fly.

| RS.4 Bobsleigh | Private Owner | G-AGOS | VZ728 | VZ728 | Restoration |

Ryan PT-22 Recruit

The Ryan PT-22 was developed in 1941 from the civilian Ryan ST.3KR series of aircraft and was the USAAC's first purpose built monoplane trainer. Powered by a slow-revving Kinner radial engine the aircraft boasted a very distinctive sound. Also included in this section is the UK-based ex-RAAF Ryan STM – effectively a PT-22 with an inline Menasco engine.

Richie Piper's PT-22 G-BTBH is currently undergoing restoration. It has been resident in the UK since 1991.
Steve Bridgewater

ST.3KR/PT-22	Harry de Vries	G-AGYY	1167	'27 USAAC'	Flyable
ST3.KR/PT-22	Richie Piper	G-BTBH	2063	'854 USAAC'	Restoration
ST3.KR/PT-22	Tracey Curtiss Taylor	G-BYPY	1001	'001 USAAC'	Stored
ST3.KR/PT-22	Andrew Montgomery	G-CIRR	1711		Restoration
ST3.KR/PT-22	Robert Fleming	G-RLWG	1716		Flyable
ST3.KR/PT-22	Flying Heritage Inc	N1344	2086		Stored
ST3.KR/PT-22	Flying Heritage Inc	N56421	1539	'855 USAAC'	Stored
STM-S2	Hisey Aviation	NC17343	A50-17	RAAF	Flyable

Tracey Curtiss Taylor's PT-22 G-BYPY flies in the colours of a typical USAAC PT-22 complete with '001' fuselage codes. Steve Bridgewater

PT-22 N1344 was operated by Bob Mitchell's PT Flight in the 1980s and is believed to now be in storage at Sleap airfield. Steve Bridgewater

The PT Flight's second PT-22 Recruit was N56421, which flew as aircraft '855.' It too is believed to be in storage at Sleap. Steve Bridgewater

50 | WARBIRD DIRECTORY

Spartan Executive

The single-engined Spartan 7W Executive was as an executive business aircraft in the late 1930s and was with affluent buyers worldwide. The RAF used four examples (AX666, KD100, KD101 and KD102) and 16 were impressed into the USAAF as the UC-71. Among the latter was Nigel Pickard's Little Gransden based example.

UC-71 Executive	Nigel Pickard	N17633	42-38367 (Impressed)	-	Airworthy

SNCAN Stampe SV.4

The Stampe et Vertongen SV.4 is a Belgian two-seat trainer/tourer. Only 35 aircraft were built before the company was closed during World War Two but after the end of hostilities the successor company Stampe et Renard built a further 65 aircraft between 1948 and 1955 for the Belgian Air Force. A licensed SV.4C version was built in France by SNCAN and these were widely used by French military units as a primary trainer. The Stampe is a very capable aerobatic machine and in high demand with display and competition pilots.

Stampe SV.4	Clive Butler & Gary Ferriman	G-AHXC	293 French AF	Flyable
Stampe SV.4	John Henny (Belgium)	G-AIYG	21 French AF	Flyable
Stampe SV.4	Thomas Harris	G-AMPI	213 French AF	Flyable
Stampe SV.4	John Beaty	G-ASHS	265 French AF	Flyable
Stampe SV.4	Austin Trueman	G-ATIR	1047 French AF	Flyable
Stampe SV.4	Richard Buchanan	G-AWEF	549 French AF	Flyable
Stampe SV.4	Bianchi Aviation Film Services	G-AWXZ	360 French AF	Flyable
Stampe SV.4	Carolyn Grace	G-AXNW	381 French AF	Flyable
Stampe SV.4	Christopher & Charles Manning	G-AXRP	554 French AF	Flyable
Stampe SV.4	Charles & Anna Huke	G-AYCK	1139 French AF	Flyable
Stampe SV.4	Lee & Susan Proudfoot	G-AYGE	242 French AF	Flyable
Stampe SV.4	David Savage	G-AYIJ	376 French AF	Flyable
Stampe SV.4	Francis & Joanna Esson	G-AYJB	560 French AF	Flyable
Stampe SV.4	Simon Carrel	G-AYWT	1111 French AF	Flyable
Stampe SV.4	Martin Coward (Monaco)	G-AZCB	140 French AF	Flyable
Stampe SV.4	Tiger Airways	G-AZGE	576 French AF	Flyable
Stampe SV.4	Martin Holloway	G-BAKN	348 French AF	Flyable
Stampe SV.4	Bianchi Aviation Film Services	G-BNYZ	200 French AF	Flyable
Stampe SV.4	Christopher Jesson	G-BPLM	1004 French AF	Flyable
Stampe SV.4	Terry Brown	G-BRXP	678 French AF	Flyable
Stampe SV.4	Acebell G-BWEF Syndicate	G-BWEF	208 French AF	Flyable
Stampe SV.4	Akbar Wajih	G-EEUP	451 French AF	Flyable
Stampe SV.4	Tiger Airways	G-FORC	665 French AF	Flyable
Stampe SV.4	Philip Meeson	G-FORD	129 French AF	Flyable
Stampe SV.4	Hugh Smith	G-HJSS	1101 French AF	Flyable
Stampe SV.4	Tiger Airways	G-NIFE	156 French AF	Flyable
Stampe SV.4	G-OODE Flying Group	G-OODE	500 French AF	Flyable
Stampe SV.4	Jonathan Keighley	G-SVIV	475 French AF	Flyable
Stampe SV.4	David Ashley	G-AZGC	120 French AF	Restoration
Stampe SV.4	Bob Mitchell	G-AWIW	532 French AF	Stored
Stampe SV.4	Tiger Airways	G-AYCG	59 French AF	Stored
Stampe SV.4	James Ashley	G-AYDR	307 French AF	Stored
Stampe SV.4	Dave & Tricia Fenton	G-AYZI	15 French AF	Stored
Stampe SV.4	Ian Noakes	G-AZNK	290 French AF	Stored
Stampe SV.4	Michael Dolman	G-AZSA	64 French AF	Stored
Stampe SV.4	Tiger Airways	G-BEPF	424 French AF	Stored
Stampe SV.4	Tiger Airways	G-BHFG	45 French AF	Stored
Stampe SV.4	David Hicklin	G-BHYI	18 French AF	Stored
Stampe SV.4	Strathgadie Stampe Group	G-BKRK	57 French AF	Stored
Stampe SV.4	Charles Bailey & Jeffrey Carr	G-BKSX	61 French AF	Stored
Stampe SV.4	Guy Valvekens (Luxembourg)	G-BWRS	437 French AF	Stored
Stampe SV.4	Philip Greenhalgh	G-BXSV	556 French AF	Stored
Stampe SV.4	Bianchi Aviation Film Services	G-BYDK	55 French AF	Stored
Stampe SV.4	George Stinnes	G-GMAX	141 French AF	Stored
Stampe SV.4	Andrew & Philippa Solleveld	G-SPIP	303 French AF	Stored
Stampe SV.4	Anthony Thorne	G-STMP	241 French AF	Stored
Stampe SV.4	Geoffrey Lynch	G-SVGL	516 French AF	Stored

Stampe SV.4 G-AWEF was an integral part of the Tiger Club at Headcorn for many years but is now owned by Richard Buchanan.

Charlie and Anna Huke purchased Stampe SV.4 G-AYCK from The Real Flying Company at Shoreham in March 2017.
Steve Bridgewater

Stinson AT-19 Reliant

Designed as a three-seat civil aircraft the Reliant first flew in 1933. During World War Two the type was used by the USAAF as the UC-81 and the RAF and Royal Navy as the AT-19. Three ex-military AT-19s are now flying in the UK.

AT-19 Reliant	Sopwith Court Ltd	G-BUCH	FB653/43-44094	-	Flyable
AT-19 Reliant	Paul Kehoe	N69745	42-46703/FX877	FX877	Flyable
AT-19 Reliant	Private Owner	NC50238	FL161	-	Flyable

Paul Kehoe, Managing Director of Birmingham International Airport, has recently acquired 1942-built AT-19 Reliant FX877. The aircraft is one of over 500 transferred to the Royal Navy (under the Lend–Lease arrangement) for use as navigational trainers and communications aircraft. This aircraft is now registered N69745. Via Birmingham International Airport

Stinson AT-19 Reliant NC50238 was built for the Royal Navy as FL161 and after it returned to the USA was purchased by Gen Curtis LeMay and several of his officer colleagues in 1952. The men based it at the home of Strategic Air Command, Offut AFB in Omaha, Nebraska and used it for hunting trips across the border to Canada!

Stinson L-5 Sentinel

The L-5 Sentinel was liaison aircraft used by the RAF and all branches of the US military. Unlike other types used in the liaison role it was purpose-built for military use and had no civilian counterpart. Just one example flies in the UK in 2017.

▶ Stinson L-5 Sentinel N6438C was built for the USAAF as 42-98177 and has recently been restored to flight. It is the sole example flying in the UK.

| L-5 Sentinel | Paul Bennett & Mike Nice | N6438C | 42-98177 | 42-98177/8-R | Flyable |

Stinson L-1 Vigilant

The Vigilant was designed in response to a 1938 USAAC competition for a two-seat light observation aircraft with very short take off and landing capabilities. The aircraft was capable of stopping in less than its own length, and could maintain stable flight at just 27kts (31mph). One example is being restored to fly in th UK.

| L-1 Vigilant | Garth & Patricia Turner | G-CIGB | 40-283 | | Restoration |

Vultee Valiant

The Vultee Valiant was the second basic trainer flown by most American pilots during the war. After primary training in PT-17 Stearman or PT-19 Cornell the student pilot moved to the more complex Valiant before completing his training on the T-6 Texan.

Valiant N58566 was operated by Bob Mitchell's PT Flight but has not flown for many years. After a period of storage at RAF Cosford it has moved to RAF Sleap. Steve Bridgewater

BT-15 Valiant	Flying Heritage Inc	N58566	10670	Stored

Westland Lysander

Named after the mythical Spartan general the Lysander was an army co-operation and liaison aircraft produced during the early part of World War Two. After becoming obsolete in the army co-operation role, the aircraft's remarkable short-field performance enabled clandestine missions to take place using small, unprepared airstrips behind enemy lines to drop off or recover agents.

Lysander IIIA	Shuttleworth Trust	G-AZWT	V9552/1582 RCAF	'V9367'/MA-B	Flyable
Lysander IIIA	Propshop Ltd	G-CCOM	V9312		Restoration

The Shuttleworth Collection's Lysander was originally built for the RAF as V9552 but went to Canada in 1942 as a target tug for the RCAF. In 1971 it was returned to the UK by the Strathallan Collection in Scotland and returned to flight by 1979 as G-AZWT. Grounded in 1986 it was purchased for the Shuttleworth Collection in 1998. A year later, with the aid of a donation from the family of Peter Vaughan Fowler who had flown with 161 Sqn on Lysander operations during the war G-AZWT was repainted black with the markings of his aircraft (V9367). A fixed ladder was installed to allow rapid access to the rear cockpit – as fitted to facilitate picking up agents - and a dummy long range fuel tank was also attached below the fuselage. Steve Bridgewater

Left: When it was restored at Strathallan G-AZWT was painted in standard RAF camouflage with markings to represent 309 (Polish) Sqn while operating from bases in Scotland between 1940 and 1942. Steve Bridgewater **Right:** Built by Westland at Yeovil in January 1941 Lysander V9312 served with 225, 613 and 4 Sqns before being shipped to Canada in 1942 to fly with the Commonwealth Air Training Plan in Saskatchewan. The remnants were discovered at a farm in 1972 and acquired by Harry Wherreat, who sold them to US collector Kermit Weeks in 1988. The project was registered N3093K but no restoration work was undertaken until it was purchased by the Aircraft Restoration Company in 2003. The aircraft is now registered G-CCOM and is making steady progress at Duxford towards a first flight. Alan Longstaff

GREAT SUBSCRIPTION OFFERS FROM KEY

SUBSCRIBE
TO *YOUR* FAVOURITE MAGAZINE
AND SAVE

UK WARBIRDS DIRECTORY

Britain's Top-Selling Aviation Monthly
FlyPast is internationally regarded as the magazine for aviation history and heritage. Having pioneered coverage of this fascinating world of 'living history' since 1980, **FlyPast** still leads the field today. Subjects regularly profiled include British and American aircraft type histories, as well as those of squadrons and units from World War One to the Cold War.

www.flypast.com

History in the Air
Aeroplane traces its lineage back to the weekly The Aeroplane launched in June 1911, and is still continuing to provide the best aviation coverage around. **Aeroplane** magazine is dedicated to offering the most indepth and entertaining read on all historical aircraft.

www.aeroplanemonthly.com

The Past, Present and Future of Flight

As Britain's longest established monthly aviation journal, **Aviation News** is renowned for providing the best coverage of every branch of aviation. Each issue has the latest news and in-depth features, plus firsthand accounts from pilots putting you in the cockpit and illustrated with the very best photography. Now incorporating JETS magazine, **Aviation News** brings you the best of both magazines.

www.aviation-news.co.uk

Britain's best selling military history monthly

Britain at War is dedicated to exploring every aspect of Britain's involvement in conflicts from the turn of the 20th century through to modern day. Readers are able to re-live decisive moments in Britain's history through fascinating insight combined with rare and previously unseen photography.

www.britainatwar.com

ALSO AVAILABLE DIGITALLY:

Available on iTunes | Available on the App Store | Available on Google play | Available on BlackBerry | Available on kindle fire | Available on PC, Mac & Windows 10

Available on PC, Mac, Blackberry and Windows 10 from **pocketmags.com**

FOR THE LATEST SUBSCRIPTION DEALS

VISIT: www.keypublishing.com/shop

PHONE: (UK) 01780 480404 (Overseas) +44 1780 480404

THE HEAVIES Multi-Engined Aircraft of World War Two

The largest, often most complex and normally most expensive of all World War Two machines still operating in the 21st century are the multi-engined bombers, transports and communications aircraft. Yet through the dedicated of groups both small and large, the UK is blessed with a diverse and active range of 'heavies.'

Avro Lancaster

The Avro Lancaster is, perhaps, the most famous British bomber of World War Two. Powered by four iconic Rolls-Royce Merlin engines the aircraft flew more than 156,000 sorties and dropped more than 600,00 tonnes of bombs between between 1942 and 1945. Of the 7,377 built just 17 remain and of those just two fly – one of which is based in the UK.

| Lancaster I | Battle of Britain Memorial Flight | - | PA474 | PA474 | Flyable |
| Lancaster VII | Lincolnshire Aviation Heritage Centre | G-ASXX | NX611 | NX611 | Ground Runner |

◀ The Lincolnshire Aviation Heritage Centre's Lancaster NX611 *Just Jane* is maintained in ground-running condition by the Panton family at their base in East Kirkby. The Lancaster regularly taxies around the former bomber base during the summer months and each winter more work is completed towards the long-term goal of returning the aeroplane to the air. NX611 was built in April 1945 and was destined as part of the RAF's Tiger Force in the Far East. However, Japan's surrender meant she was bought by the French and flew with the Aéronavale in the South Pacific. In 1964, the French presented her to the Historical Aircraft Preservation Society who overhauled her in Australia and flew her back to Britain as G-ASXX in 1965. In 1983, after a period as a gate guard at various airfields, the airframe was purchased by the Panton family to commemorate the death of their brother Chistopher who was killed on the Nuremburg Raid in March 1944. Steve Bridgewater

Boeing B-17 Flying Fortress

The four-engined Boeing B-17 developed a reputation as an effective bomber and dropped more bombs than any other US aircraft in World War Two. Of the 1.5 million tonnes of bombs dropped on Germany and its occupied territories by US aircraft, 640,000 tonnes were dropped from B-17s. Today just ten B-17s are left in flyable condition – and just one of those is located outside the USA.

| B-17G | B-17 Preservation Ltd | G-BEDF | 44-86784 | '41-24485/Sally B' | Flyable |

Bristol Beaufighter

Although it was conceived as a heavy fighter variant of the Bristol Beaufort the Beaufighter served as a multi-role aircraft. It proved to be well suited to the night fighter role and was also used on anti-shipping and coastal command duties. No examples currently fly anywhere in the world.

| Beaufighter I | Skysport Engineering | G-DINT | X7677 | - | Stored |
| Beaufighter 21 | Patina/The Fighter Collection | - | - | 'A19-144' | Restoration |

Bristol Blenheim

The Bristol Blenheim light bomber was originally developed as the civil-orientated Type 142 in response to Lord Rothermere's challenge to produce the fastest commercial aircraft in Europe. First flying in April 1935, the Air Ministry was shocked to learn it flew faster than their fighters and quickly ordered the type as a bomber. The Blenheim was one of the first British aircraft to feature an all-metal stressed-skin construction, retractable landing gear, flaps, a powered gun turret and variable-pitch propellers. Today just one example is flyable in the world – a Canadian-built Bolingbroke that has been converted to Blenheim I standard.

| Blenheim I (Bolingbroke) | Blenheim (Duxford) Ltd | G-BPIV | L6739 | L6379 | Flyable |

In its Blenheim I guise G-BPIV represents the type of bomber available to Britain at the start of World War Two. The Mk I nose had been donated to the team and had an interesting history in its own right having been converted to an electric-powered car in the 1950s. The data-plate on the nose revealed it to be L6739, which was issued to 23 Sqn on September 2, 1939. It fought throughout the Battle of Britain as a night fighter before being struck off charge in December 1940 after being damaged. Today G-BPIV flies as L6739 and wears its original YP-Q codes carried when it was based at Wittering in February 1940. Jamie Ewan

The world's only flyable Blenheim owes its existence to Graham Warner's decision in the 1970s to restore an example of 'the forgotten bomber.' The first Blenheim project, a Canadian Bolingbroke (licence-built Blenheim Mk IV) flew after a twelve years restoration in May 1987 but was wrecked in an accident just a month later, through no fault of the aeroplane. The determined team found another airframe and spent another five years restoring this example to flying condition. G-BPIV flew again in May 1993 and flew successfully for a decade, initially in the markings of 'W5722/WM-Z'; a night fighting Blenheim IV attached to 68 Sqn.

Left: G-BPIV wearing the QY-C codes of an air/sea rescue/coastal command Blenheim IV of 254 Sqn. The aircraft gained these markings in 1998 and wore them until early 2000. **Right:** In early 2000 G-BPIV had her port side temporarily painted into 43 Sqn markings, complete with the codes UX-N, to take part in an air-to-air photo shoot for a calendar. Later that season the entire aeroplane gained the same 43 Sqn markings to depict R3821'. In August 2003 it was badly damaged in a landing accident – again through no mechanical fault with the aircraft. The badly damaged airframe was taken back into the hangar for a restoration and this time the decision was made to convert it to short-nose Blenheim I configuration. After another eleven years of painstaking work, G-BPIV flew once again on November 20, 2014 with John Romain and engineer James Gilmour at the controls.

Consolidated Catalina

The amphibious Consolidated PBY Catalinas (and Canadian built Cansos) were one of the most widely used seaplanes of World War Two. The type was used for anti-submarine warfare, patrol bombing, convoy escorts and search and rescue missions (especially air-sea rescue).

PBY-5A Canso/Catalina	Plane Sailing	G-PBYA	11005 RCAF	'44-33915/*Miss Pick Up*'	Flyable

Left: G-PBYA was originally ordered for the Royal Canadian Air Force as a Canso A amphibian (the equivalent to the US Navy PBY-5A). It was taken on charge by the RCAF as 11005 on October 27, 1943 and initially saw service with 9 (Bomber Reconnaissance) Squadron at Bella Bella on the British Columbia coast between Vancouver and Prince Rupert. It remained on RCAF charge until it was retired in 1961 and became a fire bomber as C-FNJF. Used both in Canada and France until the 1990s, it was acquired by an organisation that planned to use it for tourist flights in Zimbabwe. In 2004 it was acquired by Plane Sailing and flown to the UK where it is now based at Duxford and registered G-PBYA. Today the 'Cat' flies in the markings of a USAF OA-10A search and rescue aircraft called *Miss Pick Up*. Steve Bridgewater
Right: After its arrival from Canada in 2004 the Catalina flew its first season in its original yellow, red and green fire bombing markings giving rise to the 'Rasta Cat' nickname.

de Havilland DH.89A Dragon Rapide/Dominie

The de Havilland DH.89 Dragon Rapide was a 1930s British short-haul biplane airliner for up to eight passengers. At the start of World War Two a number of Rapides were impressed by the British armed forces for passenger and communications duties. Over 500 more were built for military use and as Dominies, powered by improved Gipsy Queen engines. Dominies were mainly used by the RAF and Royal Navy for radio and navigation training.

Mark and David Miller's Gradon Rapide G-AGJG wears the camouflage markings it wore when impressed into service with Scottish Airways to fly a skeleton service to remote destinations in the Highlands during World War Two. G-AGJG was built by Brush Coachworks in 1941 and joined the RAF as X7344 but then transferred to Glasgow in 1943 as G-AGJG. In 1947, it was acquired by BEA at Northolt and later served with Mediterranean Air Services in Cyprus before it ended up giving joyrides at Heathrow in the 1950s. Its restoration at Duxford took an incredible 27 years and it now appears regularly at airshows and events around the UK. Steve Bridgewater

DH.89A	Mark & David Miller	G-AGJG	X7344	-	Flyable
DH.89A	Techair London Ltd	G-AGSH	NR808	-	Flyable
DH.89A	Ben Cox	G-AGTM	NF875	-	Flyable
DH.89A	Scillonia Airways Ltd	G-AHAG	RL944	-	Flyable
DH.89A	Private Owner	G-AHGD	NR786	'Z7258'	Stored
DH.89A	Cirrus Aviation Ltd	G-AIDL	TX310	TX310	Flyable
DH.89A	Private Owner	G-AIUL	NR749	-	Stored
DH.89A	Spectrum Leisure Ltd	G-AIYR	HG691	HG691	Flyable
DH.89A	Private Owner	G-AYBJ	NF894	-	Stored
DH.89A	Airborne Taxi Services Ltd	G-AKIF	NR750	-	Flyable
DH.89A	Private Owner	G-AKOE	X7484	-	Stored
DH.89A	Eaglescott Dominie Group	G-AKRP	RL958	-	Restoration
DH.89A	Private Owner	G-ALAX	RL948	-	Stored

Left: G-AGSH joined the RAF as NR808 is May 1945 and two months later it passed to Channel Islands Airways in Jersey as G-AGSH. In 1947 it transferred to British European Airways (BEA) with whom it flew until 1956. The aircraft later passed through various owners before it returned to BEA in 1962. In 1965 it joined the RAF Sport Parachute Association at RAF Abingdon and plied its trade there until 1973 when it was sold into civilian hands. In 1989 G-AGSH was acquired by Phillip Meeson's Techair London Ltd and repainted into BEA colours with the name *Jemma Meeson* added to the nose. Today Phillip bases the aeroplane at the Shuttleworth Collection's airfield at Old Warden, Bedfordshire. Steve Bridgewater **Right:** G-AGTM rolled off the production line in 1944 as NF875 and was immediately taken on charge by the RAF. Like many of the Dragon Rapides produced in the latter stages of the war NF875 was already surplus to requirements when it was manufactured and appears never to have left storage until June 1945 when it was sold at auction to Airwork General Trading Ltd. It was registered G-AGTM and sold to the Iraq Petroleum Transport Co Ltd, based in Haifa, Palestine. Steve Bridgewater

Douglas C-47 Skytrain/Dakota

The Douglas DC-3 was the airliner that revolutionised air transport in the 1930s. The all-metal, twin-engined monoplane was faster, larger and more comfortable than its forebears and the DC-2 was able to cross the continental United States, making transcontinental flights and worldwide flights possible. In fact the DC-3 was considered the first airliner that could make money by carrying passengers alone. Civil production ended in 1942 but the type's suitability for military operations meant more than 16,000 were built as C-47 Skytrain (designated the Dakota in RAF Service). Today it is thought around 2,000 are still flyable, including seven in the UK.

C-47A Dakota	Battle of Britain Memorial Flight	-	ZA947	ZA947	*Kwicherbichen*	Flyable
DC-3C Dakota	RVL Aviation	G-AMPY	KK116	KK116		Flyable
DC-3C Dakota	Forderverein Rosinenbomber EV (Germany)	G-AMRA	XE280	-		Flyable
DC-3C Dakota	Rajeev Chandrasekhar	G-AMSV	KN397	-		Flyable
DC-3C Dakota	RVL Aviation	G-ANAF	KP220	-		Flyable
DC-3C Dakota	Aces High	N147DC	TS423	42-100884/L4-D		Flyable
DC-3C Dakota	Paddy Green	N473DC	42-100882	42-100882/3X-P	*Drag-Em-Oot*	Flyable
DC-3C Dakota	Yorkshire Air Museum	G-AMYJ	KN353	'KG247'		Ground Runner
C-47A Dakota	Membury Airfield Memorial Flight	N308SF	42-100521	42-100521	*Night Fright*	Restoration
DC-3C Dakota	RAF Transport Command Memorial	G-AMHY	KG651	KG651		Restoration

▶ The Battle of Britain Memorial Flight's C-47 Dakota was manufactured in the USA in March 1942 and transferred to the Royal Canadian Air Force (RCAF). It was declared surplus in 1971 and acquired by the Royal Aircraft Establishment (RAE) at Farnborough as a trials aircraft. It was allocated the UK military serial number KG661, as it had carried the serial 661 with the Canadians. Research later showed that the serial KG661 had previously belonged to a Dakota that had been destroyed in an accident so the aircraft was re-registered as ZA947. When it became surplus to requirements in 1993 the aircraft was taken on charge with the BBMF. ZA947 is now painted to represent Dakota FZ692 of 233 Sqn, around the D-Day period in 1944. This aircraft, which was named *Kwicherbichen* by her crews, was involved in Para-dropping operations on the eve of D-Day and subsequently in re-supply and casualty evacuation missions into and out of forward airfields in the combat areas. *Steve Bridgewater*

◀ Having seen operational service in Burma during World War Two and having played a vital part in the Berlin Airlift in the immediate post-war year Douglas DC-3 G-AMPY is one of the most historically important aeroplanes flying today. The aircraft was built in 1943 for the USAAF as 43-49308 but joined the RAF's 435 Sqn as KK116 on November 10, 1944. It later flew as OFM-T with the squadron during the Berlin Airlift and was then stored before being sold to Starways Ltd in Liverpool as G-AMPY in 1952. A sale to Jordan failed to go through in 1957 (although the aircraft was registered JY-ABE) and the aircraft stayed with Starways until 1964 when it transferred to Aviation Overhauls Ltd. In 1970 the aircraft joined the Intra Airways fleet in Jersey and in 1982 it joined the Air Atlantique group. In the ownership of the Coventry-based airline it flew passengers and cargo and was also used to spray detergent on oil spills at sea. It currently flies in military markings and is operated by RVL Ltd. *Steve Bridgewater*

Douglas C-54 Skymaster

The Skymaster was a four-engined transport aircraft used by the USAAF in World War Two and the Korean War. Like the C-47 Skytrain, the Skymaster was derived from a civilian airliner (the Douglas DC-4) and besides cargo (notably coal during the Berlin Airlift), the type also carried presidents and prime ministers in VIP configuration. The type was also used for air-sea rescue, research fights and even missile tracking. During the Berlin Airlift it hauled coal and food supplies to West Berlin.

Douglas	C-54 Skymaster	Aces High	N44914	BuNo 56498	56498 USAAF	Stored

Ace's High's Douglas C-54 Skymaster arrived at North Weald with a view to making a film about the Berlin Airlift. The film never came to be and the aircraft has been in open storage for a number of years. In early 2017 the Save a Skymaster group began 'crowd-funding' to try to acquire and return the aircraft to the skies. *Tim Badham*

WARBIRD DIRECTORY | 59

In Focus

Boeing B-17G Flying Fortress G-BEDF

Since 1989 G-BEDF has flown in the markings she wore during the filming of the motion picture *Memphis Belle*. Smoke systems were fitted to the port engines during filming and are routinely used during the aircraft's displays around the UK and Europe. Steve Bridgewater

B-17 Preservation Ltd's Boeing B-17G Flying Fortress has become one of the UK's most iconic historic aeroplanes and now flies as a memorial to the 79,000 Allied airmen who lost their lives in Europe during World War Two.

This particular B-17 was one of the last to be constructed by the Lockheed-Vega plant at Burbank, California and was accepted by the United States Army Air Force (USAAF) on June 19, 1945, meaning it was too late to see wartime service.

It was therefore converted into a TB-17G for training purposes and later modified to become an EB-17G research aircraft.

In 1954, the aircraft was sold to the French Institut Geographic National (IGN) for survey and mapping work. Based at Creil, it became F-BGSR and served until 1975, when it was sold to British-based businessman and pilot Ted White.

Ted had the aircraft transferred to the US register as N17TE and in March 1975 it arrived at the Imperial War Museum's airfield at Duxford, which would be its home for the next 40+ years.

Ted named his newly acquired Fortress *Sally B* after his long-time companion Elly Sallingboe. In 1980, Ted and Elly formed the *Sally B* Supporters Club, in order to raise much-needed funds to keep the aircraft in the skies. Over the years the club has produced a loyal and hardworking band of supporters, which has become the life-blood of the operation.

However, tragedy struck in 1982 when Ted was killed after his T-6 Harvard (G-ELLY) crashed during an air rally in Malta. Devastated by the disaster, Elly

In the late 1970s Sally B was routinely flown by Don Bullock and Keith Sissons, initially in the markings of the 457th BG, USAAF 8th AF, based at Glatton during World War Two, but retaining her original serial number 485784.

and the team vowed to keep *Sally B* flying in memory of the man who saved the B-17 from the scrap man less than a decade earlier. The decision was also made to paint the aircraft's starboard inner engine cowling with the same black and yellow chequered markings worn by Ted's Harvard – a tradition that is retained to this day.

C-47A Dakota	Battle of Britain Memorial Flight	-	ZA947	ZA947	*Kwicherbichen*		Flyable
DC-3C Dakota	RVL Aviation	G-AMPY	KK116	KK116			Flyable
DC-3C Dakota	Forderverein Rosinenbomber EV (Germany)	G-AMRA	XE280	-			Flyable
DC-3C Dakota	Rajeev Chandrasekhar	G-AMSV	KN397	-			Flyable
DC-3C Dakota	RVL Aviation	G-ANAF	KP220	-			Flyable
DC-3C Dakota	Aces High	N147DC	TS423	42-100884/L4-D			Flyable
DC-3C Dakota	Paddy Green	N473DC	42-100882	42-100882/3X-P	*Drag-Em-Oot*		Flyable
DC-3C Dakota	Yorkshire Air Museum	G-AMYJ	KN353	'KG247'			Ground Runner
C-47A Dakota	Membury Airfield Memorial Flight	N308SF	42-100521	42-100521	*Night Fright*		Restoration
DC-3C Dakota	RAF Transport Command Memorial	G-AMHY	KG651	KG651			Restoration

▶ The Battle of Britain Memorial Flight's C-47 Dakota was manufactured in the USA in March 1942 and transferred to the Royal Canadian Air Force (RCAF). It was declared surplus in 1971 and acquired by the Royal Aircraft Establishment (RAE) at Farnborough as a trials aircraft. It was allocated the UK military serial number KG661, as it had carried the serial 661 with the Canadians. Research later showed that the serial KG661 had previously belonged to a Dakota that had been destroyed in an accident so the aircraft was re-registered as ZA947. When it became surplus to requirements in 1993 the aircraft was taken on charge with the BBMF. ZA947 is now painted to represent Dakota FZ692 of 233 Sqn, around the D-Day period in 1944. This aircraft, which was named *Kwicherbichen* by her crews, was involved in Para-dropping operations on the eve of D-Day and subsequently in re-supply and casualty evacuation missions into and out of forward airfields in the combat areas. Steve Bridgewater

◀ Having seen operational service in Burma during World War Two and having played a vital part in the Berlin Airlift in the immediate post-war year Douglas DC-3 G-AMPY is one of the most historically important aeroplanes flying today. The aircraft was built in 1943 for the USAAF as 43-49308 but joined the RAF's 435 Sqn as KK116 on November 10, 1944. It later flew as OFM-T with the squadron during the Berlin Airlift and was then stored before being sold to Starways Ltd in Liverpool as G-AMPY in 1952. A sale to Jordan failed to go through in 1957 (although the aircraft was registered JY-ABE) and the aircraft stayed with Starways until 1964 when it transferred to Aviation Overhauls Ltd. In 1970 the aircraft joined the Intra Airways fleet in Jersey and in 1982 it joined the Air Atlantique group. In the ownership of the Coventry-based airline it flew passengers and cargo and was also used to spray detergent on oil spills at sea. It currently flies in military markings and is operated by RVL Ltd. Steve Bridgewater

Douglas C-54 Skymaster

The Skymaster was a four-engined transport aircraft used by the USAAF in World War Two and the Korean War. Like the C-47 Skytrain, the Skymaster was derived from a civilian airliner (the Douglas DC-4) and besides cargo (notably coal during the Berlin Airlift), the type also carried presidents and prime ministers in VIP configuration. The type was also used for air-sea rescue, research fights and even missile tracking. During the Berlin Airlift it hauled coal and food supplies to West Berlin.

Douglas	C-54 Skymaster	Aces High	N44914	BuNo 56498	56498 USAAF	Stored

Ace's High's Douglas C-54 Skymaster arrived at North Weald with a view to making a film about the Berlin Airlift. The film never came to be and the aircraft has been in open storage for a number of years. In early 2017 the Save a Skymaster group began 'crowd-funding' to try to acquire and return the aircraft to the skies. Tim Badham

IN FOCUS   Avro Lancaster I PA474

PA474 is repainted regularly and is seen here wearing the 'PM-M²' codes of 103 Sqn Lancaster ED888 in 1990. For the 2017 season PA474 is due to reappear in a dual scheme commemorating two different Lancasters. The left-hand side will be painted as 460 (RAAF) Sqn Lancaster 'W5005/AR-L' (complete with nose art of a bagpipe playing kangaroo!) and the right side will carry the 50 Sqn letters 'VN-T', representing the Lancaster flown by FO Douglas Millikin DFC – grandfather of the BBMF's current Officer Commanding, Sqn Ldr Andy Millikin, on operation 27 of his first tour of 30.

Lancaster PA474 rolled off the production line at Hawarden, Chester on May 31, 1945, just after the war in Europe came to an end. By the time she could be prepared to join Tiger Force in the Pacifc the Japanese had also surrendered so PA474 was converted for photo-reconnaissance work and assigned to 82 Sqn for aerial survey duties in East and South Africa.

On her return to the UK in February 1952 PA474 was loaned to Flight Refuelling Ltd at Tarrant Rushton to be used as a pilotless drone. Fortunately, before the conversion started, PA474 was reprieved and transferred to the Royal College of Aeronautics at Cranfield where she was used as a trials platform. Various experimental aerofoil sections were mounted vertically on her upper fuselage for airborne testing.

In 1964 the Lancaster was adopted by the Air Historical Branch with a view to displaying it as the proposed RAF Museum at Hendon. She was painted in a camouflage paint scheme (although still devoid of turrets) and it was at this time that she appeared in the films *Operation Crossbow* and *The Guns of Navarone*.

Later in 1964, she was moved to RAF Henlow and grounded but a year later Wg Cdr D'Arcy (the Commanding Officer of 44 Sqn flying Vulcans at RAF Waddington) asked permission for PA474 to be transferred into the care of his unit. This was granted and over the coming years the aircraft was renovated with turrets etc. Permission to fly PA474 regularly was granted in 1967 and in 1973 44 Sqn gifted the aeroplane to the Battle of Britain Memorial Flight – with whom it has remained ever since.

Left: Until the end of the 2016 season PA474 was painted to represent Lancaster 'DV385/*Thumper Mk III*' of 617 (Dambuster) Sqn, with the code letters 'KC-A'. This aircraft was one of the brand-new standard Lancasters issued to the squadron as replacements after the Dams Raid. Although the real *Thumper Mk III* flew a total of 50 'ops', the 'bomb log' under the cockpit on PA474 displays 35 missions, as shown in a wartime photograph. The original aeroplane also took part in the two raids against the battleship *Tirpitz* in Tromso Fjord in 1944. PA474 is seen here welcoming the Canadian Warplane Heritage Museum Lancaster to Biggin Hill in August 2014. *Steve Bridgewater* **Right:** PA474 during her time flying as a aerial test-bed at the Cranfield College of Aeronautics – complete with a Folland Midge wing mounted atop the fuselage.

60 | WARBIRD DIRECTORY

When operated by 44 Sqn at Waddington (which was also the first unit to be equipped with Lancasters during the war) PA474 was painted in the markings of 'R5508/KM-B'. This 44 Sqn aeroplane was flown by Sqn Ldr John Nettleton VC on the famous low level raid against the Augsburg U-Boat engine factory in April 1942.

In the late 1960s both front and rear turrets were refitted but no mid-upper turret could be found. Following the 1979 season, PA474 was flown to Lyneham, where it was given the markings of 'ED932/AJ-G' the Lancaster famously flown by Wg Cdr Guy Gibson VC DSO* DFC* during the 'Dambusters' raid in May 1943.

Left: After major servicing at Kemble during the winter of 1983-84, PA474 was re-painted to represent 'SR-D', a Lancaster B.1 from Ludford Magna based 101 Sqn. **Right:** Over the winter of 1987-88 PA474 was sent to Exeter for major servicing. When she reappeared she had gained the 'PM-M²' markings of ED888, a Lancaster flown by both 103 and 576 Sqns. The real 'PM-M²' flew 140 missions – more than any other Lancaster.

Left: The Lancaster emerged in the markings of 9 Sqn's famous 'PM-M2' W4964/WS-J' after servicing at St Athan in 1994. The nose art depicted the distinctive Johnnie Walker whiskey logo and 'Still Going Strong' slogan. **Right:** After a major service by Air Atlantique in Coventry during the winter of 2006-07, PA474 was repainted into the markings of EE139, along with *Phantom of the Ruhr* nose art. The original EE139 flew 30 'ops' with 100 Sqn at 'HR-W' and then a further 91 missions with 550 Sqn as *BQ-B*. PA474 wore the 100 Sqn markings on the port side and the 550 Sqn colours on the starboard. Steve Bridgewater

WARBIRD DIRECTORY | 61

IN FOCUS

Boeing B-17G Flying Fortress G-BEDF

Since 1989 G-BEDF has flown in the markings she wore during the filming of the motion picture *Memphis Belle*. Smoke systems were fitted to the port engines during filming and are routinely used during the aircraft's displays around the UK and Europe. Steve Bridgewater

B-17 Preservation Ltd's Boeing B-17G Flying Fortress has become one of the UK's most iconic historic aeroplanes and now flies as a memorial to the 79,000 Allied airmen who lost their lives in Europe during World War Two.

This particular B-17 was one of the last to be constructed by the Lockheed-Vega plant at Burbank, California and was accepted by the United States Army Air Force (USAAF) on June 19, 1945, meaning it was too late to see wartime service.

It was therefore converted into a TB-17G for training purposes and later modified to become an EB-17G research aircraft.

In 1954, the aircraft was sold to the French Institut Geographic National (IGN) for survey and mapping work. Based at Creil, it became F-BGSR and served until 1975, when it was sold to British-based businessman and pilot Ted White.

Ted had the aircraft transferred to the US register as N17TE and in March 1975 it arrived at the Imperial War Museum's airfield at Duxford, which would be its home for the next 40+ years.

Ted named his newly acquired Fortress *Sally B* after his long-time companion Elly Sallingboe. In 1980, Ted and Elly formed the *Sally B* Supporters Club, in order to

In the late 1970s Sally B was routinely flown by Don Bullock and Keith Sissons, initially in the markings of the 457th BG, USAAF 8th AF, based at Glatton during World War Two, but retaining her original serial number 485784.

raise much-needed funds to keep the aircraft in the skies. Over the years the club has produced a loyal and hardworking band of supporters, which has become the life-blood of the operation.

However, tragedy struck in 1982 when Ted was killed after his T-6 Harvard (G-ELLY) crashed during an air rally in Malta. Devastated by the disaster, Elly and the team vowed to keep *Sally B* flying in memory of the man who saved the B-17 from the scrap man less than a decade earlier. The decision was also made to paint the aircraft's starboard inner engine cowling with the same black and yellow chequered markings worn by Ted's Harvard – a tradition that is retained to this day.

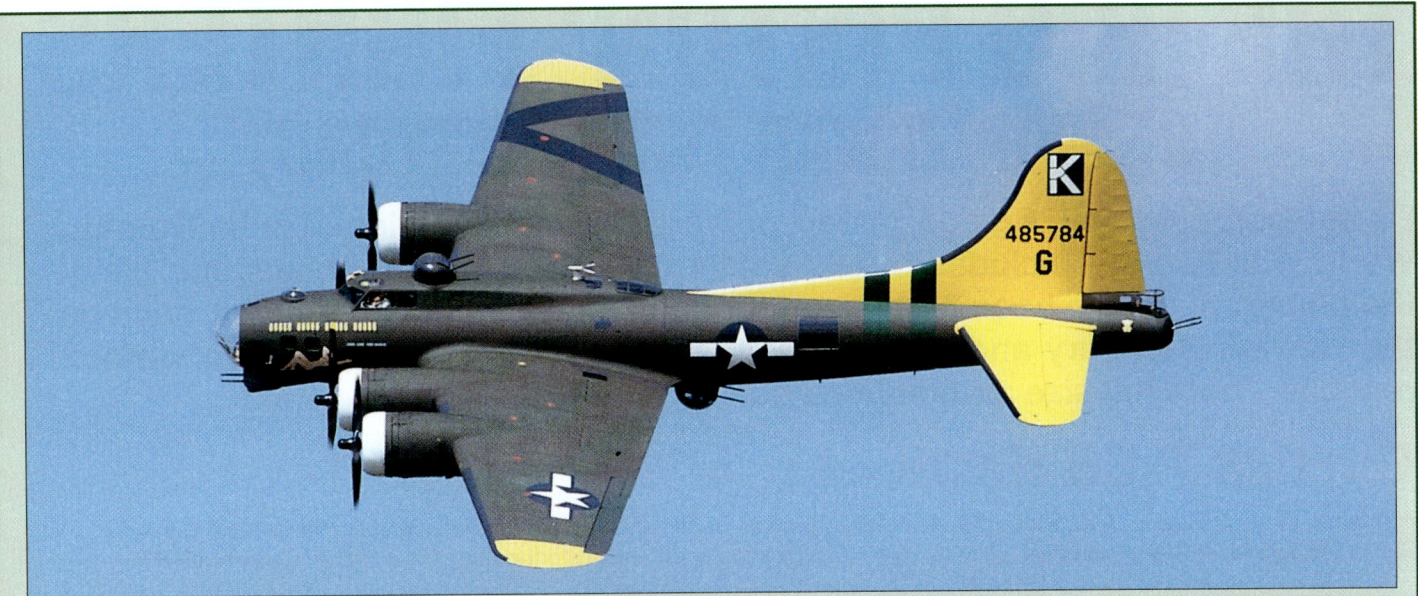

In order to protect the airframe from the damp British weather, *Sally B* (by now re-registered in the UK as G-BEDF) shed her bare metal scheme over the winter of 1983–84 and gained an olive drab and neutral grey colour scheme with a yellow tail depicting an aircraft of the 447th BG when flying from Rattlesden, Suffolk. She would retain this scheme until 1989.

Left: In 1981 *Sally B* appeared in the London Weekend Television series *We'll Meet Again*, which told the story of an American bomb group stationed in East Anglia during 1943. *Sally B* appeared both as herself and as *Ginger Rogers* (by applying different names on either side nose). The filming also enabled the operators to acquire and fit a full set of gun turrets, something that she had lacked since her military days. Awyr Aviation Archives. **Left:** For many years Sally B operated under sponsorship from the Imperial War Museum as the official aeroplane of the American Air Museum at Duxford. Steve Bridgewater

In the summer of 1989, *Sally B* was one of five B-17s contracted to take a starring role in the *Memphis Belle* feature film. Fitted with engine smoke canisters and configured to fire 'gas guns' from the rear and ball turrets, she also shed her chin turret to more accurately represent a B-17F and was repainted into the colours of the 91st BG's 324th Bomb Squadron to represent the *Memphis Belle* and other aircraft. After filming it was decided to retain the *Memphis Belle* markings although the chequered cowling and nose turret were reinstated, along with the original *Sally B* artwork on the starboard side of the nose. Steve Bridgewater

WARBIRD DIRECTORY | 63

THE 'BIG PISTON' FIGHTERS
OF WORLD WAR TWO (& BEYOND)

For the purposes of this guide, piston-powered 'fighters' designed or built during World War Two are included in this section. For the sake of consistent 'filing' the boundaries have been extended to include certain post-war types, such as the Hawker Sea Fury and Douglas AD-4 Skyraider. Also included are various replicas – both full size and reduced scale.

Curtiss P-36 Hawk

Formed by Glenn Curtiss in 1916, the Curtiss Aeroplane Company is perhaps best remembered for its range of Hawk fighters. Two of the earliest surviving examples of the family fly from Duxford under the custodianship of The Fighter Collection (TFC).

| Hawk 75A | Patina Ltd/The Fighter Collection | G-CCVH | 82 French AF 38-210 | 82 French AF 38-210 | Flyable |
| P-36C Hawk | Patina Ltd/The Fighter Collection | G-CIXJ | | | Flyable |

◀ TFC's Hawk 75A G-CCVH is one of the batch of aircraft sent to the Armée de l'Air in April 1939. It flew with the 1ére Escadrille, Groupe de Combat II/5 Lafayette at Reims and Toul during the Battle of France and then moved to Oran in Algeria to fly with Vichy forces before the Armistice in 1942. It returned to the Armée de l'Air at the end of the war and was used as an advanced trainer until 1949 when it was sold. After storage with a variety of private owners TFC acquired the airframe in 1995 and following restoration in the USA and New Zealand it made its Duxford debut in 2005. It wears its authentic Armée de l'Air scheme. Steve Bridgewater

▶ TFC's P-36C was the last example to roll off the production line. Delivered to Selfridge Field, Michigan in May 1939 she participated in that year's Cleveland Air Races wearing experimental camouflage prior to participating in the War Games at Maxwell Field in September. In 1942 the P-36C was sent to a variety of technical colleges prior to being acquired by a Pratt & Whitney instructor who shipped it to his home in Canada. The aircraft resided there until a Florida collector acquired it and passed it to TFC. Restoration began in 2011, under the leadership of Matt Nightingale at Chino, California, and the aircraft arrived at Duxford four years later. Darren Harbar

Curtiss P-40 Warhawk & Kittyhawk

The Fighter Collection fly a Curtiss P-40C Warhawk and Rolls-Royce Merlin-powered P-40F from Duxford and the Hangar 11 Collection's late-war P-40M Kittyhawk G-KITT flies from North Weald, Essex. A further, privately owned, P-40M remains in storage. NB: as these words closed for press it was announced that G-KITT has been sold to the USA, however as it still appeared on the UK register at the time of going to print it has been retained in this directory.

P-40C Warhawk	Patina Ltd/The Fighter Collection	G-CIIO	41-13357	'39-160'	Flyable
P-40F Warhawk	Patina Ltd/The Fighter Collection	G-CGZP	41-19841	41-19841/'X1-7 Lee's Hope'	Flyable
P-40M Kittyhawk	Hangar 11 Collection	G-KITT	43-5802	2104590/'44 Lulu Belle'	Flyable
P-40N Kittyhawk	Private Owner	N9950	44-79834	4-7983	Stored

TFC's P-40C was one of a pair of aircraft acquired from the former Soviet Union in the 1990s (the other now based in Seattle with the Flying Heritage Collection). 41-13357 was accepted by the USAAC in April 1941 and flew coastal and anti-submarine patrols before it was overhauled and sent to the Soviet Union as part of the Lend-Lease programme. Nothing more is known of its history until it was recovered. It was sent to the USA for restoration in 2011 and has been finished to represent a P-40 based at Chanute Field, Kansas in 1940. Aircraft 39-160 was stripped of its olive drab camouflage paint and used as a personal 'hack' for base commanders. The restored aircraft arrived at Duxford in the summer of 2014. Steve Bridgewater

◀ TFC's Merlin-engined P-40F is one of only two left airworthy anywhere in the world. It was built in late 1942 and shipped to the Thirteenth Air Force in the Southwest Pacific on Christmas Eve. Unfortunately her service career remains a mystery but the aircraft was discovered in a dump on the Vanautu's islands, Espiritu Santo in the 1970s. TFC acquired it many years later and the restoration was undertaken at Wangaratta, Australia. Due to the lack of information on her service history, the P-40F wears the scheme of *Lee's Hope* from the 85th Fighter Squadron, 79th Fighter Group, which was flown by Lt Robert J Duffield from Capodichino airfield, southern Italy in early 1944. It has been based at Duxford since the summer of 2011.

Steve Bridgewater

Douglas Skyraider

The Douglas Skyraider was developed as a dive bomber/attack aircraft but World War Two was almost over by the time it first flew in March 1945. However, the type went on to serve US and overseas forces extensively, most notably in the Korean and Vietnam Wars. The sole UK example is operated by Kennet Aviation and carries the markings its wore in service aboard the USS Princeton CV-37 in the 1950s.

| AD-4NA Skyraider | Orion Enterprises Ltd | G-RADR | BuNo7792 | 126922/H-503 | Flyable |

◀ Skyraider G-RADR was built in 1948 and served with the USN until 1960 including ditching off the carrier USS *Princeton* due to engine trouble on July 25, 1953. The aircraft now carries the colour scheme worn at that time but it also saw service with the French Armée de l'Air and the Gabonese Air Force. It was recovered from Gabon in 1985 by French organisation Aero Retro and was restored to fly as F-AZED.
Steve Bridgewater

IN FOCUS

Curtiss P-40M Kittyhawk G-KITT

G-KITT currently wears the markings of P-40N-1 Warhawk 44-2104590 *Lulu Belle*, flown by 2nd Lieutenant Philip R Adair of the USAAF's 89th FS, 80th FG of the 10th Air Force in the China Burma India Theatre. It is an exact reproduction of the first of two P-40s to bear Adair's markings. The American flew 113 missions in *Lulu Belle*, including one sortie on December 19 in which he singlehandedly attacked an incoming raid of 24 Japanese 'Sally' bombers and 40 Japanese fighters sent to bomb the US air base at Nagaghuli, India. Adair managed to shoot down one bomber and one 'Oscar' fighter, but his relentless harassment scattered the formation so that they ended up bombing inaccurately, causing only minor damage at the strategically important airfield. Adair's aircraft was hit 16 times in the action, but managed to return to base. Lt. Adair was awarded the Silver Star for his actions that day and went on to fly a total of 139 combat missions, before returning to the USA at the end of the war. Darren Harbar

Curtiss P-40M Kittyhawk G-KITT has been an integral part of the British warbird scene almost constantly since 1985.

The aircraft was built at the Curtiss plant at Buffalo, New York in October 1943 and issued the serial 43-5802 – however, she was diverted to the Royal Canadian Air Force. The aircraft was assigned the RCAF code 840 and assigned to 5 Operation Training Unit for the entirety of the war. The Kittyhawk was struck of charge in 1947 and sold to Vance B Roberts who registered her as N1233N.

From 1951 until 1954 she was based at Oregon State University as an instructional airframe but then transferred to Bob Sturges of Columbia Airmotive, Troutdale, Oregon who used the aircraft as an eye catching advertising display at Troutdale Airport.

The P-40 remained at the airport until 1979 when she was discovered by P-40 enthusiast Tommy Camp. He deemed it suitable for restoration to fly and after acquiring the aircraft he shipped it to Livermore, California and spent the next three years restoring it to airworthy condition. For certification reasons the airframe was given the false ID and paperwork belonging to P-40N N1009N/43-23494/RCAF 877, which had been scrapped and in 1984 the 'new' N1009N was acquired by Stephen Grey and shipped across the Atlantic.

The aircraft arrived at Duxford on Valentine's Day 1985 and flew again on February 27 of that year. It was subsequently painted to represent an RAF Desert Air Force Kityhawk III (FR870/GA-S) of 112 Sqn.

In July 1994 the Kittyhawk was sold to French collector Christophe Jacquard, who registered is F-AZPJ and painted into a 'Flying Tigers' scheme. It returned to TFC in 1998 and was allocated the appropriate civilian registration G-KITT. Around the same time it was painted in the colours of the 343rd Fighter Group 'Aleutian Tigers' that operated in Alaska during 1942-43 under the command of John 'Jack' Chennault, the son of General Claire Chennault who commanded the famous Flying Tigers in China.

TFC retained the aeroplane until December 2005 when it was acquired by Peter Teichman's Hangar 11 Collection at North Weald, Essex. It retained its Aleutian Tigers scheme until 2009 when it was repainted to take part in the film *Red Tails*. The temporary markings, depicting P-40M 42-10855, assigned to 1st Lieutenant Robert W Diez of the 99th FS, 332nd FG based at Madna, Italy in early 1944 were retained (with various modifications) until 2012 when the aircraft flew to Biggin Hill, Kent for a repaint. It emerged in the colours warn by P-40N-1 Warhawk 44-2104590 *Lulu Belle*, flown by 2nd Lieutenant Philip R Adair of the USAAF's 89th FS, 80th FG of the 10th Air Force in the China Burma India Theatre.

As these words were committed to print in June 2017 news emerged that the aircraft had been sold. It is not yet known whether the aircraft is destined to depart UK shores.

Stephen Grey taxies N1009N at Duxford in February 1984. The aircraft had been restored in the USA by Tommy Camp.

66 | WARBIRD DIRECTORY

Between 1984 and 1994 the aircraft was painted to represent RAF Desert Air Force Kittyhawk III FR870/GA-S of 112 Sqn. The real FR870 crash-landed at Santa Maria Nuova, near Rome on November 3, 1943 after being damaged by an explosion caused by her own bombs.

From 1994 until 1997 the P-40 was registered F-AZPJ and based at Dijon, France with Christophe Jacquard. During this time it was painted to represent 'P-8196/34' of the USAAC AVG, the famed 'Flying Tigers'.

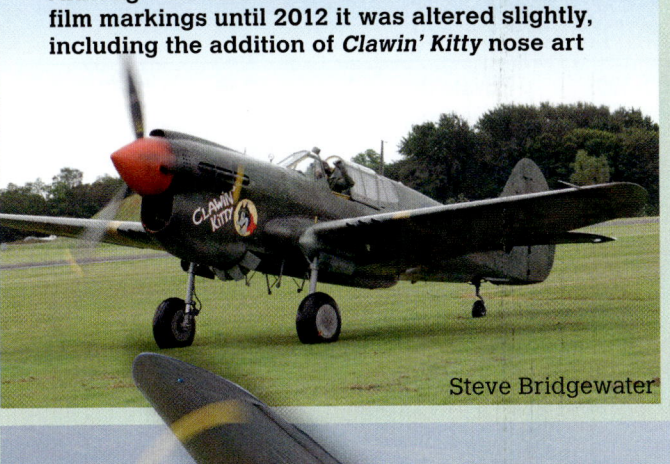

Although the aircraft retained the *Red Tails* film markings until 2012 it was altered slightly, including the addition of *Clawin' Kitty* nose art

Steve Bridgewater

For the 2009 film *Red Tails* G-KITT was repainted into temporary markings depicting P-40M 42-10855, assigned to 1st Lieutenant Robert W Diez of the 99th FS, 332nd FG based at Madna, Italy in early 1944. Darren Harbar

After it had been re-registered as G-KITT in 1998 the P-40 was painted in the colours of the 343rd Fighter Group 'Aleutian Tigers' that operated P-40s in Alaska in 1942-43 under the command of John 'Jack' Chennault, the son of General Claire Chennault who commanded the famous Flying Tigers in China. The aircraft retained this scheme when it was sold to the Hangar 11 collection in 2005. Darren Harbar

WARBIRD DIRECTORY | 67

The Skyraider was acquired by The Fighter Collection in 1991 and initially wore US Navy markings as '26922/JS-937.' During this time it was registered G-RAID. It is seen here at the 1992 Great Warbird Air Display. Neil Taylor via Awyr Aviation Communication

TFC subsequently repainted the Skyraider into a new scheme, depicting '26922/AK-402', before it was sold to Kennet Aviation in October 2003. It was then re-registered as G-RADR and later repainted into its original USS *Princeton* scheme. Darren Harbar

EKW D-3801

During World War Two the Swiss Federal Construction Works Eidgenössische Konstruktionswerkstätte (EKW) developed the D-3801 from the French-built Morane-Saulnier MS406 fighter. Three examples of the 1,060hp Hispano-Suiza 12Y-51-powered aircraft are stored in Northamptonshire pending future restoration.

D-3801	Private Owner	-	J-146	-	Stored
D-3801	Private Owner	-	J-95	-	Stored
D-3801	Private Owner	-	TBC	-	Stored

EKW C-3605

The Swiss Federal Construction Works – (EKW) constructed 175 examples of the C-3603 fighter during World War Two. Many of these remained in service until the 1950s and in the late 1960s some 24 were converted to turboprop power to act as target tugs for the Swiss Air Force. Two examples exist in the UK, one being restored and one stored pending sale.

| C-3605 | William Tomkins Ltd | G-CCYZ | C-558 | Swiss AF | - | Restoration |
| C-3605 | Robert Gray | G-DORN | C-552 | Swiss AFC | 552 Swiss AF | Stored |

Fairey Firefly

The carrier-borne Fairey Firefly served the Royal Navy as a fighter and ant-submarine aircraft from 1943 to 1956. Since the tragic loss of the Fleet Air Arm Historic Flight's Firefly WB271 in 2003 the UK has been without an airworthy example of this classic naval aircraft, but former Swedish target tug DT989 is now being restored to fly at Duxford.

▶ Firefly TT.1 DT989 was acquired by the Svensk Flygtjänst in 1950 for use as a target tug and was registered SE-BRG. It was withdrawn from service in 1963 and in 1969 it joined the Technical Museum at Arlanda, Stockholm. It remained at the collection until 1985 when it was sold to Bjorn Lowgren, who stored it in a barn at Ska Edeby along with SE-CAU. Plans to restore both aircraft failed to materialise and in 2004 they were sold to the Aircraft Restoration Company/Propshop Ltd. SE-CAU has since been sold on but SE-BRG was registered G-CCYD in 2011 when restoration began. Steve Bridgewater

| Firefly TT.1 | Propshop Ltd | G-CCYD | DT989 | - | Restoration |

Fiat CR.42

More than 1,800 examples of the Italian Fiat CR.42 – considered by some to be the most advanced military biplane to enter service – were built, but just a four of the aircraft remain. Of those just one is being restored to fly. G-CBLS arrived at Duxford in 2006 and is making rapid progress towards the day it flies again.

▶ Just four Fiat CR.42s are thought to survive and TFC's ex-Swedish AF example will be the sole airworthy example when it takes to the skies. G-CBLS was built for Swedish Air Force as a J11 and carried the serial Fv2542 and individual markings 'F9-10'. It crashed near Kiruna, Sweden in April 1943 and the wreck was recovered in 1983. Restoration began in Italy in 1994 and TFC acquired it a year later. It arrived at Duxford in 2006 and work has continued on this rare airframe ever since.

Steve Bridgewater

CR.42	Patina Ltd/The Fighter Collection	G-CBLS	Fv2542 (SwAF)	-	Restoration

Focke-Wulf Fw 190

Although it is one of the most famous fighters of World War Two just one airworthy example of Kurt Tank's Fw 190 remains airworthy (in the USA). Although at least one example of the 'new-build' Flugwerk FW190 examples was based in the UK for some years it never flew and the closest British enthusiasts can get to a flying Fw 190 are the various scale replicas flying or under construction by avid homebuilders.

Fw 190 (WAR Replica)	Shaun Freeman	G-BSLX	-	'4+1'	Stored
Fw 190 (WAR Replica)	David Conway	G-CCFW	-	'9'	Flyable
Fw 190 (WAR Replica)	Ashley Collins	G-SYFW	-	'2+1'	Flyable
Fw 190 (WAR Replica)	Bernard Hunter	G-WULF	-	'1'	Flyable
Fw 190 (Jurca Replica)	Stanley Howes	G-KURT	-		Restoration

Grumman F8F Bearcat

The prototype Grumman F8F Bearcat had not flown by the time World War Two ended but the type went on to serve in the French Indochina War. Considered by many to be the epitome of the piston-powered fighter the Bearcat could reach 421mph (366kts) in combat and a highly modified post-war air racing example set a world speed record for piston-powered aircraft at 528.33mph (455.25kts). The Fighter Collection's example has been based in the UK since 1982.

F8F-2P Bearcat	Patina Ltd/The Fighter Collection	G-RUMM	BuNo121714121714/'201/B'	Flyable

G-RUMM wears the markings of Lt Cdr D C 'Whiff' Caldwell, Commander of VF-20. Darren Harbar

Grumman F8F Bearcat (Continued)

In June 1981 John Crocker ferried the Bearcat from the USA to Stephen Gery's then base in Geneva. It would soon make Duxford its home and was painted in the markings of '121714/S-100' of the Red Rippers. It joined the UK register in 1998, at which point it was repainted into its current VF-20 scheme.

TFC's Bearcat was built in 1948 and was converted to F8F-2P photo-reconnaissance configuration in 1952. It was struck off charge in 1957 and passed to Ed Maloney's The Air Museum who registered it as N4995V. It later passed to Harold 'Bubba' Beal and Charles 'Chubb' Smith, who re-registered it as N1YY and, later, N700H and N700HL.

Grumman F4F/FM-2 Wildcat

The Grumman Wildcat was the only effective 'modern' fighter available to the US Navy at the start of World War Two. The Fighter Collection's example has been the sole UK-based flyer since it arrived at Duxford in 1993 but in recent years has been joined by a number of restoration projects.

FM-2 Wildcat	Patina Ltd/The Fighter Collection	G-RUMW	BuNo86711	'JV579'/F	Flyable
FM-2 Wildcat	Thomas Harris	G-KINL	BuNo86690		Restoration
FM-2 Wildcat	Wildcat WP Ltd/Bygone Engineering Ltd	G-WCME	BuNo55585		Restoration
FM-2 Wildcat	Wildcat WP Ltd/Bygone Engineering Ltd	G-WCMI	BuNo86750		Restoration
FM-2 Wildcat	Wildcat WP Ltd/Bygone Engineering Ltd	G-WCMO	BuNo55404		Restoration

◄ TFC's Wildcat was built for the US Navy by the General Motors Corporation (Eastern Aircraft Division) at Trenton, New Jersey in 1945. However, it was immediately placed into storage at Tillamook Naval Air Station, Oregon and was struck off charge in February 1946. It passed through a series of civilian owners until it moved to the Chennault Air Museum, California in 1975. In 1992 it moved to Chino for overhaul to airworthy condition by Fighter Rebuilders and it flew again in January of the following year. The aircraft arrived at Duxford in April 1993 and although it was initially painted as USN 86711/84 it was quickly re-sprayed into Fleet Air Arm markings to depict Wildcat V JV579 embarked on HMS *Tracker* in 1944. It was re-registered as G-RUMW in 1998 and remains an integral part of the TFC fleet.

Steve Bridgewater

► Thomas Harris' Wildcat, G-KINL, previously flew as a crop spraying aircraft in the USA with both underwing and wingtip tanks. In the late 1970s it passed to Jack Lenhardt who painted N20HA in a USMC scheme. It subsequently passed through various hands before it was placed on loan to the Museum of Flight in Seattle in 2006 as N49JC. In 2011 it was acquired on behalf of the Shuttleworth Collection (where it is seen here) but it was subsequently sold in 2016 and is now under restoration to fly at Duxford. Steve Bridgewater

Hawker Hurricane

Often overshadowed by the Spitfire the Hurricane has seen something of a resurgence in recent years and there are now nine flyable examples on the UK register (albeit one of those is normally based in Germany). One more aircraft is expected to fly again before the end of 2017.

Type	Owner	Reg	Serial	Codes	Status
Hurricane I	James Brown	G-HUPW	R4118	R4118/UP-W	Flyable
Hurricane I	Anglia Aircraft Restorations Ltd	G-ROBT	P2902	P2902/DX-R	Flyable
Hurricane I	Hugh Taylor	G-HITT	P3717	P3717/SW-P	Flyable
Hurricane IIB	Karl-Friedemann Grimminger	G-CBOE	5487 RCAF	'AG244'	Flyable
Hurricane IIB	Hangar 11 Collection	G-HHII	5403 RCAF	'BE505'	Flyable
Hurricane IIC	BBMF	-	LF363	LF363/'GN-F'/'SD-A'	Flyable
Hurricane IIC	BBMF	-	PZ865	PZ865/'EG-S'	Flyable
Hurricane X	Peter Monk/Biggin Hill Heritage Hangar	G-CHTK	AE977	'P2921/GZ-L'	Flyable
Hurricane XII	Historic Aircraft Collection Ltd	G-HURI	5711 RCAF	'P3700/RF-E'	Flyable
Sea Hurricane IB	Shuttleworth Trust	G-BKTH	Z7015	Z7015/7-L	Flyable
Hurricane I	Hawker Restorations Ltd	G-HRLI	V7497	-	Restoration
Hurricane IIB	Karl-Friedemann Grimminger	G-BYDL	Z5207	-	Restoration
Hurricane IIB	Hawker Restorations Ltd	-	Z5053	-	Restoration
Hurricane I	Cambridge Bomber & Fighter Society	-	L1639	-	Stored
Hurricane I	Hawker Restorations Ltd	-	L1866	-	Stored
Hurricane II	Patina Ltd/The Fighter Collection	-	Ex Soviet AF	-	Stored
Hurricane IIB	Biggin Hill Heritage Hangar	-	BH238	-	Stored
Hurricane IV	Robs Lamplough	-	KZ191	-	Stored
Sea Hurricane XIIA	Kevin Wheatcroft	G-BRKE	BW853	-	Stored

◀ When Peter Vacher discovered Hurricane I R4118 in India in 1982 he had no idea how important a find it was – in fact the aircraft is described by many as the most historic fighter aircraft to have survived the war. R4118 flew 49 sorties from Croydon and shot down five enemy aircraft during the Battle of Britain and later saw further combat over the North Sea before being shipped to India as a training aircraft. However it was never needed and remained in its packing case in Bombay until 1947 when it was struck off charge and donated to a university for engineering instruction. There it remained, unassembled, until Peter Vacher began negotiating to return it to the UK in 1996. Five years later the aircraft finally arrived in the UK and it took to the air again on December 23, 2004 as G-HUPW. In 2015 Peter sold R4118 to James Brown's Hurricane Heritage and the Hurricane was moved to Old Warden. It flies in its original UP-W codes. Steve Bridgewater

▶ Hurricane I P3717 was delivered to 253 Sqn at Kirton in Lindsey before being transferred to RAF Kenley on August 29, 1940. However, the aircraft's Battle of Britain was brief – the day after it arrived at Kenley P3717 was scrambled with P/O Samolinski at the controls. Samolinski was credited with the destruction of a Bf 110 over Surrey but P3717 was so badly damaged that she had to be returned to Hawkers for significant repairs. Upon completion of repairs the aircraft was sent to Russia to serve with the Soviet Air Force as DR348. It was from here that she was recovered in the late 1990s by Jim Pearce and the long road to returning to airworthiness started. Hugh Taylor acquired P3717 in 2004 and after a complete rebuild by Hawker Restorations it returned to the skies on March 21, 2017. The aircraft is now based at Old Warden alongside Hurricane Heritage's R4118 and the Shuttleworth Collection's Z7015.
Darren Harbar

Karl-Friedemann Grimminger's Hurricane IIB began life in Canada as a Hurricane XII registered RCAF 5487. The aircraft crashed in 1942 and the remnants were subsequently shipped to the UK for restoration by Thruxton-based Classic Aero Engineering for Peter Tuplin and Paul Portelli. Following Portelli's death the project was sold to Phillip Lawton and Classic Aero Engineering returned it to the skies for him as G-CBOE on July 16, 2014. The aircraft has been rebuilt to Mk IIB standard and initially flew in Finnish AF markings as 'HC-465' before being repainted in an unusual silver Rhodesian AF scheme depicting 'AG244'. In 2015 the aircraft was sold to Karl-Friedemann Grimminger and although it remains on the UK register it is now based in Germany.

Steve Bridgewater

The Hangar 11 Collection's Hurricane IIB has been restored to 'Hurri-Bomber' configuration, although it doesn't actually fly with under-slung bombs. This aircraft began life in Canada where she was built in 1942 by the Canadian Car & Foundry Company and coded RCAF 5403. It served the RCAF until the end of the war when it was acquired by a farmer and 'robbed' of spare parts. It was acquired by collector Jack Arnold in the 1970s and eventually passed to Tony Ditheridge of Hawker Restorations Ltd. Restoration work began in 2005 and Hangar 11 Collection acquired it in 2007, registering it G-HHII and commissioning it to be restored to depict BE505, a Manston based Mk IIB operated by 174 (Mauritius) Sqn in 1942. G-HHII returned to the skies on January 27, 2009. Steve Bridgewater

The Biggin Hill Heritage Hangar's Hurricane X began life as Hurricane IB AE977. The aircraft was converted to Sea Hurricane standard in July 1942 but was involved in a mid-air collision in the December. The wreckage was excavated in 1960 and passed through various owners before it arrived with Hawker Restoration for rebuild for Sir Tim Wallis and Tony Ditheridge. It returned to the skies, appropriately registered G-TWTD, on June 7, 2000 wearing the codes LE-D. A year later it was sold to Tom Friedkin's Chino Warbirds Inc and it resided in California until it was shipped to Biggin Hill in the summer of 2012. Upon its return it was initially painted in 'Eagle Squadron' markings to depict 'P3886/UF-K' but in 2015 it was resprayed to represent 'P2921/L-GZ'. Both Steve Bridgewater

Left: In May 2015 G-HURI was repainted again, this time to depict 'P3700/RF-E' of 303 (Polish) Sqn. The original P3700 was abandoned by Sgt Kazimierz Wunsche over Kent on September 9, 1940 after sustaining damage from a Bf 109 during combat. Steve Bridgewater **Right:** For many years the only Hurricanes flying in the UK were the RAF owned examples flown by the Battle of Britain – but then Stephen Grey's The Fighter Collection began the restoration of Hurricane XII RCAF 5711. The remains of the former RCAF fighter were shipped to Duxford in 1982 and components from various other airframes were incorporated in the restoration, which took place at Duxford, Coventry and Coningsby. It flew again in 1989 and was painted in an Eagle Squadron scheme depicting 'Z7381/XR-T'

In 2002 G-HURI joined the Historic Aircraft Collection fleet at Duxford and in although it retained its XR-T scheme for a short time it was repainted as 'Z5140/HA-C' in 2004. This was an accurate depiction of a 126 Sqn Hurricane IIB flown during the siege of Malta and the aircraft was flown to the island to help commemorate the conflict.
Steve Bridgewater

In 1968 Z7015 was used as a static airframe in the film Battle of Britain but it was not until 1986 that thought was given to returning her to flyable condition. The aircraft was moved to Duxford and it would be almost ten years before the Sea Hurricane, now registered G-BKTH, returned to the skies on September 16, 1995. The aircraft flies in the colours of 880 NAS, Fleet Air Arm embarked on HMS *Indomitable* during 1942.
Steve Bridgewater

◀ Hurricane I P2902, was built by Gloster Aircraft and first flew in October 1939. During the Battle of Britain P2902 flew with 245 Sqn and was coded DX-B but it force landed on a beach in Dunkirk in 1940 after engaging two Bf 109s. There it remained until recovered by French enthusiasts in 1988. It was later obtained by warbird operator Rick Roberts, who sent it to Hawker Restorations with instructions to return it to flight as G-ROBT. In 2016 the aeroplane was sold to Anglia Aircraft Restorations Ltd and the aircraft flew again on June 19, 2017. It is thought it will ultimately be based at Duxford. Darren Harbar

Hawker Sea Fury

The Sea Fury was the last piston-powered fighter to serve with the Fleet Air Arm and was powered by the powerful but complex 3,000hp Bristol Centaurus 18-cyilinder radial engine giving it a top speed of around 460mph (400kts). The engine has been the type's 'Achilles Heel' in recent years, with a number of engine failures resulting in the type being a rarely seen warbird. As these words were written The Fighter Collection was embarking on a project to re-engine WG655 with a US-built Pratt & Whitney R2800.

Sea Fury/ISS Fury	Anglia Aircraft Restorations Ltd	G-CBEL	315 Iraqi AF	'SR661/P'	Flyable
Sea Fury FB.11	Patina Ltd/The Fighter Collection	G-BUCM	VX653	VX653	Restoration
Sea Fury FB.11	Royal Navy Historic Flight	-	VR930	VR930	Stored
Sea Fury T.20	Nicholas Grey/The Fighter Collection	G-CHFP	WG655	WG655/910-GN	Restoration
Sea Fury T.20	Naval Aviation Ltd	G-RNHF	VX281	VX281	Restoration
Sea Fury T.20	Patina Ltd/The Fighter Collection	-	VX345	VX345	Restoration

Anglia Aircraft Restorations Ltd's Hawker ISS Fury G-CBEL was delivered to the Iraqi Air Force in 1953 and served as IAF 315 until 1979 when it was acquired by Ed Jurist and David Tallichet (along with the rest of the Iraqi Fury fleet) and shipped to Florida. It was restored to fly by the Coleman Warbird Museum in Texas in the late 1980s and was sold to Concorde pilot John Bradshaw in the UK in 1991. It remained in the UK until 2009 when it was sold to Australia and re-registered as VH-SFW. The aircraft returned to the UK in 2016 and has been painted to represent SR661 – the prototype Hawker Sea Fury.
Darren Harbar

IN FOCUS

Hawker Hurricane IIC LF363

Between 2014 and 2016 LF363 was painted to represent Hurricane Mk 1 P3395 'JX-B', the personal aircraft of Sgt Pilot Arthur 'Darkie' Clowes DFM, of No 1 Squadron, during the Battle of Britain. The aircraft is seen here departing on September 15, 2015 from Goodwood for the 75th anniversary of the Battle. *Steve Bridgewater*

Hawker Hurricane LF363 is believed to be the last Hurricane ever to enter service with the RAF. LF363 was built at the Hawker factory at Langley near Slough and first flew on January 1, 1944. It was delivered to 5 MU on January 28 that year - and has been in continuous RAF service from then until today.

The aircraft served with 63 Sqn at Turnhouse, 309 (Polish) Sqn at Drem (where it was used on shipping protection patrols off the Scottish coast) and 26 Sqn with whom it flew naval artillery spotting and reconnaissance sorties.

At the end of the war LF363 was placed into open storage at Langley, waiting to be scrapped, but in mid-1949 it was spotted by Air Commodore (later Air Vice Marshal) Stanley Vincent CB, DFC, AFC. Vincent requested that LF363 be made airworthy and on September 15 he led the Battle of Britain flypast over London in LF363.

The aircraft's on-going survival then fell to the various front line squadrons and station flights it passed through before it returned to Hawkers in 1956 for a major refurbishment. The following year it became a founding aircraft of the Historic Aircraft Flight, the forerunner of the Battle of Britain Memorial Flight (BBMF) and has been allocated to the unit ever since.

Sadly LF363 cannot claim to have an unbroken flying history though, because on September 11, 1991 it suffered an engine failure and forced landed at RAF Wittering, Cambridgeshire. The aircraft was seriously damaged by the impact and the ensuing fierce fire but fortunately the pilot escaped with 'just' a broken ankle and minor burns.

Spitfire PR.XIX PS853 was sold to help fund LF363's subsequent rebuild and the Hurricane was despatched to Historic Flying Ltd (then at Audley End, Essex) in 1994 for a complete restoration and flew again in 1998 – some seven years after it had force landed.

Over the years LF363 has worn a variety of colour schemes to honour a number of pilots, units and squadrons – a selection of those schemes are shown here.

Seen at Langley in the mid-1950s LF363 wears the silver scheme requested by Air Commodore Vincent.

▲ During filming of the *Battle of Britain* movie LF363 wore various schemes, including 'H3421/MI-D'.

◀ When LF363 was handed over to the RAF's Historic Aircraft Flight in 1957 LF363 was painted in a generic RAF green and brown camouflage, but was devoid of unit codes. It is seen here visiting RAF Stradishall in the mid-60s. *Richard Cousens via Awyr Aviation Archives*

Between 1969 and 1972 LF363 wore a scheme based on the aircraft flown by Douglas Bader, complete with LE-D codes.

LF363 gained a dramatic 85 Sqn night-fighter scheme, complete with VY-X codes, in 1983 and carried these markings until 1986.

In 1987 LF363 returned to a day-fighter scheme when it gained the NV-L codes of a 79 Sqn Hurricane.

After crashing at RAF Wittering following engine failure in 1991 LF363 was despatched to Historic Flying Ltd at Audley End for a complete rebuild to airworthy condition.

After its rebuild following crash and fire damage LF363 was, fittingly, painted in the markings of 56 Sqn – whose emblem is the Phoenix. Here the aircraft makes its post-restoration airshow debut at Duxford in October 1998.

In March 2006 LF363 was repainted to represent 17 Sqn Hurricane I P3878/YB-W, the aircraft of F/O Harold 'Birdy' Bird-Wilson during the Battle of Britain. He fought continuously through the Battle of France and the Battle of Britain, achieving six confirmed kills, sharing in the destruction of several others and being awarded a DFC. On September 24, 1940 when he became Adolf Galland's 40th victim and had to bale out of a flaming YB-W over the channel. *Steve Bridgewater*

For the 2017 season LF363 was repainted with different markings on each side to pay tribute to two surviving Battle of Britain pilots. The port side of the fuselage wears the GN-F codes of Tom Neil's 249 Sqn Hurricane and the starboard side is marked up with SD-A, representing one of the 501 Sqn Hurricanes flown by Paul Farnes. *Both Steve Bridgewater*

WARBIRD DIRECTORY | 75

IN FOCUS

Hawker Hurricane IIC PZ865

In 1998 PZ865 was repainted into a RAF Desert Air Force scheme – depicting aircraft 'J' of 261 Sqn in Malta in September 1940. Steve Bridgewater

In July 1944 Hawker Hurricane PZ865 was the last of 14,533 examples of the iconic fighter to roll off the production line. Wearing 'The Last of the Many' titling the aircraft was purchased back from the Air Ministry by Hawkers and initially placed in storage at the Langley factory.

At the end of the war PZ865 was brought out of storage, painted in a smart blue civilian colour scheme and used as both a communications aeroplane and 'chase-plane' by Hawker Aviation. It was eventually given the civil registration G-AMAU and Hawkers allowed it to be used for air racing – most notably in 1950 when it was entered in the King's Cup Air Race by HRH Princess Margaret. Flown by Group Captain Peter Townsend it achieved second place.

To make it more competitive PZ865 was modified for racing with the removal of its cannons and the installation of two 'overload' wing fuel tanks but in the 1960s PZ865 was repainted into camouflage once again. In this guise, in addition to being used as a company 'hack', the Hurricane appeared at various airshows – often in the hands of test pilot Bill Bedford. In 1968 it was used in the film *Battle of Britain* and then, following a complete overhaul by Hawker Siddeley, was donated to the RAF Historic Aircraft Flight at RAF Coltishall in March 1972. For many years the aircraft appeared as 'The Last of the Many' but eventually the decision was made to repaint the aircraft in frequently changing colour schemes to honour different pilots and units. A variety of those schemes appear here.

PZ865 at Langley in the summer of 1944.

In May 1950 PZ865 was painted into Hawker's 'house colours' of Oxford Blue and gold. Around this time the cannon stubbs were also removed. The aircraft is seen here preparing to start the 1950 Kings Cup air race with Group Captain Peter Townsend at the helm.

Between 1972 and 1977 PZ865 wore the markings of Sqn Ldr Bob Stanford-Tuck's 257 Sqn Hurricane DT-A.

Left: In 1982 PZ865 returned to its original camouflage and regained the 'Last of the Many' slogan below the cockpit. **Right:** To celebrate the 50th anniversary of the Battle of Britain PZ865 was painted to represent RF-U – a 303 Sqn Hurricane flown in the Battle by Josef Frantisek. *John Dibbs*

Left: In 1998 PZ865 was painted to pay tribute to the pilots of South East Asia Command. It wore the markings of a 5 Sqn Hurricane II coded 'Q' until it was repainted again in 2004. For many years PZ865 flew without cannons but fund raising by the Lincolnshire's Lancaster Association enabled these to be refitted in 1996 to restore the aircraft's appearance to that of a Hurricane IIC. **Right:** Between 2005 and 2010 PZ865 gained a night-fighter scheme representing Flt Lt Karel Kuttelwascher's 1 Sqn Hurricane BE581/JX-E. *Steve Bridgewater*

▶ Since 2010 PZ865 has worn a South East Asia Command scheme in tribute to Flt Lt Jimmy Whalen, who flew HW840/EG-S with 34 Sqn in 1944. Sadly, Jimmy lost his life on April 18, 1944, five days before his 24th birthday, during the Battle for Kohima. He had carried out 176 sorties against the enemy, 107 being over enemy territory and 23 at night. He had to his credit three Bf 109s destroyed and another damaged whilst flying from England and three Japanese Navy *Val* Type 99s destroyed over Ceylon. *Aeroplane Monthly Archive*

WARBIRD DIRECTORY | 77

Hawker Sea Fury
(continued)

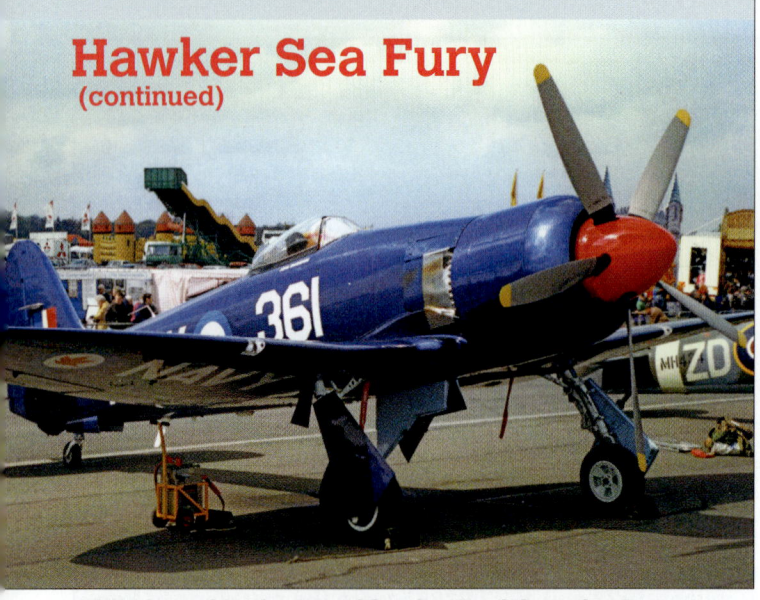

While based in the UK with John Bradshaw the Sea Fury operated as both N36SF and G-CBEL and flew in a metallic blue scheme adorned with Dutch, Canadian and Australian roundels. It is seen here at the 1992 Fighter Meet at North Weald, Essex. Neil Taylor via Awyr Aviation

Sea Fury FB.11 VX653 has been under long-term restoration at Duxford for The Fighter Collection. Now registered G-BUCM it had previously been on display at the RAF Museum, Hendon. Steve Bridgewater

Sea Fury FB.11 VR930 first flew from Kingston on February 23, 1948 and spent much of its career at the RN Fleet Requirements Unit at Hurn. It then spent a while in storage before joining the RAF museum and then the Fleet Air Arm Museum. Restoration to flying condition for the Fleet Air Arm Historic Flight began in 1990 and the aircraft flew again on March 1, 2001 wearing a Korean War-era paint scheme. The engine failed on August 21 but the pilot managed to land safely. After an engine rebuild VR930 flew again on September 13, 2004 – by which time it had been repainted into an earlier scheme. In recent years engine problems and certification issues have kept the aircraft ground-bound at its base at RNAS Yeovilton. Richard Freail

The Fighter Collection's Sea Fury T.20 G-CHFP began life as WG655 with the Fleet Air Arm. It later joined the Deutsche Luftfahrt-Berantungdienst in Cologne as a target tug and was painted red and registered D-CACU. In 1976 it was donated to the Fleet Air Arm Historic Flight and was operated until it was damaged after hitting a tree following an engine failure on July 15, 1990. The wreckage was sold and eventually restored to fly in the USA by Chuck Greenhill – albeit with the aid of an ex-Iraqi Fury fuselage centre section and wing. It flew again in May 2005 and was sold to Nick Grey in 2009. In the summer of 2017 the aircraft was being re-engined with a Pratt & Whitney R2800. Steve Bridgewater

◀ Naval Aviation Ltd's Sea Fury T.20 G-RNHF was built for the Royal Navy as VX281 in 1957 but in 1963 it was converted to a target tug for the Deutsche Luftfahrt-Berantungdienst in Cologne. It was painted red and registered D-CACO. In 1974 D-CACO was returned to the UK by collector Doug Arnold and subsequently sold to Spencer Flack as G-BCOW. It was later sold to the USA and passed through various owners before it was purchased from Wally Fisk's Amjet Aircraft Corp and shipped to the UK to be operated on behalf of the Fleet Air Arm Historic Flight as G-RNHF. On July 31, 2014 the aircraft was damaged in a forced landing following engine failure during the RNAS Culdrose Airshow. Lt Cdr Chris Gotke received the Air Force Cross for landing the aircraft with minimal damage and the Sea Fury is expected to fly again during the summer of 2017. Steve Bridgewater

Hawker Tempest

Although more than 1,700 Tempests were built, and the aircraft served extensively with air arms around the world, the type is yet to fly in civilian hands. G-TEMT and G-PEST have been under restoration with several owners since they were recovered from India in the late 1970s. The forward fuselage of G-TMPV was recovered from a scrapyard and is being reconstructed to ultimately fly with a Napier Sabre liquid-cooled H-24 sleeve-valve engine 'up front'.

Tempest II	Anglia Aircraft Restorations Ltd	G-PEST	MW401	-	Stored
Tempest II	Anglia Aircraft Restorations Ltd	G-TEMT	MW763	-	Restoration
Tempest V	Richard Grace	G-TMPV	JN658	-	Restoration

Hawker Typhoon

Perhaps one of the most eagerly awaited restorations in recent years is the Hawker Typhoon Preservation Group's reconstruction of Typhoon IB RB396, which force landed on April 1, 1945. The project was unveiled in October 2016 and the plan is to have the aircraft airworthy in time to celebrate the 80th anniversary of D-Day in 2024.

Hawker Typhoon IB RB396 was delivered to 174 'Mauritius' Sqn on January 4, 1945 and coded XP-W. The aircraft was lost on operations behind enemy lines on April 1 but pilot Flt Lt Chris House survived and evaded capture long enough to return to safety. After the war the fuselage was rescued by a local chemical company, with a view to using it as a chemical wash tank. Fortunately this conversion was never completed and the fuselage sat in the factory until saved by local historians. RB396 was then displayed in the museum at Twenthe in the Netherlands but in 2013 it was passed to the group that would become the Hawker Typhoon Preservation Group. The aircraft will be restored to fly complete with a 2,200hp Napier Sabre liquid-cooled H-24 engine. HTPG

Typhoon IB	Hawker Typhoon Preservation Group	-	RB396	-	Restoration

Ilyushin Il-2 Shturmovik

Although a combined 42,330 Ilyushin Il-2 and Il-10 aircraft were manufactured - making it the single most produced military aircraft design in aviation history - just one example has been restored to airworthy condition (in Russia for a US owner). A UK-based project had aimed to put one Shturmovik back in the air and restore a second example to static condition – however, work on the aircraft has now been shelved. The aircraft remain on the civil register but are now in storage.

Il-2 Shturmovik	Ronald Cooper/Steven Swallow	G-BZVW	1870710	-	Stored
Il-2 Shturmovik	Ronald Cooper/Steven Swallow	G-BZVX	1878576	-	Stored

Lavochkin La-11

Developed from the wartime La-9 as a long-range escort fighter the La-11 first flew in May 1947. No examples are currently airworthy although a number are on display in museums in Russia and China

▶ The Fighter Collection acquired its Lavochkin La-11 from Central Museum of the Air Forces at Monino, Russia in the in early 1990s. It remains in storage pending a future rebuild to airworthy condition. Steve Bridgewater

La-11	Patina Ltd/The Fighter Collection	-	20 Soviet AF	-	Stored

Lockheed P-38 Lightning

The twin-boom, twin engined P-38 was one of the most distinctive fighters of World War Two. The last example to fly in the UK was N3145X, which was lost in a fatal accident on July 14, 1996. However, in September 2014 the former-Classic Jets Fighter Museum owned P-38H 42-66841 was shipped to the UK from Australia for restoration to airworthy condition.

P-38H Lightning	Private Owner	-	42-66841	-	Restoration

Messerschmitt Bf 109/Hispano Buchón

World War Two-era Luftwaffe aircraft have always been relatively rare warbirds in UK skies. For many years Spanish-built, Merlin-engined Hispano Buchóns provided the only chance to see 'German' aircraft at airshows but in recent years more accurate Daimler-Benz-powered airframes have began to emerge from restoration. Biggin Hill Heritage Hangar's authentic Bf 109E flew for the first time in the UK on June 13 and was expected to make its UK airshow debut during 2017.

Hispano HA-1112 M1L Buchón	Historic Flying Ltd	G-AWHK	C4K-102	'Yellow 10'	Flyable
Messerschmitt Bf 109E-4	Biggin Hill Heritage Hangar Ltd	G-CIPB	WrkNr 3579	White 14	Flyable
Hispano HA-1112 M1L Buchón	Air Leasing Ltd	G-AWHM	C4K-99	-	Restoration
Hispano HA-1112 M4L Buchón	Air Leasing Ltd	G-AWHC	C4K-112	-	Restoration
Messerschmitt Bf 109E	Rare Aero Ltd	G-CDTI	WrkNr 4034	Black 6	Restoration
Messerschmitt Bf 109E-3	Charleston Aviation Services	-	WrkNr 0854	-	Restoration
Messerschmitt Bf 109E-3	Private Owner	-	WrkNr 1983	-	Restoration
Messerschmitt Bf 109G-2	Mark Oliver	G-JIMP	WrkNr 13605	Yellow 12	Restoration

In 2009 G-BWUE was transferred to Historic Flying Ltd and the following year it was returned to the colours and specification it wore while filming the *Battle of Britain* movie. In 2014 the aircraft reverted to its original G-AWHK registration. In June 2017 - as these words were being committed to print - it was repainted again, this time to represent Bf109 E-7 'Black 8' of JG-27 flown by Lt Werner Schroer based at Ain El Gazala, Libya in April 1941.
Steve Bridgewater

◀ Hispano HA-1112 M1L Buchón C4K-102 flew in the *Battle of Britain* film as 'Yellow 10' and was registered G-AWHK. At the end of filming it passed to Wilson 'Connie' Edwards and in 1971 it was sold to the Confederate Air Force as N9938. In 1993 the aircraft was sold to the Alpine Fighter Collection in Wanaka, New Zealand but the restoration to flying condition was not completed and in 1995 it was sold to the Old Flying Machine Company at Duxford, becoming G-BWUE. In 1997 the aircraft was sold to Robert Fleming who moved it to the Real Aeroplane Company at Breighton, Yorkshire for rebuild – it is seen here in 2001.
Steve Bridgewater

▲ Following restoration at Breighton G-BWUE returned to the skies on May 19, 2006 wearing the markings of 'Red 1'. The aircraft was later sold to Tom Blair's Spitfire Ltd and relocated to Duxford. Steve Bridgewater

◀ In 2016 G-AWHK was temporarily painted as 'Black 2' and used in the film *Dunkirk*. It is seen here preparing to take off from Duxford in May of that year. Steve Bridgewater

Left: Former Spanish Air Force Hispano HA-1112 M1L Buchón C4K-99 appeared in the *Battle of Britain* film as G-AWHM, coded as 'Yellow 7.' At the end of the filming the aircraft was acquired by Wilson 'Connie' Edwards and shipped to his ranch in Big Spring, Texas. It remained in his hangar until 2014 when it was one of five Buchóns sold to Swiss collector Paul Boschung. The aircraft is now under restoration at Sywell along with the unique two-seat Hispano HA-1112 M4L Buchón G-AWHC. Andy O'Dell **Right:** Bf 109E-3 'White 14' was being flown by JG2 when it was shot down and belly-landed near Calais, France during the Battle of Britain on September 2, 1940. It was then rebuilt as a Bf 109E-7 (coded 'White 7') and sent to the Eastern Front where it was shot down by Russian Hurricanes on August 2, 1942. The wreck was recovered in 1991 and sold to David Price's Museum of Flying in Santa Monica, California. Restoration was undertaken in the UK by Craig Charleston and the aircraft flew for the first time, from Chino, California as N81562, on September 29, 1999. In 2004 it was sold to Canadian collector Ed Russell, becoming CF-EML, and in 2014 it was acquired by the Biggin Hill Heritage Hangar and registered G-CIPB. It performed its first flight in the UK on June 13, 2017 and its airshow debut is eagerly awaited. Darren Harbar

Nakajima Ki-43 Hayabusa

No original examples of the Japanese Army Air Force's Ki-43 'Oscar' are currently flyable, although replicas have been constructed in the USA. The original airframe held by The Fighter Collection arrived in the 1990s but remains in storage pending a future restoration.

Ki-43 Hayabusa	Patina Ltd/The Fighter Collection	-	TBC	-	Stored

North American P-51 Mustang

In recent years the UK has traditionally boasted a healthy population of airworthy Mustangs, but exports and losses have reduced this figure of late. A number of restoration projects continue and numbers have been temporarily bolstered with the arrival of Comanche Fighters' P-51D N357FG to perform at the 2017 Flying Legends airshow at Duxford. Maurice Hammond's popular P-51D *Janie* was severely damaged in a landing incident in October 2016 but as it remains on the UK civil register it is listed here. Likewise, a number of replica 'Mustangs' now grace the UK register and are included here for the sake of completeness.

◀ G-BIXL retained her Memphis Belle markings until 2000 when research revealed her true identity. She was therefore repainted in her original blue nose 352th FG livery complete with HO-M codes and the name *Miss Helen*. In 2015 the aircraft was sold to Robert Tyrrell.

Type	Owner	Reg	Serial	Markings	Name	Status
P-51B Mustang	Comanche Fighters	N515ZB	43-24837	'43-24823/B6-O'	Berlin Express	Flyable
P-51D Mustang	Robert Tyrrell	G-BIXL	44-72216	44-72216/HO-M	Miss Helen	Flyable
P-51D Mustang	Pelham Ltd	G-BTCD	44-13704	'44-13704/'B7-H'	Ferocious Frankie	Flyable
P-51D Mustang	Sharkmouth Ltd	G-SHWN	44-73877	'KH774/GA-S'		Flyable
P-51D Mustang	Hangar 11 Collection	G-SIJJ	44-72035	44-72035/A3-3	Tall in the Saddle	Flyable
P-51D Mustang	Comanche Fighters	N357FG	44-12852	'44-13318/C5-N'	Frenesi	Flyable
TF-51D Mustang	Anglia Aircraft Restorations Ltd	G-TFSI	44-84847	'44-14561/CY-D'	Miss Velma	Flyable
P-51D Mustang	Iceni International Ltd (France)	G-CEBW	44-72181	44-72181/VF-S	Sunny VIII	Restoration
P-51D Mustang	Phil Earthey (France)	G-CITN	44-73196	44-73196		Restoration
P-51D Mustang	Philip Warner	G-UAKE	44-13954	44-13954/CL-U	Da Quake	Restoration
P-51D Mustang	Private Owner	N51CK	44-64005	E9-Z	Mary Mine	Restoration
P-51D Mustang	Maurice Hammond	G-MSTG	45-11518	'44-14419/LH-F'	Janie	Stored

REPLICAS

Type	Owner	Reg	Serial	Markings	Status
P-51D Mustang (Jurca MJ-77)	Paul Carlton & Denis Finan	G-PSIR	-	'474008/VF-R'	Flyable
P-51D Mustang (Stewart S-51)	Kevin Armstrong	G-CGOI	-	'413926/E2-S'	Flyable
P-51D Mustang (Titan T-51)	Benedict Chester-Master	G-CIFD	-	'2106638/E9-R'	Flyable
P-51D Mustang (Titan T-51)	John Gammidge	G-CIXK	-	KH570'/5J-X	Flyable
P-51D Mustang (Titan T-51)	John Carey	G-CMPC	-	'36922 USAAF'/WD-Y	Flyable
P-51D Mustang (Titan T-51)	David Houghton	G-DHYS	-	'414907 USAAF'/CY-S	Flyable
P-51D Mustang (Titan T-51)	Alexander Wordsworth	G-FION	-	'441968 USAAF'/VF-E	Flyable
P-51D Mustang (Titan T-51)	Alan Bales	G-MUZY	-	'472218 USAAF'/WZ-I	Flyable
P-51D Mustang (Titan T-51)	Alan Evans	G-MZTG	-	-	Restoration
P-51D Mustang (Titan T-51)	Benedict Chester-Master	G-TSIM	-	CY-G	Flyable

◀ Comanche Fighters' F-6K photo-reconnaissance Mustang 44-12852 is being shipped to the UK this summer to take part in the Flying Legends Airshow at Duxford. The aircraft was sold surplus after the war and registered as NX66111 to take part in the 1946 Cleveland Air Races as racer No.80 *Full House*. However, it engine failed and was it was forced to crash-land. The aircraft was then sold to Jack Hardwick in the early 1950s, who rebuilt it and sold it to the Dominican Air Force. It served the South American air arm as FAD 1900 until it was sold into private ownership in the USA in 1984. Registered N21023 the aircraft flew again in 1990 and was sold to the Beasley family, who painted it as *Frenesi*, the personal mount of 357th FG ace Gen Tommy Hayes. The aircraft has just been completely restored for Dan Friedkin's Comanche Fighters and re-registered as N357FG but retains the markings of *Frenesi*. Comanche Fighters

◀ Over the winter of 2015/16 G-SIJJ was repainted into original 332nd FG 'Red Tail' markings complete with the name *Tall in the Saddle*. Research showed that the aircraft had been flown by both Capt Wendell Lucas and Lt Col George Hardy – the latter a combat veteran who flew 21 sorties and was a recipient of the Air Medal. Darren Harbar

Left: When it was first restored G-BIXL flew as 472216/HO-L and carried the name *Silver Dollar*, but in 1989 the aircraft was repainted in olive drab and gained the codes AJ-L and the name *Miss L* to appear in the feature film *Memphis Belle*. **Right:** P-51D Mustang 44-72035 was built in late 1944 and in March of the following year she arrived in Italy to be assigned to the 332nd FG, the famed 'Tuskegee Airmen.' Little is known of her squadron service but she returned to the USA in September 1945 and put into storage before joining the Oklahoma Air National Guard in 1948. In 1950 she was assigned to the Nevada Air National Guard but was finally retired in October 1956. The following year she was sold into civilian hands becoming N5411V and she remained with the same owner for 24 years before moving to Humberto Escobar in Colombia as HK-2812P (later HK-2812X). In August 1989 the aircraft arrived in France for new owner Jacques Bourret, who registered it as F-AZMU and painted it in the colours of Lt Jacques E Young's 44-640076 *Jumpin' Jacques*. The aircraft arrived in the UK for Peter Teichman's Hangar 11 Collection in 2003 and was originally operated in *Jumpin Jacques* markings as G-SIJJ. Both Steve Bridgewater

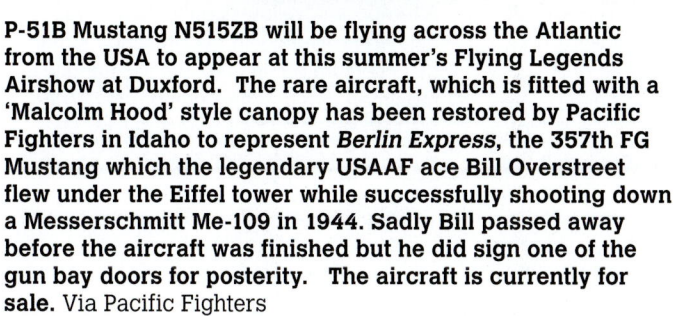

P-51B Mustang N515ZB will be flying across the Atlantic from the USA to appear at this summer's Flying Legends Airshow at Duxford. The rare aircraft, which is fitted with a 'Malcolm Hood' style canopy has been restored by Pacific Fighters in Idaho to represent *Berlin Express*, the 357th FG Mustang which the legendary USAAF ace Bill Overstreet flew under the Eiffel tower while successfully shooting down a Messerschmitt Me-109 in 1944. Sadly Bill passed away before the aircraft was finished but he did sign one of the gun bay doors for posterity. The aircraft is currently for sale. Via Pacific Fighters

Dual-control TF-51D Mustang was built as a P-51D (44-84847) and was one of the last Mustangs constructed at the North American plant in Dallas, Texas. Details of her service career are sparse but at least one photograph shows her serving with the 45th Tactical Reconnaissance Squadron at Kimpo, South Korea, during the Korean War. She was shipped back to the USA in 1951 and served with Air National Guard units until 1956 when she disappears. In January 1999 the aircraft reappeared as a restoration project and was acquired by The Fighter Collection and rebuild to TF-51 configuration began at Chino. Darren Harbar

WARBIRD DIRECTORY | 83

IN FOCUS

North American P-51D Mustang G-BTCD

Alistair Kay taxies G-BTCD in after a display at Duxford. The aircraft currently wears the colours of 44-13704/B7-H as flown by Maj Wallace E Hopkins. Hopkins – who was Deputy Commander of the 374th FS and flew a total of 76 combat missions with the unit (and was credited with eight victories and one and a 'half' damaged) named the aircraft *Ferocious Frankie* after his wife.   Steve Bridgewater

North American P-51D G-BTCD was the first military painted Mustang warbird to fly in the UK and has been based at Duxford for more than 35 years.

The aircraft was built as 44-73149 by North American Aviation at Inglewood, California and delivered to the USAAF on February 27, 1945. Some reports suggest the aircraft was stationed in the UK with the USAAF 8th AF for eleven months in late 1945/early 1946 but it seems more likely that the aircraft was retained 'Stateside' and used by various training units.

In April 1947 the aircraft was passed to the Royal Canadian Air Force, with whom it flew as RCAF 9568 until 1953 when it was placed into open storage at Carberry, Manitoba. The aircraft was officially struck off charge in February 1957 and acquired by civilian owners James H Defuria and Fred J Ritts, who registered it as N6340T. In 1962 it was transferred to Ernest W Beehler and in 1965 it made a wheels-up landing at Lexington, Missouri. The aircraft was restored for Charles Beck and Edward J Modes in California who painted it red and raced it as *Candyman* from 1974 to 1976.

In 1980 Stephen Grey acquired the aeroplane and arranged for it to be ferried to the UK. Legend has it that Stephen wanted a Spitfire but while he was waiting for his example (ML417) to be restored he acquired a Bearcat and Mustang to fly. He loved both types so much that he kept them when the Spitfire was completed – forming the nucleus of what would become The Fighter Collection.

Fitted with drop tanks John Crocker flew

The Mustang shows off her newly applied *Moose* markings following a repaint at Stansted in the late 1980s. The original scheme was applied by British Airways engineers at Heathrow and was based on the P-51D flown by Lt M A 'Moose' Becraft. Stephen Grey ideally wanted a scheme that included his initials and originally considered painting his Mustang as a 112 Sqn RAF Mustang KH774/GA-S – although he rejected that scheme it would later appear on P-51D G-SHWN more than 30 years later!

N6340T across the Atlantic via Reykjavik, Prestwick and Gatwick to Stephen's then base in Geneva – arriving on August 20, 1980. Less than a year later the aeroplane moved to Duxford, where it would remain based for the next 35 years. The aircraft's British airshow debut was at the 1981 Biggin Hill Air Fair (in the hands of Ray Hanna), by which time it had been painted to represent P-51D 44-63221/GA-S *Moose*, flown by Lt M A 'Moose' Becraft with the 357th FG.

In 1986 the registration changed to N51JJ and in 1991 it was finally placed on the UK register, becoming G-BTCD. Over the coming years the Mustang appeared in various temporary paint schemes for filming projects but always reverted back to its *Moose* colours until 1999 when it was sold to the Old Flying Machine Company. A temporary 'yellow nose' scheme was applied for work with the Breitling Fighters display team but in 2002 the Mustang was repainted into the markings of 44-13704/B7-H *Ferocious Frankie* as flown by Maj Wallace E Hopkins with the 374th FS, 361st FG.

Today the aircraft remains in the care of the Old Flying Machine Company and is a regular airshow attendee.

84 | WARBIRD DIRECTORY

Although the colour scheme for the original 44-63221 filled the owner's requirements (a military scheme to include his initials) that particular Mustang flew in bare metal. This was not considered ideal for operations in wet European skies so the decision was made to paint the airframe olive drab but retain the G4-S codes and distinctive nose art. Here, *Moose* departs La Ferte Alais in the early 1990s.

In homage to the aircraft's air racing history Stephen Grey elected to keep the *Candyman* name on the starboard side of the nose. This, combined with the olive drab paint and non-standard yellow rudder made for a very unauthentic scheme – but it was eye-catching, memorable and very popular.

When the Mustang appeared in the 1987 film *Empire of the Sun* it was repainted as *My Dallas Darlin'*. It was now registered as N51JJ ad appeared alongside Stephen Grey's second P-51D (G-PSID), the latter flying as *Tugboat*.

◀ When G-BTCD passed to the OFMC in 1999 it was given a temporary repaint into the markings of 463221/E2-Z. The yellow nose was chosen to fit in with the remainder of the Breitling Fighters display team - all of which were adorned with the same coloured spinners or cowlings.

For the 1989 film *Memphis Belle* the P-51D was painted olive drab but, unlike the other aircraft used for filming, retained its individual nose art.

WARBIRD DIRECTORY | 85

IN FOCUS — North American P-51D Mustang G-SHWN

Laas Ness flies P-51D Mustang G-SHWN in 2016. The aircraft is painted to represent an Mustang IV belonging to 112 Sqn RAF, complete with GA-S codes and dramatic shark's mouth nose art. *Steve Bridgewater*

North American P-51D 44-73877 was built in 1945 and too late to see active service during World War Two. The aircraft was therefore delivered straight into storage and she remained there until January 1951 was it was transferred to the Royal Canadian Air Force as RCAF 9279.

The aircraft served with 403 (Auxiliary) Sqn at Calgary, Alberta until 1958 when it was struck off charge and sold to New Yorkers James H Defuria and Fred J Ritts. In turn, they sold it back to Canada in 1960 when it joined Neil McClain in Strathmore, Alberta as CF-PCZ.

On April 29, 1968 the Mustang was acquired by Paul D Finefrock and flown to Oklahoma where it was registered as N167F. Just over a year later the aircraft was damaged while taxiing at the Euless Air Races in Texas when it collided with P-51D N2870D. The wreckage was subsequently stored until 1980 when it was sold to Anders Saether's Scandinavian Historic Flight (SHF) in Norway. Vintage Aircraft at Fort Collins, Colorado were commissioned to restore the aeroplane and it flew again in 1985.

N167F arrived in Norway in June 1986, by which time it had been painted to represent Clarence 'Bud' Anderson's 357th FG Mustang B6-S *Old Crow* – although it retained its original tail number 44-73877.

The aircraft was a regular visitor the UK and wore a variety of colour schemes during its time with the SHF (and on lease to the Old Flying Machine Company) but in 2015 the aircraft was sold to UK-based Sharkmouth Ltd and re-registered as G-SHWN. It is now painted to represent an RAF 112 Sqn Mustang IV coded GA-S and carrying a distinctive shark's mouth motif on the nose.

◀ **For much of its time in Europe the Mustang wore a silver-based scheme representing the P-51 flown by 357th FG 'Triple Ace' Clarence 'Bud' Anderson. As part of the 'Yoxford Boys' at Leiston, Suffolk 'Bud' shot down 16 ¼ victories flying the original Old Crow. The 357th FG was credited with shooting down 609 ½ enemy aircraft in only 15 months and produced 42 Aces.** *Steve Bridgewater*

86 | WARBIRD DIRECTORY

In 1993 N167F was leased to the Old Flying Machine Company and temporarily painted as 19 Sqn RAF Mustang IV KM272/QV-S *Dooley Bird*. The aircraft is seen here in the hands of Mark Hanna at the 1993 North Weald Fighter Meet. Neil Taylor via Awyr Aviation Communication

Left: For her role in the 1989 film *Memphis Belle* N167F was painted olive drab and wore the name *Cisco* on the nose. All the Mustangs in the film wore AJ- codes with the individual aircraft letter chosen to represent the owner – as such the Norwegian based SHF aeroplane became AJ-N. Likewise, Ray Hanna's P-51 became AJ-H, Charles Church's aeroplane was AJ-C, Robs Lamplough's was AJ-L and Stephen Grey's example was AJ-S. **Right:** Between 1998 and 2001 N167 was painted to represent Lt Urban L Drew's Mustang 44-14164/ E2-D *Detroit Miss*. The original 375th FS, 361st FG aircraft was based at Bottisham, Cambridgeshire and Drew was credited with six victories including two Me-262 jets in a single mission.

For the 2001 Flying Legends Airshow at Duxford N167F was painted into an authentic olive drab version of its *Old Crow* markings (complete with white wall tyres!) and 'Bud' Anderson was able to fly in the rear seat overhead Leiston one final time.

WARBIRD DIRECTORY | 87

Supermarine Spitfire/Seafire

The Spitfire is, without doubt, the most popular warbird fighter in UK skies – both in terms of number flying and the universal adoration it receives from the general public. As of June 2017 there were 33 Spitfires and Seafires flying in the UK with several others very close to returning to the skies. Airworthy examples range from early Mk Is to Rolls-Royce Griffon-powered Mk XVIII and XIXs. Numbers are also bolstered by a number of replica airframes – of differing levels of authenticity.

Spitfire I X4650 made its first flight from Eastleigh on the October 23, 1940 before joining 54 Sqn at RAF Catterick, Yorkshire two days later. The aircraft was involved in a mid-air collision in December 1940 and the wreckage was discovered on the banks of the River Lever in 1976. The remains were acquired by Peter Monk in 1995 and restoration work soon commenced. The aircraft flew again for the first time (from Biggin Hill, Kent) in March 2012 as G-CGUK and the aircraft is now owned by Houston, Texas-based Comanche Fighters and lives at Duxford. It wears its original 54 Sqn KL-A unit codes. Steve Bridgewater

Spitfire I	Imperial War Museum	G-CFGJ	N3200	N3200/QV-	Flyable
Spitfire I	Comanche Warbirds Ltd	G-CGUK	X4650	X4650/KL-A	Flyable
Spitfire IA	Spitfire The One Ltd	G-AIST	AR213	'P7308/XR-D'	Flyable
Spitfire IIA	BBMF	-	P7350	P7350/'QJ-G/QV-E'	Flyable
Spitfire VB	BBMF	-	AB910	AB910/'SH-F'	Flyable
Spitfire VB	Historic Aircraft Collection Ltd	G-MKVB	BM597	BM597/JH-C	Flyable
Spitfire VB	Patina Ltd/The Fighter Collection	G-LFVB	EP120	EP120/AE-A	Flyable
Spitfire VB	Comanche Warbirds Ltd	G-CISV	EP122	EP122/GL-B	Flyable
Spitfire VC	Fairfax Spitfires LLP	G-IBSY	EE602	EE602/DU-V	Flyable
Spitfire IX	Merlin Aviation Ltd	G-ASJV	MH434	MH434/ZD-B	Flyable
Spitfire IX	BBMF	-	MK356	MK356/'QJ-R'	Flyable
Spitfire IX	Martin Phillips	G-BRSF	RR232	RR232/'PV181/RAB'	Flyable
Spitfire IX	Peter Monk	G-PMNF	TA805	TA805/'FX-M'	Flyable
Spitfire T.VIII	Paul Andrews	G-AIDN	MT818	MT818	Flyable
Spitfire T.9	Warbird Experiences Ltd	G-BMSB	MJ627	MJ627/9G-Q	Flyable
Spitfire T.9	Air Leasing Ltd	G-LFIX	ML407	ML407/OU-V	Flyable
Spitfire T.9	Keith Perkins/Aero Legends	G-CICK	NH341	NH341/DB-A	Flyable
Spitfire T.9	Historic Flying Ltd	G-CCCA	PV202	PV202/'5R-H'	Flyable
Spitfire T.9	Anthony Hodgson	G-CTIX	PT462	PT462/'SW-A'	Flyable
Spitfire T.9	Boultbee Vintage LLP	G-ILDA	SM520	SM520/'KJ-I'	Flyable
Spitfire PR.XI	Hangar 11 Collection	G-MKXI	PL965	PL965/R	Flyable
Spitfire XIV	Anglia Aircraft Restorations Ltd	G-SPIT	MV293	'MV268/JE-J'	Flyable
Spitfire XVI	Downlock Ltd	G-PBIX	RW382	RW382/3W-P	Flyable
Spitfire XVI	Spitfire Ltd	G-OXVI	TD248	TD248/'CR-S'	Flyable
Spitfire XVI	Keith Perkins/Aero Legends	G-CGYJ	TD314	TD314/FX-P	Flyable
Spitfire XVI	Stephen Stead	G-MXVI	TE184	TE184/'9N-B'	Flyable
Spitfire XVI	BBMF	-	TE311	TE311/'SZ-G'	Flyable

Type	Owner	Registration	Serial	Markings	Status
Spitfire XVIII	Spitfire Ltd	G-BUOS	SM845	SM845/'R'	Flyable
Spitfire PR.XIX	BBMF	-	PM631	PM631	Flyable
Spitfire PR.XIX	Rolls-Royce PLC	G-RRGN	PS853	PS853/C	Flyable
Spitfire PR.XIX	BBMF	-	PS915	PS915	Flyable
Seafire IIIC	Air Leasing Ltd	G-BUAR	PP972	PP972/11-5N	Flyable
Seafire XVII	Kennet Aviation	G-KASX	SX336	SX336/VL	Flyable
Spitfire I	Peter Monk Ltd	G-CDGU	X4276	-	Restoration
Spitfire IA	Mark One Partners LLC	G-CFGN	P9373	-	Restoration
Spitfire IIA	Mark Oliver	G-CGRM	P8088	-	Restoration
Spitfire IIA	Martin Phillips	G-TCHZ	P7819	-	Restoration
Spitfire IIB	Retro Track & Air	G-RRFF	P8208	-	Restoration
Spitfire VA	Peter Wood	-	AD540	-	Restoration
Spitfire VB	George Farrant	G-CHVJ	AD189	-	Restoration
Spitfire VB	Peter Wood	-	BL688	-	-Restoration
Spitfire VB	Ian Ward	G-SSVB	BM539	-	Restoration
Spitfire VC	Shuttleworth Trust	G-AWII	AR501	AR501/A-NN	Restoration
Spitfire VC	Aero Vintage Ltd	G-CDGY	EF545	-	Restoration
Spitfire VIII	Aviation Heritage Foundation Ltd	G-CFGA	A58-441 (RAAF)	-	Restoration
Spitfire VIII	Composite Mast Engineering & Technology Ltd	G-RAAF	JF872	-	Restoration
Spitfire VIII	Alec Wilson	-	MD338	-	Restoration
Spitfire IX	Peter Monk Ltd	G-BRRA	MK912	MK912/SH-L	Restoration
Spitfire IX	Hangar 11 Collection	G-BYDE	PT879	PT879/Soviet AF	Restoration
Spitfire IX	Mervyn Aldridge	G-CBNU	ML411	ML411	Restoration
Spitfire IX	Historic Flying Ltd	G-CGJE	RK858	-	Restoration
Spitfire IX	Mark Bennett	G-CGZU	LZ842	LZ842/'EF-F'	Restoration
Spitfire IX	Boultbee Vintage LLP	G-IRTY	MJ271	-	Restoration
Spitfire IX	Peter Monk	G-JGCA	TE517	-	Restoration
Spitfire IX	Mark Collenette	G-MCDB	MA764	-	Restoration
Spitfire IX	Paul Andrews	G-SDNI	ML119	-	Restoration
Spitfire IX	Martin Phillips	G-TCHO	EN179	-	Restoration
Spitfire IX	Mark Bennet-	SM639	-	-	Restoration
Spitfire IX	Martin Cobb	VH-IXT	TE566	-	Restoration
Spitfire IX	Pay's Flying Museum (Australia)	-	BS548	-	Restoration
Spitfire T.9	Warbird Experiences Ltd	G-ACAV	MJ772	MJ772	Restoration
Spitfire T.9	Martin Phillips	G-TCHI	BS410	-	Restoration
Spitfire PR.XI	Propshop Ltd	G-PRXI	PL983	-	Restoration
Spitfire XII	Air Leasing Ltd	G-FXII	EN224	-	Restoration
Spitfire XVI	Aero Engineering Ltd	G-SAEA	SL611	-	Restoration
Spitfire XVI	Peter Monk Ltd	-	TB885	-	Restoration
Spitfire F22	Kennet Aviation	-	PK664	-	Restoration
Seafire XV	Tim Percy	G-TGVP	SR462	-	Restoration
Seafire XVII	Seafire Displays Ltd	G-RIPH	SX300	-	Restoration
Seafire F46	Craig Charleston	G-CFZJ	LA543	-	Restoration
Seafire F46	Seafire Displays Ltd	G-FRSX	LA546	-	Restoration
Spitfire PR.IV	Peter Arnold	G-PRIV	BP926	-	Stored
Spitfire VC	Martin Cobb	-	LZ844	LZ844/'UP-X'	Stored
Spitfire IX	Private Owner	-	NH238	NH238/'D-A'	Stored
Spitfire IX	Airframe Assemblies	-	EN570	-	Stored
Spitfire XIV	Rolls-Royce PLC	G-ALGT	RM689	-	Stored
Spitfire XIV	Paul Andrews	G-DBKL	RM694	-	Stored
Spitfire XIV	Paul Andrews	G-JNMA	RM927	-	Stored
Spitfire XVI	Airframe Assemblies	-	TB382	-	Stored
Spitfire XVI	Private Owner	-	SL542	-	Stored
Spitfire XVIII	Airframe Assemblies	-	TP298	-	Stored
Spitfire F22	Peter Arnold	G-SPXX	PK519	-	Stored
Spitfire F22	Patina Ltd/The Fighter Collection	-	PK624	-	Stored
Seafire IIC	Mark One Partners LLC	G-CFGI	MB293	-	Stored
Seafire IIIC	Aircraft Spares & Materials Ltd	G-BWEM	RX168	-	Stored

◀ Spitfire I N3200 was taken on strength by 19 Sqn at Duxford in April 1940 and on May 26 was being flown by the squadron's commanding officer, Sqn Ldr Geoffrey Dalton Stephenson, during the evacuation of Dunkirk. N3200 was hit by ground fire and one bullet holed the radiator. With his engine seized, Stephenson put the stricken Spitfire down on the beach at Sangatte, where he was picked up by the Germans and became a POW. The Spitfire sank into the beach, where it remained for 46 years until it was discovered in 1986 and excavated by a group of enthusiasts. The remains were put on public display until 2000 when the aircraft was acquired by Simon Marsh and Tom Kaplan. IWM

REPLICAS					
Isaacs Spitfire	Alan Harpley	G-CGIK	-	'EN691/SD-X'	Flyable
Isaacs Spitfire	Alan James	G-ISAC	-	'TZ164/OI-A'	Flyable
Isaacs Spitfire	Stephen Vince	G-BBJI	-	'RN218'	Stored
Jurca Spitfire	Timothy Major	G-CHBW	-	'AD370/PJ-C'	Stored
Spitfire Mk 26 (Replica)	Cokebusters Ltd	G-CCGH	-	'AB196'	Flyable
Spitfire Mk 26 (Replica)	Paul Whitaker & Michael Hanley	G-CCJL	-	'PV303/ON-B'	Flyable
Spitfire Mk 26 (Replica)	David Bishop	G-CEFC	-	'RB142/DW-B'	Flyable
Spitfire Mk 26 (Replica)	Angela Jones	G-CENI	-	'W3257/EF-Y'	Flyable
Spitfire Mk 26 (Replica)	Steven Marsh	G-CEPL	-	'P9398/KL-B'	Flyable
Spitfire Mk 26 (Replica)	Bertha Property LLP	G-CGWI	-	'BL927/JH-I'	Flyable
Spitfire Mk 26 (Replica)	Andrew Counsell	G-CIEN	-	'PL788'	Flyable
Spitfire Mk 26 (Replica)	Stephen Markham	G-CIXM	-	'PL793'	Flyable
Spitfire Mk 26 (Replica)	G-ENAA Syndicate	G-ENAA	-	'EN130/FN-A'	Flyable
Spitfire Mk 26 (Replica)	Wright Grumman Aviation Ltd	G-HABT	-	'BL735/BT-A'	Flyable
Spitfire Mk 26 (Replica)	Richard Collenette	G-PIXY	-	'RK855/FT-C'	Flyable
Spitfire Mk 26 (Replica)	Stephen Hall	G-SMSP	-	'JG241/ZX-J'	Flyable
Spitfire Mk 26 (Replica)	Robert Parnall	G-CJWO	-	'BL688'	Restoration
Spitfire Mk 26 (Replica)	Martin Overall	G-CJWW	-	-	Restoration
Spitfire Mk 26 (Replica)	David Whitmore	G-CJYY	-	-	Restoration
Spitfire Mk 26 (Replica)	Bertha Property LLP	G-RORB	-	-	Restoration

Restoration of N3200 began in 2007 with Historic Flying Ltd undertaking the work at Duxford in conjunction with Airframe Assemblies and RetroTrack & Air. The aircraft took to the skies again on March 26, 2014 (registered G-CFGJ) and the following year it was donated to the Imperial War Museum. It is now based at Duxford and wears the same QV – codes it wore in May 1940 (it was shot down before an individual unit letter could be allocated to the aeroplane). *Steve Bridgewater*

Left: Spitfire IA AR213 was built at the Westland Aircraft Factory in Yeovil in 1941. By now more modern Spitfire variants were available and AR213 was relegated to training duties and sent to 7 OTU at Harwarden, near Chester. Following a number of landing accidents she was struck off charge in November 1945 but she was acquired (for £10!) by Grp Capt Allan Wheeler in October 1946 as a spares source for his Spitfire G-AISU. The aircraft was placed in storage at Old Warden until 1963 and in 1967 it was restored to airworthy condition to take part in the *Battle of Britain* film. Today the aircraft is owned by Spitfire The One Ltd/Comanche Warbirds LLC and is painted to represent 'P7308/XR-D.' *Steve Bridgewater* **Right:** Following its appearance in the *Battle of Britain* movie AR213 was fully restored at Booker and flew again as QG-A.

Left: In 1974 AR213 was sold to the Hon Patrick Lindsay, who operated it for five years until it passed to Victor Gauntlett and Peter Livanos. It was eventually repainted into the PR-D codes of 609 Sqn and is seen here running up its engine at Booker. **Right:** In 1996 AR213's port fuselage was adorned with 19 Sqn markings to depict George 'Grumpy' Unwin's QV-H.

Following an extensive restoration by Personal Plane Services at Booker AR213 flew again on November 12, 2007 in the JZ-E codes it wore with 7 OTU in 1941. Steve Bridgewater

▶ Spitfire VB BM597 was built at Castle Bromwich and delivered to 315 Sqn in May 1942 at RAF Woodvale. In September it transferred to 317 Sqn (also at Woodvale) and flew a number of combat missions with the unit. It was damaged several times during the war but survived to be retired in October 1945. It was then used as an instructional airframe at RAF St Athan before being allocated to 'gate guardian' duties. It was also the aircraft from which the moulds were taken to produce the fibreglass replica Spitfires for the *Battle of Britain* film. In 1989 it was acquired by Tim Routsis, the founder of Historic Flying, and he sold it to the Historic Aircraft Collection in 1993. Historic Flying completed the restoration to original specification BM597 (now G-MKVB) took to the air again on July 19, 1997 in its original 317 Sqn markings (albeit in an earlier camouflage paint scheme).
Steve Bridgewater

◀ Spitfire VB EP120 is one of the most credited historic aircraft left anywhere in the world with an impressive seven confirmed kills – six of which were scored by Sqn Ldr Geoffrey Northcott. The aircraft was built at the Castle Bromwich factory in 1942 and assigned to 501 Sqn in June of that month. A ground collision saw her returned to Castle Bromwich for repair following which she was allocated to 19 Sqn in Cornwall. In April 1944 she was taken on charge with 402 Sqn 'City of Winnipeg' RCAF, coded AE-A, which are the colours she wears today. After the war EP120 served as a gate guard at a number of RAF stations and was used as a static aircraft in the *Battle of Britain* movie. The Fighter Collection discovered EP120 in storage at St. Athan in 1993 and acquired it for restoration. Following a full restoration, EP120 returned to the skies as G-LFVB on September 12, 1995.
Steve Bridgewater

WARBIRD DIRECTORY | 91

IN FOCUS: Supermarine Spitfire IIa P7350

For the BBMF's 60th anniversary year in 2017 P7350 has been repainted into a 'dual' scheme to pay tribute to two of "the few" who took part in the Battle of Britain and are still with us to this day. The aircraft's port side is marked up as QJ-G, representing Geoffrey Wellum's 92 Sqn aircraft. The starboard side is marked up as QV-E, to commemorate Ken Wilkinson and his 19 Sqn Spitfire. Both Steve Bridgewater

The Battle of Britain Memorial Flight's 'Baby Spit' (P7350) was built in August 1940 as a Mk IIa. It was the 14th of 11,939 Spitfires constructed at the Castle Bromwich 'Shadow' factory and it was test flown by famous test pilot Alex Henshaw.

With the Battle of Britain raging over the south coast, P7350 was allocated to 266 Sqn on September 6 and coded UO-T before joining the battle at Martlesham Heath. On October 17, the aircraft was transferred to 603 (City of Edinburgh) Sqn at Hornchurch and it re-coded XT-W. On 25 October, whilst being flown by Polish pilot Ludwik Martel, P7350 was force landed after being shot at by a German Bf 109.

The aircraft was repaired and allocated to 616 (County of South Yorkshire) Sqn at Tangmere in March 1941 and the following month it joined 64 Sqn with whom it flew fighter sweeps over occupied Europe. It was damaged in a landing accident in August and following repairs it was issued to various training units.

Amazingly, P7350 survived both the war and the post-war scrapping programme and in 1948 scrap merchants Messrs John Dale and Sons Ltd realised the historical importance of the aircraft and donated it to the museum at RAF Colerne.

In 1968 it was brought back to flying status for the *Battle of Britain* movie and at the end of filming it was donated to the BBMF at Coltishall. It has flown with the unit ever since and continues to delight crowds at events across the UK each summer.

Until the start of the 2017 season P7350 had spent the last few years painted to represent N3162/EB-G – a 41 Sqn Spitfire 1a flown by the top-scoring Battle of Britain fighter ace Eric Lock when he destroyed three enemy aircraft in a single sortie on September 5, 1940. *Darren Harbar*

Between 1997 and 2000 P7350 appeared in the BA-Y codes of 277 (Air Sea Rescue) Sqn. *Steve Bridgewater*

P7350 wore the RN-S codes of 72 Sqn between 1993 to 1997.

Left: P7350 wearing the QV-B codes of 19 Sqn in 1980. The aircraft has been repainted regularly during its time with the BBMF to pay tribute to as many pilots, units and squadrons as possible. **Right:** Between 2000 and 2001 P7350 was overhauled at St Athan. When it reappeared it had been painted to represent XT-D of 603 (City of Edinburgh) Sqn. In May 2006 the scheme changed slightly to represent XT-W and the following year it was altered again to depict XT-L, the aircraft flown by ace Gerald 'Stapme' Stapleton.

WARBIRD DIRECTORY | 93

IN FOCUS ▶ Supermarine Spitfire Vb AB910

AB910 is currently painted to represent Spitfire Mk Vb BM327/SH-F, named *PeterJohn1*, which was the personal aircraft of Flt Lt Tony Cooper, one of the flight commanders on 64 Sqn in 1944. Steve Bridgewater

The Battle of Britain Memorial Flight's Spitfire Vb AB910 flew a remarkable 143 operational missions during a career that lasted almost three years of continual 'ops'.

The aircraft was allocated to 222 (Natal) Sqn at North Weald in August 1941 ad then moved to 130 Sqn at Perranporth, Cornwall flying convoy protection patrols and escorting daylight bombing raids. In June 1942, AB910 was delivered to 133 (Eagle) Sqn at Biggin Hill and flew 29 'ops', including four Operation *Jubilee* sorties during the Dieppe Raids. On one of those trips Flt Sgt 'Dixie' Alexander was credited with destroying a Dornier 217 bomber in AB910.

AB910 continued to fly operationally up to July 1944, serving with 242, 416 and 402 (RCAF) Sqns. With the latter it flew numerous patrols over the D-Day invasion beachheads on June 6, 1944 and afterwards.

The aircraft was then relegated to support duties and, famously, on Valentines Day 1945 it flew with Margaret Horton on its tail! The WAAF ground-crew fitter, was sitting on the tail whilst the aircraft taxied out to the take-off point (as was standard practice in rough weather). Pilot Flt Lt Neil Cox DFC hadn't realised she was there and took off with her clinging to the tail. Luckily he managed to land safely with the shaken WAAF still wrapped around the fin!

Post-war AB910 was 'demobbed' and sold to Allen Wheeler, who raced her as G-AISU until 1953 when it was returned to Vickers-Armstrong. Here it was refurbished and displayed regularly by the renowned Spitfire test pilot Jeffrey Quill until being donated to the BBMF in 1965.

▼ Post-war, AB910 was 'demobbed' and flew as an air racer for six years before being returned to Vickers-Armstrong for refurbishment in 1953. After this it was displayed regularly by the renowned Spitfire test pilot Jeffrey Quill and given his initials in lieu of squadron codes.

94 | WARBIRD DIRECTORY

In 2003 AB910 was repainted into the desert camouflage scheme of Spitfire Vb AB502, which was the personal aircraft of Wg Cdr Ian 'Widge' Gleed DSO DFC when he became the Wing Leader of 244 Wing in Tunisia in 1943.

AB910 at the 2009 Kemble Air Day in the RF-D codes of 303 (Polish) Sqn's Sqn Ldr Jan Zumbach.
Steve Bridgewater

In 1997 AB910 was painted in Eagle Squadron markings and shipped to the USA where it took part in the USAF 50th anniversary celebrations at Nellis AFB, Nevada.

Left: Upon its return from the USA AB910 was repainted in 222 (Natal) Sqn markings with the codes ZD-C.
Steve Bridgewater **Right:** : In 1986 AB910 was repainted into 457 Sqn markings as BP-O. It also bore the inscription 'In Memory of RJ Mitchell' beneath the cockpit. It is seen here at the 1989 PFA Rally at Cranfield.
Neil Taylor via Awyr Aviation Communication

WARBIRD DIRECTORY | 95

◀ Spitfire VB EP122 was built in early 1942 and crated for shipment to the North African theatre of operations. It arrived in Gibraltar on June 12 and delivered to Malta the following month where it was immediately pressed into service in defence of the island. EP122 was flown by 19-year old American volunteer, Sgt Claude Weaver III of Oklahoma City, who shot down two Bf 109s on July 22, followed by another pair the next day and a half-share in a Ju 88 the day after that! EP122 then became the regular mount of 185 Sqn's Wg Cdr JM Thompson and wore his personal code of JM-T. Thompson was leading a flight of eight Spitfires on October 14, 1942 when he shot down a Ju 88. EP122 eventually joined 1435 Sqn and was coded GL-B but on March 27, 1943 it crash-landed on the edge of the cliff at Dwejra Bay, Gozo. The wreckage was pushed over the cliff-edge into the bay shortly but was recovered from the seabed in the mid 1970s. The aircraft was subsequently restored at Biggin Hill for Comanche Warbirds Ltd and flew again on May 5, 2016. *Steve Bridgewater*

▶ Spitfire VC EE602 first flew on September 11, 1942 and joined 66 Sqn and then 129 (Mysore) Sqn. During her time with the unit EE602 completed more than 100 combat sorties, including escorting the B-17 Flying Fortress *Memphis Belle* back to the English coast after its now famous 25th mission. EE602 was christened 'Central Railways Uruguayan Staff' in recognition of the £5,000 donated by members of the company. In July 1943 the Spitfire was wrecked when it was struck by another aircraft, and the remains were sent to a local scrapyard. These remnants were later recovered and in 2011 they were registered as G-VMIJ to Ian D. Ward/ VMI Engineering Services Ltd. Restoration began in Aldershot but the project passed to Chris Fairfax/ Fairfax Spitfires LLP in 2012 and the aircraft was re-registered G-IBSY. Restoration continued at Audley End and Biggin Hill and the aircraft flew again – wearing its 129 Sqn DV-V markings – on May 16, 2015. This rarely seen aeroplane now resides with the Biggin Hill Heritage Hangar (BHHH) collection. *BHHH*

◀ In March 1944 MK356 was allocated to the newly formed 443 'Hornet' Sqn, Royal Canadian Air Force and coded 21-V. On April 14, 1944 it flew its first operational mission as part of a 'Rodeo' fighter sweep over occupied France. In its 60 day wartime career MK356 flew 60 operational sorties and was damaged by enemy fire on three occasions. On D-Day+1 (June 7, 1944) during a beachhead cover patrol MK356 destroyed a Bf 109G but on June 14 the aircraft was badly damaged in a wheels up landing and shipped back to the UK. Post war, MK356 was used as an instructional airframe and between 1992 and 1997 it was restored for the BBMF. For its first few years it wore its original 21-V codes but in 2016 it was repainted into the 126 Sqn 5J-K codes to depict ML214 flown by Sqn Ldr 'Johnny' Plagis. For the 2017 season MK356 is expected to re-appear in the QJ-R codes of a 92 Sqn Spitfire flown by Neville Duke in Africa in 1943.

In 2008 MK356 was repainted to represent MJ250/UF-Q of 601 (County of London) Sqn. The original aircraft was flown by Flt Lt Desmond Ibbotson on fighter bomber missions over the Balkans from bases in Southern Italy. Ibbotson, who shot down eleven enemy aircraft and survived being shot down by the enemy three times was eventually killed on a routine test flight when MJ250 crashed close to Assisi, Italy in November 1944. *Steve Bridgewater*

Martin Phillips' Spitfire IX RR232 was built in Castle Bromwich by Vickers Armstrong and delivered to the RAF in October 1944 as a HF.IX high altitude fighter. In 1948 it was sold to the South African Air Force (SAAF) as SAAF 5632 and flew until 1954 when it was damaged and sent to a Johannesburg scrapyard. The remnants were subsequently used to help restore Spitfire MA793 and what was left was sold to Australia in 1976 and incorporated into a static restoration. RR232 finally made it back to the UK in 1986 when it was purchased by Charles Church, who in turn sold the airframe to Jim Pearce who then sold it to Martin Phillips in 2001. The epic restoration was finally completed in 2012 when RR232, now registered G-BRSF, took off from Filton on its maiden flight – in doing so becoming the last aircraft to take off from the airfield before it closed. RR232 is now operated by the Boultbee Flight Academy at Goodwood but in the summer of 2017 was leased to Norwegian Spitfire Foundation and was temporarily painted as in Norwegian Air Force markings as 'PV181/RAB'.

Spitfire IX TA805 was built at Castle Bromwich in 1944 but did not join her first operational unit (183 Sqn at Chilbolton) until June 1945. A month later the aircraft transferred to 234 Sqn at RAF Bentwaters before being placed in storage. In 1949 the aircraft was sold to the South African Air Force but was scrapped in 1954. The remains of the aircraft were discovered in a scrapyard in 1977 and returned to the UK by Steve Atkins in 1989. In 1995 the project was shipped to the Isle of Wight for restoration and a year later it was sold to Peter Monk and Mike Simpson. TA805 moved to Duxford in 2003 for completion by the Aircraft Restoration Company and the aircraft flew again on December 7, 2005. The aircraft is painted in the FX-M codes she wore with 234 Sqn and now resides with the Biggin Hill Heritage Hangar collection. On occasion the aircraft has been adorned with temporary D-Day markings to help celebrate significant anniversaries.

MK627 was built as a single-seat Spitfire LF.IXC and flew on November 8, 1943 but did not join its first operational unit (441 RCAF) Sqn until September 1944. She joined the unit in Belgium and was coded 9G-Q for operations over occupied Europe. On September 27 P/O Bregman took off in MJ627 to patrol the Arnhem area and engaged a flight of 15 Bf 109s and Fw 190s – shooting down one of the Messerschmitts. The squadron was relocated to Skeabrae, Orkney Islands, Scotland in December for defence of the Naval Fleet and on March 9 the following year MJ627 was damaged when it force landed after an engine problem. By September it had been repaired but the aircraft went straight into storage until it was sold to Vickers Armstrong in July 1950 to be converted into a Tr.9 trainer aircraft for the Irish Air Corps. MK627 served as IAC 158 until 1960 when she was retired and sold to Film Aviation Services and robbed of parts to keep MH434 aloft. In September 1964 Tim Davies bought what remained and stored the components until they were purchased in 1976 by Maurice Bayliss. Registered G-BMSB the aircraft flew again on November 8, 1993, exactly 50 years since its last maiden flight, and was finished in number 441 Sqn colours, and coded '9G-P' with invasion stripes In 2014 the Bayliss family sold MJ627 to Warbird Experiences Ltd at Biggin Hill and the two-seat Spitfire has been kept busyprovided Spitfire 'experiences' ever since. Over the winter of 2015/2016 it was repainted into its original 9G-Q markings. Steve Bridgewater

The 'Grace Spitfire' was built as a single-seat LF.IX variant registered ML407 in early 1944. The aircraft served in mainland Europe throughout the last twelve months of World War Two with six different allied Squadrons of the RAF's 2nd Tactical Air Force. In fact, ML407 flew 176 operational combat sorties and an impressive 319 combat hours – including being the 485 (NZ) Sqn mount of F/O Johnnie Houlton DFC who was accredited, whilst flying ML407, with the first enemy aircraft shot down over the Normandy beachhead on D-Day. Steve Bridgewater

In December 1944 ML407 was transferred to 341 (Free French) Sqn and flown by Sergeant Jean Dabos in the codes NL-D. The aircraft also served with 308 (Polish) Sqn, 349 (Belgian) Sqn, 345 (Free French) Sqn, 332 (Norwegian) Sqn and back to 485 (NZ) Sqn at the end of hostilities. ML407 was then selected by Vickers Armstrong for conversion to the two seat Tr.9 configuration for the Irish Air Corps. It flew as IAC 162 until 1968 when it was sold to Sir William Roberts for his museum in Strathallan, Scotland.

WARBIRD DIRECTORY | 97

IN FOCUS

Supermarine Spitfire IX MH434/G-AJSV

Although MH434 has worn various markings over the past five decades it is most commonly seen in its original 222 Sqn ZD-B codes.

Perhaps the most famous of all Spitfires flying today, MH434 was built as a LF.IX at Castle Bromwich in 1943 and test flown by Alex Henshaw on August 3.

Later that month the Spitfire joined 222 (Natal) Sqn and was allocated to South African pilot Flt Lt Henry Lardner-Burke. On August 27, the duo downed a Focke-Wulf Fw 190 (and damaged a second) near St Omar, France. On September 5, a second Fw 190 fell to MH434's guns and three days later Lardner-Burke claimed a half share in a Bf 109G over Northern France.

The following year MH434 transferred to 350 Sqn at Hornchurch before being returned to 222 Sqn and re-allocated to Flt Sgt Alfred 'Bill' Burge. He flew another 12 operational sorties in the aircraft and by the time MH434 was retired in March 1945 it had amassed 80 operational sorties.

After the war the aircraft was sold to the Royal Netherlands Air Force in 1947 (serving as H-105) and it later transferred to the Belgian Air Force as SM-41. Between 1956 and 1963 it served as a target tug with the civilian operated COGEA Nouvelle organisation (registered OO-ARA) and in 1963 it was sold to Tim Davies and returned to the UK. Tim registered MH434 as G-ASJV and following overhaul at Elstree it took part in its first film – *Operation Crossbow* – in 1964.

This would mark the start of a long and successful film career and in 1967 MH434 joined the fleet of aircraft used in the *Battle of Britain* movie. In 1968 MH434 was sold to Sir Adrian Swire, Chairman of Cathay Pacific Airways, who had the Spitfire painted in 1944 camouflage colour scheme with his initials AC-S, as squadron codes. It was in these colours that MH434 appeared in the film *A Bridge Too Far*.

In April 1983 MH434 was sold at auction to Ray Hanna (Nalfire Aviation Ltd) and it became one of the Old Flying Machine Company's founding aircraft. It has been based at Duxford ever since.

Tim Davies painted MH434 in a stylish civilian scheme when it was first overhauled at Elstree in 1964.

It was Sir Adrian Swires who returned MH434 to camouflage – albeit with his initials as code letters.

98 | WARBIRD DIRECTORY

In perhaps her most famous TV/film role MH434 was on of six Spitfires to appear in the 1988 ITV series *Piece of Cake*. In one scene Ray Hanna flies MH434 under a 'French' bridge – that was actually in Tyneside. For much of the filming MH434 (and the other Spitfires) flew devoid of unit markings or codes. Neil Taylor via Awyr Aviation Communication

Left: For her role in *Agatha Christie's Poirot* MH434 appears as the 'Mayfield Kestrel' fighter prototype. The Spitfire was repainted in an all-over anonymous light Grey colour scheme with no other markings for the episode, which was filmed on the former Battle of Britain airfield at West Malling. **Right:** Following her role in *Poirot* MH434's grey paint was altered into an RAF high-altitude scheme in 1989.

Left: The next evolution of MH434's grey scheme saw the addition of Norwegian Air Force markings for a visit to Scandinavia in the summer of 1989. **Right:** For the 1990 TV series *Perfect Hero*, which starred Nigel Havers as a badly burned Battle of Britain pilot MH434 was painted in 1940-style markings along with the codes CK-D. After filming this was later modified into a Belgian Air Force scheme.

WARBIRD DIRECTORY | 99

Supermarine Spitfire IX MH434/G-AJSV (Continued)

In 1993 MH434 was painted into a 1941-style 121 'Eagle' Sqn colour scheme – complete with AV-H codes – to appear in *The Diamond Swords*. The movie was based on the life of Luftwaffe ace Hans Joachim Marseille and MH434 was flown by Rolf Meum for filming. Steve Bridgewater

To appear in the late 1990s BBC series *Over Here*, based on experiences on the arrival of USAAF B-17 bomber groups in Britain MH434 was repainted into camouflage again and wore the fictitious codes WO-A.

In 1996 MH434 appeared in the markings of Grp Capt Aleksander Gabszewicz's SZ-G from 131 (Polish) Wing. This scheme is also to be worn by TE311 of the BBMF during the 2017 season. Steve Bridgewater

For her part on the Breitling Fighters display team MH434 retained her 222 (Natal) Sqn codes but gained a yellow spinner.

In June 1998 MH434 had her unit codes removed and special markings added to celebrate the 60th anniversary of the opening of the Castle Bromwich Aeroplane Factory.

MH434 was repainted into PK-K codes on the opening morning of the Cranfield Classic Jet & Fighter Display in August 1998. It only wore these markings for a very short period. Steve Bridgewater

Left: MH434 where she's best known – at low level during a Duxford flying display. **Right:** The late, great and much missed Ray and Mark Hanna operated MH434 for many years but even after their passing the aeroplane is still looked after by the Hanna family and the Old Flying Machine Company formed by Ray in 1983.

WARBIRD DIRECTORY | 101

IN FOCUS

Supermarine Spitfire Tr.9 PV202/G-CCCA

PV202 leads ML407 into the skies at Duxford – ably showing the difference in the original canopy design and the more streamlined Grace conversion. PV202 now wears her original 33 Sqn codes as 5R-H. Steve Bridgewater

Spitfire PV202 was built as an LF.IX at Castle Bromwich in 1944 and delivered to 33 Sqn on October 19 the same year. The following January the airframe moved to 412 (Canadian) Sqn and she operated in Europe until it returned to the UK for storage in May 1945.

Post-war PV202 was sold back to Vickers-Armstrong (in July 1950) and converted to two-seat Tr.9 trainer configuration for the Irish Air Corps – with whom she served as IAC 161 from 1951 until December 1960. Upon retirement the aircraft made its way back to the UK and was sold to Sir William Roberts in April 1970 for his collection at Strathallan, Scotland. PV202 then remained in storage until August 1979 when she was sold to Nick Grace and then to Steve Atkins, who registered her G-TRIX in July 1980.

In 1990 G-TRIX was sold to Richard Parker and on February 23 of that year the aeroplane made its maiden flight as a civilian aircraft, complete with VZ-M codes, World War Two camouflage and the Grace in-line canopy conversion. In late 1991 she was sold to Rick Roberts and in 2000 it was sold to South African Greg McCurragh. Unfortunately PV202 crashed at Goodwood, West Sussex, on April 8 of that year killing McCurragh and instructor Norman Lees.

In 2002 Historic Flying Ltd began restoring PV202 and when she returned to flight on January 13, 2005 (registered G-CCCA) she was painted in her former Irish Air Corps colours as IAC-161. The aircraft has since worn various schemes and been essential in the training of countless new Spitfire pilots.

When she first returned to the skies in 1990 she wore her original 412 (Canadian) Sqn codes of VZ-M.

102 | WARBIRD DIRECTORY

After her second rebuild – and re-register as G-CCCA – PV202 wore her original Irish Air Corps markings as IAC 161.

Left: Following sale to Rick Roberts PV202 was eventually repainted into 33 Sqn marks as 5R-Q.
Right: For a period between 2007 and 2010 G-CCCH operated in Royal Netherlands Air Force markings as 'H-98', the aircraft in which Prince Bernhard of the Netherlands made his last Spitfire flight. Steve Bridgewater

Left: From 2010 until 2015 G-CCCA flew as a representation of a Duxford-based 19 Sqn Spitfire I – complete with 'QV-I' codes. **Right:** Today PV202 carries out training of future Spitfire pilots but is also operated on 'pleasure flying' operations enabling members of the public to sample the legendary fighter in the air. Steve Bridgewater

WARBIRD DIRECTORY | 103

◀ In late 1979 ML407 was sold to Nick Grace who restored it to airworthy condition as G-LFIX. Nick kept it two-seat configuration but incorporated amore streamlined canopy - the so-called 'Grace In-Line Canopy Conversion.' The aircraft flew again on April 16, 1985 with Nick at the controls and his wife Carolyn in the rear seat. Tragically, Nick was killed in a car accident in 1988 leaving Carolyn with two children, Olivia (5) and Richard (4) and a Spitfire to care for. Carolyn went solo in ML407 in 1990 the aircraft is now regularly displayed by Richard. The story of ML407 really is a family story. Here the aircraft sports D-Day stripes to mark the 70th anniversary of its famous D-Day 'kill'. Darren Harbar

Left: Spitfire NH341 was built at Castle Bromwich as a Spitfire Low Level Fighter (LF.IXE) and joined 411 (Grizzly Bear) Sqn RCAF on 22, June 1944. Seven days later NH341 downed a Bf 109 near Caen, France and the following evening another example fell to NH341's guns. However, on July 2 NH341 was shot down by Fw 190s from JG26 while flying a morning patrol. Pilot W/O 'Jimmy' Jeffrey baled out and successfully evaded capture and the remains of the Spitfire lay undiscovered until 1996 when it was excavated and placed on display in Bayeux. The wreckage was acquired by Aero Legends in 2011 and the aircraft was restored to fly as a two-seat T.9 variant in order to offer rides from its base at Headcorn. Registered G-CICK the aeroplane took to the skies again on March 11, 2017 wearing its original 411 Sqn DB-E codes and the name *Elizabeth*. Darren Harbar **Right:** Today G-AIDN/MT818 is based at Biggin Hill and is one of the two-seat Spitfires used for experience flights at the Biggin Hill Heritage Hangar. It was the prototype two-seat Spitfire and first flew in 1947. Tim Badham

Left: Spitfire PT462 was built as a HF.IX variant in July 1944 and shipped to the Mediterranean Allied Air Force where it served with 253 Sqn and was coded SW-A. At the end of the war PT462 was transferred to the Italian Air Force as MM4100 and in 1952 it was acquired by the Israeli Air Force. After being withdrawn from Israeli service the aircraft was donated to a Kibbutz in the Gaza Strip for use in their playground and it remained there until 1983 when it was discovered by Robs Lamplough and brought back to the UK. The remnants were sold to Charles Church in 1985 and he decided to rebuild it as a two-seat trainer using the Grace In Line Canopy Conversion. It flew again (as G-CTIX) on July 25, 1987 but following Church's death in 1988 it was sold by Dick Melton before it was sold to the USA in 1994 as N462JC. It would remain in the USA for four years, during which is shed this distinctly blue 'hue' and gained an interpretation of its 253 Sqn markings. **Right:** When Steve Boultbee-Brooks began to search for an authentic RAF scheme for his two-seat Spitfire he discovered that the first, and probably only, two-seater in RAF service was an unofficial conversion of a former South African Spitfire V (ES127). It is thought to have been converted locally in Sicily by 118 MU in 1944 and saw the front fuel tank removed and a second wind screen attached that enabled passenger and observer flights to be given. The aircraft was coded KJ-I and these markings are now worn by SM520. Steve Bridgewater

104 | WARBIRD DIRECTORY

Single-seat Spitfire HI.IX SM520 was built at Castle Bromwich in 1944 but was too late to see operational service. It went straight into storage before being sold to the African Air Force in 1948. Very little is known of its history after that but it was clearly involved in a major flying accident and the wreckage disposed of in a Cape Town scrapyard. It was later recovered by the SAAF Museum and in 1989 wa shipped to the UK by Steve Atkins. It then passed through various owners before being purchased by Paul Portelli in 2002. Paul decided to convert it to two-seat T.9 configuration and commissioned both Airframe Assemblies (on the Isle of Wight) and Classic Aero (at Truxton) to complete the project. The aircraft was registered as G-ILDA after Paul's granddaughter but his untimely death meant that on completion (in a semi-complete Royal Netherlands Air Force scheme) the aircraft was put up for auction. It was purchased by Steve Boultbee-Brooks and is now operated from Goodwood by the Boultbee Flight Academy where members of the public can purchase flights in this iconic fighter. Via Classic Aero

◀ Griffon-powered Spitfire XIV MV293 was built in late 1944 at Keevil and stored by the RAF until early 1945. It was then transferred to the Indian Air Force and nothing further is known about its history until it was discovered in Bangalore in 1978 by Doug Arnold's Warbirds of Great Britain. The aircraft returned to the UK and was registered G-SPIT in 1979 but in 1985 it was sold to The Fighter Collection. The aircraft returned to the air on August 14, 1992 in a distinctive post-war silver scheme. The Fighter Collection sold Spitfire XIV G-SPIT to Anglia Aircraft Restorations Ltd in 2016 and, to date, the aircraft has continued to wear the markings of 'MV268' and JE-J codes of AVM 'Johnnie' Johnson.

Right: Bubble-canopied Spitfire XVI RW382 was built in 1945 and served 604 Sqn RAuxAF between 1947 and 1950. It then transferred to 3 Civilian Anti-Aircraft Cooperation Unit at Exeter and the Control and Reporting School at Middle Wallop before it was retired in 1953 and allocated as an instructional airframe. It then spent a period as a gate guardian before it was acquired by Tim Routis' Historic Flying Ltd in 1988. The aircraft was sold to US collector David Tallichet in 1989 and Historic Flying returned it to the air for him on July 3, 1991 as G-XVIA. It wore 604 Sqn's NG-C markings and was operated in the UK until 1995 when it was shipped to the USA for new owners Thomas and Bernie Jackson. The aircraft flew as N382RW but crashed in California in 1998 killing Thomas Jackson. The wreckage was returned to the UK in 2001 and in 2008 it was registered G-PBIX to Pemberton-Billing LLP. The airframe was restored to 'high-back' Mk XVI configuration by the Spitfire Company (Biggin Hill) Ltd and took to the skies again on September 18, 2013 wearing the codes 3W-P. Steve Bridgewater

Left: In 2005 Spitfire XVI TD248 was re-sprayed by Spitfire Ltd into a rendition of a 74 Sqn Spitfire attached to 2 Tactical Air Force in May 1945. The aircraft wore CR-S codes in tribute to Chief Pilot Sir Cliff Spink. In 2010 Richard Lake acquired TD248 (and Spitfire Ltd) from Tom Blair but retained the aircraft's colour scheme. Steve Bridgewater **Right:** Spitfire XVI TD248 joined 695 Sqn at Bircham Newton, Norfolk in mid-1945 and was coded 8Q-T. The aircraft later passed through 2 CAACU (Civilian Anti Aircraft Co-operation Unit) at Little Snoring, Norfolk before being retired in 1954. A year later it was issued to 610 Sqn of the Royal Auxilery Air Force for static display at Hooton Park, Cheshire (coded DW-A) and from there it became a gate guardian with 1366 Squadron Air Training Corps at RAF Sealand. She remained on the gate until 1988 when she was acquired by Historic Flying and restoration began for Eddie Coventry. The aircraft was registered G-OXVI and when it returned to the air on November 10, 1992 it wore a striking silver and red livery based on a 41 Sqn Spitfire XXI that participated in the Blackpool Air races of 1948/49. The aircraft was later sold to Karel Bos in 1996 and then to Tom Blair's Spitfire Ltd in 2005. In 2010 it passed to current owner Richard Lake.

WARBIRD DIRECTORY | 105

IN FOCUS
Supermarine Spitfire PR.XI PL965/G-MKXI

Today PL965 flies in a highly accurate rendition of the original 16 Sqn photo-reconnaissance scheme it wore during operations over occupied Europe in 1944-45. Darren Harbar

Supermarine Spitfire PR.XI PL965 left the Aldermaston factory in mid 1944 as a high altitude photo-reconnaissance aircraft.

She was allocated to 16 Sqn in late 1944 and sent to the unit's forward operating base at Melsbroek near Brussels, Belgium as part of the 2nd Tactical Air Force. Here PL965 was coded 'R for Robert' and the blue painted Spitfire would go on to fly more than 40 operational missions over Germany, France and Holland before the end of the war. The RAF retired the aircraft in 1946 and it was sold to the Royal Netherlands Air Force in July 1947 for use as a ground instructional aircraft.

In 1960 she became an exhibit at the Dutch War Museum at Overloon and the aircraft remained there until 1987 when it was acquired by Nick Grace and returned to the UK.

Restoration work began in Rochester but Nick was killed in a car accident before PL965 could fly and in 1989 it was registered G-MKXI for Chris Horsley. It

When it first flew in 1992 PL965 was painted to represent a USAAF 8th Air Force Spitfire PR.XI.

would be December 23, 1992 before the aircraft flew again (in the hands of Mark Hanna), by which time it was painted in a USAAF scheme.

PL965 was operated by the Old Flying Machine Company until 1997 when it was sold to Robert Fleming and 'Taff' Smith and relocated to the Real Aeroplane Company at Breighton,

Yorkshire. From 2001 it spent three years based in Florida before being returned to the UK in 2003 and sold to Peter Teichman's Hangar 11 Collection at North Weald.

The aircraft remains at North Weald today and is unique in flying using the original Merlin engine it operated over Europe with in 1945.

106 | WARBIRD DIRECTORY

During her tenure with the Old Flying Machine Company in the 1990s PL965 was painted in a gloss blue version of its 16 Sqn markings, complete with 'R' code letter.

▲ To appear in the late 1990s BBC series *Over Here* PL965 wore camouflage and the fictitious codes WO-P. She is seen here in formation with MH434.
Richard Paver

◀ For a period in the early 2000s PL965 was painted in a distinctive pink scheme. This was a variation of the light pink markings worn by some photo reconnaissance Spitfires during the war years – although it is doubtful that any were actually this bright a shade!

WARBIRD DIRECTORY | 107

Left: The Battle of Britain Memorial Flight (BBMF) Spitfire XVI TE311 was built just after the war had ended and was placed into storage before joining the Handling Squadron of the Empire Central Flying School (ECFS) at Hullavington. In May 1951 it was allocated to 1689 Ferry Pilot Training (FPT) Flight at Aston Down before joining the Ferry Training Unit at RAF Benson. On December 13, 1954, TE311 was retired and allocated as a 'gate guardian' at RAF Tangmere until 1968 when was modified to look like a Spitfire I and made taxi-able for the film *Battle of Britain*. With filming complete TE311 was restored to its original configuration and allocated to the RAF Exhibition Flight. For over 30 years, from 1968 to 1999, TE311 was displayed as a static exhibit at airshows, regularly being dismantled and re-assembled for transportation by road. In January 2000 TE311 and TB382 were delivered to RAF Coningsby for 'spares recovery' but Chief Technician Paul Blackah MBE decided that the aircraft could be rebuilt to flying condition. Work began in October 2001 with a small team of engineers initially working on the aircraft in their own time until official approval was received from the Ministry of Defence in 2007. The aircraft flew again on October 19, 2012 and was painted to represent TB675/4D-V of 74 Sqn, the personal aircraft of Sqn Ldr AJ 'Tony' Reeves DFC, the squadron's Commanding Officer. For the 2017 display season TE311 is due to be repainted to represent TD240/SZ-G as flown by Officer Commanding No 131 (Polish) Wing, Grp Capt Aleksander Gabszewicz DSO DFC, during the last weeks of World War Two. Darren Harbar

Right: Since its most recent restoration Spitfire XVIII SM845 has carried the silver markings of 28 Sqn RAF. Steve Bridgewater

◄ Aero Legends' Spitfire XVI TD314 was one of the last high back Spitfires built before the production line switched to low back aircraft in February 1945. The aircraft was delivered to 183 (Gold Coast) Sqn at Chilbolton in June 1945. A month later it passed to 234 (Madras Presidency) Sqn at Bentwaters and was coded FX-P. It is believed it took part in the 1945 Battle of Britain flypast over London before being put into storage. In 1948 TD314 was one of 136 Spitfires sold to the South African Air Force and little is known of her subsequent career until the her remains were recovered from a Cape Town scrapyard in 1969. From there she passed through the hands of several owners in Canada before arriving in the UK in 2009. The aircraft was acquired by Aero Legends in 2011 and the it was restored at Biggin Hill as G-CGYJ. The aircraft flew again on December 7, 2013 in its original 234 Sqn FX-P codes.
Steve Bridgewater

SM845 is an early production Spitfire XVIII Spitfire built at Chattis Hill in 1945 and delivered to 39MU. In late 1945 she was shipped to Karachi, arriving early in 1946 and received by the South East Asia Air Command. The aircraft was transferred to the Indian Air Force in late 1947 and served as HS687 until the late 1950s – although little is known of her career. In 1977 Ormond and Wensley Haydon-Baillie discovered theaircraft at Kalaikunda AB in Kharagpur, where it was being used as a decoy. It was one of eight Spitfires acquired from the IAF by tender and it returned to the UK in March 1978 before immediately being sold to California. The aircraft passed through various American owners before it returned to the UK once again in 1992 for restoration to be completed. Registered G-BUOS it flew again in July 2000, initially in a bare camouflage scheme. SM845 was later given the codes GZ-J and was flown extensively by Historic Flying until it was sold to Sweden in 2009 to become SE-BIM. Sadly the aircraft crashed on August 21, 2010 killing the pilot and two years later the wreckage returned to the UK to be restored for Richard Lake's Spitfire Ltd. Steve Bridgewater

◄ Spitfire PR.XIX PM631 was built at Reading too late to see service in World War Two. It was delivered to the RAF on November 6 1945 but was stored until May 1949 when it was issued to 203 Advanced Flying School. Later, after being modified for meteorological work, she was flown by civilian pilots with the Temperature and Humidity Monitoring (THUM) Flight based at Hooton Park and Woodvale. On July 11, 1957, PM631 was flown to Biggin Hill from Duxford by World War Two fighter ace Group Captain Jamie Rankin DSO* DFC* in formation with two other THUM Flight Spitfires XIXs (PS853 and PS915) to form the Historic Aircraft Flight (which later developed into the BBMF). The aircraft has worn various colour schemes over the years, including that of 91 Sqn Spitfire XIV DL-E, which it gained in 1984.

◀ For the 2016 airshow season the BBMF Spitfire PR.XIX PS915 was repainted into a silver scheme to represent the PR.XIX flown by from Kai Tak, Hong Kong by Flt Lt Ted Powles AFC in February 1952 to establish the world altitude record for piston engine aircraft. His altitude of 51,550ft remains unbeaten today!
Darren Harbar

Left: Built at Southampton in 1945, PS915 entered service just too late to see service in World War Two, joining 541 Squadron at Benson in June 1945 before moving to the PR Development Unit to take part in tests of new cameras. In April 1947 she was assigned to No 2 Squadron at Wunstorf in Germany, flying 'Cold War' strategic reconnaissance sorties in connection with the East/West divide of Europe and during the Berlin Airlift of 1948/49. She was returned to the UK in 1951 and joined the Temperature and Humidity Monitoring (THUM) Flight at Woodvale in 1954. When it was restored in 1987 she wore a standard blue photo recce scheme typical to the breed. Neil Taylor via Awyr Aviation Communication **Right:** In 2004 MK912 was sold to Ed Russell in Canada as CF-FLC but it returned to the UK in 2011 after being acquired by Peter Monk and Paul Andrews. In 2014 the aircraft acquired D-Day stripes but it was damaged when the engine failed during take-off at Biggin Hill on August 1, 2015. It is currently being restored to fly.

Left: In 1957, PS915 became a founder member of the Historic Aircraft Flight, the forerunner of the BBMF, but she was quickly retired to gate-guardian duties. She re-joined the BBMF in 1987 after being refurbished to flying condition by British Aerospace (Warton Division) and modified to take an ex-Shackleton Griffon 58 engine with a specially-manufactured reduction gear driving a single propeller. Among the markings worn by PS915 over the years has been this depiction of a 152 Sqn SEAC Spitfire XIV, complete with pouncing panther. Steve Bridgewater **Right:** Perhaps the most striking scheme worn by PS915 since it returned to flight was this interpretation of the prototype Spitfire XIV, JF319, complete with bright yellow undersides.

Left: In 2004 PS915 was painted in the colour scheme and markings of PS888, a PR.XIX of 81 Sqn based at Seletar in Singapore during the Malaya Campaign. This aircraft conducted the last ever operational sortie by an RAF Spitfire when, April 1, 1954 it flew a photographic mission over an area of jungle in Johore thought to contain hideouts for Communist guerrillas. For this occasion the aircraft's ground crew painted the inscription *The Last!* on the left engine cowling. Steve Bridgewater
Right: Air Leasing Ltd operates Seafire IIIC PP972/G-BUAR in its original Royal Navy markings as PP972/11-5-N. Steve Bridgewater

WARBIRD DIRECTORY | 109

IN FOCUS

Supermarine Spitfire TE184/G-MXVI

The latest colour scheme worn by TE184 is 9N-B of 127 Sqn. The aircraft gained this scheme at the start of 2017 and is spending much of the year flying from Eastern Europe. Via Stephen Stead

Spitfire XVI TE184 was built as a low-back 'bubble canopy' equipped LF.XVI and delivered from Castle Bromwich to 9 MU at Cosford on May 30, 1945. It immediately went into storage and would be September 1948 before it was finally attached to a flying unit – 226 Operational Conversion Unit.

TE184 remained in service with the OCU until 1950 when it was transferred first to 607 Sqn RAuxAF and then to the Central Gunnery School at Leconfield. It was damaged in an accident on January 30, 1951 and transferred to ground instructional use with the maintenance serial 6850M.

The airframe was then assigned to an Air Training Corps unit before it was used as a static 'extra' in the *Battle of Britain* film. TE184 was then put on display at RAF Finningley before being restored and sent to RAF Aldergrove in late 1971 for storage on behalf of the Ulster Folk and Transport Museum. It spent most of the next 15 years in store before it was sold to Nick Grace in 1986, who then transferred it to Myrick Aviation Services as G-MXVI in 1989.

TE184 was then sent to Trent Aero Engineering at East Midlands Airport where it was restored to 'high-back' configuration and flew again on November 23, 1990 in a high altitude grey paint scheme. It was operated by Intrepid Aviation until 1995 it was sold to Alain de Cadenet, who repainted it in Free French Air Force markings in 2002 but flew it very little. After storage at Hurn, Halton and Duxford it was sold to Paul Andrews' G2 Trust in 2006 and following restoration by Personal Plane Services at Booker TE184 flew again in February 2009. In 2011 the aircraft was sold to Stephen Stead who continues to fly it extensively throughout Europe from its base at Biggin Hill.

While on gate guardian duties at Finningley TE184 was adorned with ME-M unit codes. It was still in its original low-back configuration at the time.

In 1999 TE184 was briefly painted in a USAAF scheme to depict a 308th FS, 31th FG Spitfire VIII flown by Lt Leland 'Tommy' Molland. Coded HL-K, and named *Fargo Express*, this was the aircraft Molland flew in January 1944 when he shot down the first two of his eventual five Fw-190s over southern Italy.

When it flew again after restoration by Trent Aero for Myrick Aviation TE184 wore an all-over grey high altitude fighter scheme.

Stephen Stead departs Goodwood in TE184 in 2015 while it was wearing the DU-N codes of 312 (Czech) Sqn.
Steve Bridgewater

While in the custodianship of Alain de Cadinet TE184 appeared in Free French markings as TE184/D.

WARBIRD DIRECTORY | 111

Left: Supermarine Seafire III PP972 was one of 250 examples built by Westland Aircraft. It left the works during September 1944 and served with 809 NAS aboard HMS *Stalker* and HMS *Attacker*. In March 1945 PP972 arrived in Ceylon aboard HMS Stalker and joined the East Indies Fleet taking part in numerous operations as part of Operation Tiderace, the British plan to retake Singapore. It later took part in operations over Malaya and Singapore before it arrived back in the UK in October 1945. The following year PP972 was transferred to the French Aeronavale but it was finally retired in 1949. It survived in storage and was privately purchased in 1970 and moved to Vannes-Meucon aerodrome where it was restored to static condition and exhibited at the Resistance Museum at St Marcel. PP972 was sold to Doug Arnold's Warbirds of Great Britain collection in 1988 as G-BUAR and a punctuated restoration to airworthy condition soon began at various locations. Following Arnold's death the aircraft was stored from 2004 until 2012 but it was then moved to Bentwaters where Air Leasing finally completed the lengthy restoration on June 15, 2015. **Right:** Peter Monk's Spitfire IX MK912 was the first Allied aircraft to land on the continent after the D-Day invasion. It was being flown by 312 (Czech) Sqn pilot M Liskutin when a flak explosion under the aircraft caused the radio to fall off its shelf inside the fuselage and land on the control cables. On June 7, 1944 Liskutin landed at the unfinished Allied airfield being prepared at Bazenville, Normandy and, after repairs, took off again for the UK. Later in its career MK912 shot down a V-1 'Doodlebug' over Kent and in saw further action over Arnhem. In 1946 it was transferred to the Royal Netherlands Air Force (as H-119, later H-59) and then passed to the Belgian AF as SM29. It spent 1955 to 1988 on a pole outside a Belgian technical school and then moved to the Musee Royal de'Armee et d'Histoire Militaire in Brussels before it was sold to Guy Black's Historic Aircraft Collection in 1989. After being sold to Karel Bos it was restored to fly by Historic Flying, taking to the air again as G-BRRA on September 8, 2000. It initially flew as MN-N but later regained its original 310 (Czech) Sqn markings as SH-L.

Left: Kennet Aviation's Seafire XVII SX336 is one of only three airworthy Seafires in the world and one of only two Griffon-powered examples. It was built by Westland at Yeovil in 1946 and delivered to the Fleet Air Arm, which flew it until 1950. In 1973 the fuselage was discovered in a scrapyard and rescued by Spitfire historian Peter Arnold. He then sold SX336 to Neville Franklin, who passed it to Craig Charleston in 1983. The project transferred to Peter Wood in 1984 and restoration continued. In 2001 the aircraft was sold yet again, this time to Tim Manna's Kennet Aviation who registered it G-KASX and funded the completion of the restoration. The aircraft finally took to the skies on May 3, 2006 watched by Tommy Thompson, the Westland test pilot who had taken SX336 into the air for the very first time, 60 years ago to the very day! Steve Bridgewater
Right: The Shuttleworth Collection's Westland-built Spitfire V (AR501) was delivered to the RAF in June 1942 and joined 310 (Czech) Sqn, where she remained until March 1943. The aircraft also flew with 504 Sqn, 312 (Czech) Sqn, 442 (Canadian) Sqn and 58 OTU before joining the RAF Central Gunnery School in April 1945. AR501 was retired in August of the same year and in 1946 she was acquired by Loughborough College and used as an instructional airframe until 1961 when it was donated to the collection. It was restored (as G-AWII) to fly in *Battle of Britain* film and was then stored until 1973 when it flew again. AR501 is currently being restored to fly and is expected to return to the skies during the summer of 2017. It will regain its original 310 (Czech) Sqn markings as A-NN. The unit was the first RAF squadron to be crewed by foreign nationals. Darren Harbar Steve Bridgewater

Left: PS853 served with the THUM Flight (Temperature and Humidity Flight) at Woodvale in July 1950 and in 1957 she became a founding member of the RAF's Historic Aircraft Flight - initially flying devoid of squadron markings. The aircraft was eventually sold to Euan English in 1995 t fund the restoration of Hurricane LF363. PS853 was registered G-MXIX but put back on the market following the owner's death in a flying accident on March 4, 1995. Rolls Royce PLC acquired her in September 1996 and her registration became G-RRGN - short for Rolls Royce Griffin. Richard Cousens via Awyr Aviation Communication
Right: Rolls-Royce PLC's Spitfire XIX PS853/G-RRGN flies in the authentic photo reconnaissance blue scheme it wore during the war years. The aircraft was delivered to the central Photographic Reconnaissance Unit at RAF Benson on January 13, 1945 and then joined 16 Sqn in Belgium and, later, at Eindhoven in the Netherlands flying missions over Germany. Steve Bridgewater

◀ Following RAF service Spitfire IX MJ271 was delivered to the Royal Netherland Air Force in 1946 as H-8 (later 3W-8). It was retired in 1954 and after a period in storage ad display with various organisations it moved to the Aviodome Museum in Amsterdam here it was restored to represent 'MH424/H-53'. In 2006 it moved to Duxford for storage with Historic Flying Ltd and in 2016 it was sold to the Boultbee Flight Academy for restoration. Steve Bridgewater

Spitfire F.22 PK624 was built in 1945 and served with the 614 (County of Glamorgan) Sqn RAuxAF until she was retired in 1950. The aircraft eventually found itself in use as a gate guardian at RAF Uxbridge, RAF Northolt and RAF Abingdon. In 1994 she was acquired by The Fighter Collection and she has been in storage at Duxford ever since.

In addition to the myriad of 'original' Spitfires and Seafires flying or under restoration in the UK in 2017 a number of replicas are airworthy or under construction by dedicated homebuilders around the country. Included in these are a fleet of Supermarine Spitfire 26 replicas – which are approximately 80% scale and built of metal and composite. Steve Bridgewater

Left: In the summer of 1988 PL983 was painted in camouflage to appear in the TV show Piece of Cake. It was then stored from 1992 until 1999 when it was sold to Martin Sargent and Justin Fleming. It was lost in a accident in Rouen, France on June 4, 2001 (claiming the life of Martin Sargent) and the wreckage was eventually acquired by the Aircraft Restoration Company. The subsequent restoration was reaching an advanced stage at Duxford in mid-2017. Steve Bridgewater **Right:** Spitfire PR.XI PL983 served the RAF prior to being loaned to the US Embassy's Civil Air Attache at Hendon as NC74138. During this time it was flown in air races by ATA pilot Lettice Curtis but in 1950 it was transferred to the Shuttleworth Collection at Old Warden, where it was displayed statically until 1975. Awyr Aviation Archive

PT879, the Hangar 11 Collection Spitfire IX, was part of the wartime 'Lend Lease' programme. She was built in August 1944 and shipped to the 2nd Sqn of the 767th Regiment, 122nd Division of the Russian Air Force. The aircraft crashed during a dogfight in early 1945 (with just 29 hours on the airframe) and the wreck was recovered in 1997 and sold to UK-based Angie Soper. Angie registered the aeroplane G-BYDE but in 2003 she sold the project to Peter Teichman's Hangar 11 Collection. The fuselage arrived at North Weald in June 2015 for final assembly. Darren Harbar

After RAF service Spitfire IX LZ842 transferred to the South African Air Force in 1948 but it was scrapped four years later. The remains ere recovered from a scrapyard in 1969 and eventually arrived in the UK with Steve Atkins in 1989. Two years later the project transferred to Australia where Ross Campbell restored the fuselage to static condition. Wings (one from the UK and one from Russia) were acquired in 2003 and the airframe moved to the UK for Peter Monk. In 2005, LZ842 was acquired by Mark Bennett and the aircraft is being restored to fly at Biggin Hill as G-CGZU. Darren Harbar

WARBIRD DIRECTORY | 113

In 1975 PL983 moved to Duxford for restoration but was sold to French collector Roland Fraissinet in 1983. He commissioned Trent Aero Engineering to restore the aircraft (at East Midlands Airport) as G-PRXI.

Spitfire F22 PK664 was acquired from the RAF Museum storage facility by Kennet Aviation in 2014, reportedly in return for work it conducted to recover an ex-RAF P-40 Kittyhawk from the Egyptian desert.

PL983 flew again on July 18, 1984 and it wore a standard photo-reconnaissance scheme until it was sold throughout Fraissinet's ownership. In 1987 it was sold to Doug Arnold's Warbird of Great Britain Collection.

Vought Corsair

The Fighter Collection's Goodyear-built Corsair is the only example of the famous 'Bent Wing Bird' currently based in the UK. The aeroplane has been based at Duxford since 1986.

FG-1D Corsair	Patina Ltd/The Fighter Collection	G-FGID Bu88297	'KD345/130-A'	Flyable

Left: The Fighter Collection's FG-1D Corsair was built under licence by the Goodyear Aircraft Corporation in Ohio in April 1945 and allocated Bu No 88297. The aircraft was initially dispatched to Guam in the Pacific but nothing more is known about her history until she is recorded as being at a Repair Depot in the Philippines in October 1945. The Corsair the returned to the USA and after flying with various US Naval Air Reserve squadrons was put up for disposal in March 1956. She was purchased by a smelter but in 1960 was sold to legendary airshow and film pilot Frank Tallman. The aircraft was retained by Tallman until 1966 then passed through three more owners before joining TFC in 1986 and being shipped to the UK. G-FGID is an extremely original example of the type as she has never been fully restored and is one of the few still flying with fabric wings. The aircraft is currently painted as KD345, a Fleet Air Arm Corsair embarked on HMS Vengeance in the Pacific in December 1945 with 1850 Naval Air Squadron. Steve Bridgewater

Right: When the TFC Corsair first arrived in the UK it was registered as N8297 and carried the 'Jolly Rogers' markings. It was re-registered as G-FGID in 1991 and in 1996 was repainted into Fleet Air Arm markings.

Yakovlev Yak-1

The Yak-1 was first in the range of Yak fighters and was constructed largely of wood. Just three examples are thought to survive. G-BTZD was recovered from Russia in 1990 and has been on extended rebuild in the UK ever since.

▶ The Historic Aircraft Collection's Yak-1 served the Soviet AF as 1342 and was recovered from a Soviet lake in 1990. The aircraft is now substantially complete with the original Klimov V-12 engine rebuilt and running and the fuselage and complex wooden wing completed. It is currently in storage and is being offered for sale.
Steve Bridgewater

| Yak-1 | Historic Aircraft Collection Ltd | G-BTZD | 1342 Soviet AF | - | Stored |

Yakovlev Yak-3

Although the Yak-3 was offered to the Soviet AF at the same time as the wooden Yak-1 it was rejected as the scarcity of aviation spec aluminium meant it would be too difficult to produce in large numbers. In 1943 the project was re-energised and by mid-1946 some 4,848 had been built. Considered by many to be the best of the Yak fighters it was a short range, agile interceptor that had such an impressive rate of roll, turn and climb that German pilots were instructed not to engage it at low level. In the early 1990s Yakovlev re-opened the Yak-3 production line at Orenberg, Russia and used original plans and jigs to produce a limited run of 'new' aircraft for warbird owners. Although very closely resembled the original aircraft the rare Klimov engines were replaced with the US-built Allison V-1710 powerplants. Three of these aircraft are now based in the UK, two of which fly on a regular basis – although G-CGXG was advertised for sale at the time of writing (June 2017).

Yak-3UA	Chameleon Technologies Ltd	G-CGXG	-	'100 Soviet AF'	Flyable
Yak-3UA	Chris Bellhouse	G-CDBJ	-	'21 Soviet AF'	Stored
Yak-3UA	Will Greenwood	G-OLEG	-	'00 Soviet AF'	Flyable

Left: G-CGXG/'White 100' was one of eleven Yak-3UA airframes ordered by the California-based Flight Magic Inc in 1993. It was delivered to Brent Hisey in Oklahoma in 1995 for assembly and two years later it was registered to Bob Hannah as N551BH. In 2002 the aircraft was shipped to Germany where it became D-FJAK with Elmar & Achim Meier and was painted as '12 Soviet AF.' In 2007 it was sold to Chris Vogelgesang who repainted it a year later as 'White 100.' The aircraft moved to the UK in 2009 and eventually joined the UK register as G-CGXG. Steve Bridgewater
Right: Will Greenwood's G-OLEG is one of a fleet of three new Yak-3UA aircraft ordered by Richard Goode Aerobatics in the UK in 2001. It was built in Russia and delivered to Maxi Gainza at North Weald in 2004 as D-FLAK. Maxi then took the aeroplane to Germany where it remained until it was sold to Will Greenwood in 2015 and placed on the UK register. It currently flies in the markings of the Normandie-Niemen squadron. Mike Shreeve

Yakovlev Yak-9

Although having a later production number than the Yak-3 the Yak-9 was actually in service earlier. The fighter was actually a derivative of the Yak-7 (itself developed from the Yak-1) but had a cut down rear fuselage and increased power. The Yak-9 would become the most mass-produced Soviet fighter of all time (16,769 built between 1942 and 1948). A number of 'new' Yak-9s were built by Yakovlev in the 1990s but G-YAKP is a very rare original airframe. The aircraft was discovered at Kubinka AB, Russia and restoration began in Russia (for a Russian owner) before it was shipped to the UK in 2006.

| Yak-9P | Mark Rijkse & Nicholas Richards | G-YAKP | TBC | - | Restoration |

Yakovlev Yak-11

Yakovlev began work on an advanced trainer version of the radial-engined Yak-3U fighter in mid-1944 but the intensity of the war meant it would be late 1945 before it first flew. The aircraft used the same all-metal wings as the Yak-3U, with a fuselage of mixed metal and wood construction. A total of 3,859 were produced, including some 707 manufactured in Czechoslovakia by LET as the C-11. A number of C-11s were sold to Egypt in the 1965s and in 1983 the entire fleet was acquired by French warbird collectors Jean Salis, Alain Capel and Jacques Bourret. Five of those aeroplanes are now on the UK civil register.

Left: Yak-11 G-BTUB was built for the Egyptian Air Force as '543' in 1956 and was discovered in open storage at El Aakha Air Base, Egypt in 1985 by Alain Capel and Jean Salis. It was shipped to La Ferté-Alais, France and a year later arrived at Booker for storage. In 1991 it was sold to Mark Jefferies of Yak UK Ltd and moved to Little Gransden for restoration to fly as G-BTUB. The aircraft returned to the skies on May 13, 1994 and was retained by Mark until 2009 whe it was sold to Glenn James. **Right:** Angie Soper's Yak 11 flew as OK-KIH in Czechoslovakia before being delivered to the Egyptian Air Force in 1964 as EAF 705. Following recovery to France in 1985 it was sold to Eddie Coventry in 1988 who had it restored to fly at Earles Colne, Essex. It flew again on November 18, 1990 but was sold to Angie Soper eight years later. Today the aircraft flies in a green scheme. Yak UK Ltd

Yak C.11	Glenn James	G-BTUB	172623	-	Flyable
Yak C.11	A Balk, R Steinberger & F Fraudienst (Germany)	G-BTZE	171312	'52 Soviet AF'	Flyable
Yak C.11	Russian Radials Ltd	G-BZMY	171314	'1 Soviet AF'	Flyable
Yak C.11	Angie Soper	G-OYAK	1701139	'9 Soviet AF'	Flyable
Yak C.11	Philip Lawton (Finland)	G-YCII	2511108	'11 Soviet AF'	Flyable

Left: Unlike most Yak-11s G-BTZE is not an ex-Egyptian airframe. It served the Czech Air Force as 171312 from 1955 to 1962 and then joined the Czech Central Aero Club aerobatic team from 1970 to 1976 as OK-JIK. In 1989 it was sold to Germany collector Hans Dittes and shipped to Booker for restoration by Personal Plane Services. In 1992 ownership transferred to PPS's Bianchi Aviation Film Services Ltd/Blue Max Movie Aircraft Museum arm and the aircraft was registered G-BTZE. In 2007 the aircraft was sold to Mark Rijske who shipped it to Hungary where the restoration was finally completed and the aircraft flew again on November 30, 2011. Darren Harbar **Right:** G-BZMY is another ex-Egyptian Yak-11, but its actual identity remains a mystery. Following recovery to France in 1985 it was sold to Paul Franceschi near Marseille and registered F-AZSF and in June 2000 it transferred to North Weald, Essex-based Egido Gavazzi as G-BZMY. It subsequently passed through various owners and was painted as 'Soviet 11' before becoming White 1 with Warwickshire-based Russian Radials Ltd.

Post War Trainers, Liaison & Support

Some of the most affordable, attainable and fun to fly warbirds fall into the post-war category. From British Chipmunk and Bulldog trainers to Russian Yaks, Chinese Nanchangs and American Bird Dogs there really is something for everybody.

Antonov An-2 *Colt*

The big Russian An-2 is the largest single-engined biplane ever to enter production. More than 18,000 were manufactured between 1947 and 2001 and the type has genuine military credentials combined with the ability to carry a lot of friends! There are currently three airworthy in the UK with several others believed to be in storage.

An-2	Hinton Skydiving Centre	HA-ANG	-	-	Flyable
An-2	The An-2 Club Ltd	HA-MKF	OM-248	-	Flyable
An-2	Martin Wiseman	SP-KTS	-	-	Flyable

Antonov An-2 HA-ANG is operated by the Hinton Skydiving Centre and appeared at the 2017 Abingdon Air & Country Show. Jamie Ewan

The An-2 Club's example of the big Russian designed biplane has been resident in the UK for many years and is based at Popham, Hampshire. Jamie Ewan

Cessna L-19 Bird Dog

Developed from the civilian Cessna 170 as a replacement for the World War Two-era Piper Cub liaison aircraft the Bird Dog entered US service in 1950 and a total of 3,431 were built for the air arms including the US Army, USAF and USMC. Four examples of this fun little aeroplane are now based in the UK.

▶ Justin Needham's L-19E Bird Dog began life as 42-4550 and now operates as G-PDOG. The aircraft is painted in South Vietnamese Air Force markings but actually served with the French Army and was previously registered F-GKCP. Steve Bridgewater

L-19 Bird Dog	BC Arrow Ltd	G-JDOG	52-4541	24541/BMG (French Army)	Flyable
L-19 Bird Dog	Justin Needham	G-PDOG	52-4550	24550/GP	Flyable
L-19 Bird Dog	James Watt	G-VDOG	52-4582	24582	Flyable
L-19 Bird Dog	Southern Aircraft Consultancy Inc	N5308G	52-2829	22829	Flyable

de Havilland DH.104 Devon

The de Havilland Devon was the military version of the DH.104 Dove short-haul airliner. The type replaced the DH89A Dragon Rapide in both the military and civilian world and was once a very common site in UK skies. However, now just a single example remains airworthy in Great Britain.

Devon	Keith Perkins/Aero Legends	G-DHDV	VP981	VP981	Flyable
Devon	Yorkshire Air Museum	G-KOOL	VP967	VP967	Ground Runner
Devon	Air Atlantique Ltd	G-BWWC	XM223	XM223	Stored
Devon	955 Preservation Group	G-DVON	VP955	VP955	Stored
Devon	Columba Aviation Ltd	G-OPLC	VP962	-	Stored
Devon	Aviation Heritage Ltd	G-SDEV	XK895	XK895	Stored

de Havilland Canada DHC-1 Chipmunk

One of the most numerous warbirds in the UK today is the venerable 'Chippie' – a type that entered RAF service in 1946 and is still in squadron service with the BBMF and the Royal Navy and Army Air Corps Historic Flights. Chipmunks are also phenomenally popular with private owners, offering a combination of affordable flying and fun handling – something that has resulted in the aircraft sometimes being referred to as "the poor man's Spitfire." More than 100 remain airworthy in the UK alone in 2017.

Type	Owner	Registration	Serial	Markings	Status
DHC-1 Chipmunk	Kenneth Large & Jean Morley	G-AKDN	-	-	Flyable
DHC-1 Chipmunk 22A	Dennis & Tricia Neville	G-ALWB	-	-	Flyable
DHC-1 Chipmunk 21	Redhill Tailwheel Flying Group Ltd	G-AMUF	-	-	Flyable
DHC-1 Chipmunk 21	Gordon Briggs	G-ANWB	-	-	Flyable
DHC-1 Chipmunk 22A	William Quinn	G-AOFE	WB702	WB702	Flyable
DHC-1 Chipmunk 22	Gerard Caubergs & Nicole Marien (Belgium)	G-AOJR	WB756	-	Flyable
DHC-1 Chipmunk 22	Steven Maric	G-AORW	WB682	-	Flyable
DHC-1 Chipmunk 22A	Peter McMillan	G-AOSK	WB726	WB726/E	Flyable
DHC-1 Chipmunk 22	Chippy Sierra Yankee Group	G-AOSY	WB585	WB585/M	Flyable
DHC-1 Chipmunk 22	Sebastian Piech	G-AOTD	WB588	WB588/D	Flyable
DHC-1 Chipmunk 22 (Lycoming)	Andrew Darby	G-AOTF	WB563	-	Flyable
DHC-1 Chipmunk 22	Steven Sykes	G-AOTR	WB604	-	Flyable
DHC-1 Chipmunk 22A	Retro Track & Air (UK) Ltd	G-AOTY	WG472	WG472	Flyable
DHC-1 Chipmunk 22	Andrew Harding	G-AOUP	WB731	-	Flyable
DHC-1 Chipmunk 22A	Stewart Davies	G-AOZP	WB734	-	Flyable
DHC-1 Chipmunk 22A	Petrus Luijken (Netherlands)	G-APLO	WB696	-	Flyable
DHC-1 Chipmunk 22	The Real Flying Company Ltd	G-APPA	WP917	-	Flyable
DHC-1 Chipmunk 22	Edward Moore	G-APPM	WB711	WB711	Flyable
DHC-1 Chipmunk 22	Paul & Janice Doyle	G-APYG	WB619	-	Flyable
DHC-1 Chipmunk 22A	John Henderson Childrens Trust	G-ARMC	WB703	WB703	Flyable
DHC-1 Chipmunk 22A	Lindsay Irvine	G-ARMG	WK558	WK558/DH	Flyable
DHC-1 Chipmunk 22A	Thruxton Chipmunk Flying Group	G-ARWB	WK611	WK611	Flyable
DHC-1 Chipmunk 22	Spartan Flying Group	G-ATHD	WP971	WP971	Flyable
DHC-1 Chipmunk 22 (Lycoming)	ATVF Syndicate	G-ATVF	WD327	-	Flyable
DHC-1 Chipmunk 22	John Beattie & Robert Scarre	G-BARS	WK520	'1377' Portuguese AF	Flyable
DHC-1 Chipmunk 22 (Lycoming)	Portsmouth Naval Gliding Club	G-BAVH	WP975	-	Flyable
DHC-1 Chipmunk 22	Ralph Steiner	G-BBMN	WD359	-	Flyable
DHC-1 Chipmunk 22	Mike Oscar Group	G-BBMO	WK514	WK514	Flyable
DHC-1 Chipmunk 22	MT Group	G-BBMT	WP831	-	Flyable
DHC-1 Chipmunk 22	Boultbee Vintage LLP	G-BBMV	WG348	-	Flyable
DHC-1 Chipmunk 22	Andrew Wilson & Gregory Fielder	G-BBMW	WK628	WK628	Flyable
DHC-1 Chipmunk 22	G-BBMZ Chipmunk Syndicate	G-BBMZ	WK548	-	Flyable
DHC-1 Chipmunk 22 (Lycoming)	Coventry Gliding Club Ltd	G-BBNA	WG417	-	Flyable
DHC-1 Chipmunk 22	Bernouilli Syndicate	G-BBND	WD286	WD286	Flyable
DHC-1 Chipmunk 22 (Lycoming)	Coventry Gliding Club Ltd	G-BBSS	WG470	-	Flyable
DHC-1 Chipmunk 22	Century Aviation Ltd	G-BCAH	WG316	WG316	Flyable
DHC-1 Chipmunk 22 (Lycoming)	Charlie X-Ray Syndicate Ltd	G-BCCX	WG481	-	Flyable
DHC-1 Chipmunk 22	Gopher Flying Group	G-BCEY	WG465	WG465	Flyable
DHC-1 Chipmunk 22	Henlow Chipmunk Group	G-BCGC	WP903	WP903	Flyable
DHC-1 Chipmunk 22	Shropshire Soaring Ltd	G-BCHL	WP788	WP788	Flyable
DHC-1 Chipmunk 22	Peter Richie	G-BCIH	WD363	WD363/5	Flyable
DHC-1 Chipmunk 22	Michael Diggins	G-BCOI	WP870	WP870/12	Flyable
DHC-1 Chipmunk 22	The Loweth Flying Group	G-BCOU	WK522	WK522	Flyable
DHC-1 Chipmunk 22 (Lycoming)	Coventry Gliding Club Ltd	G-BCOY	WB762	-	Flyable
DHC-1 Chipmunk 22	Paul Green	G-BCPU	WP973	WP973	Flyable
DHC-1 Chipmunk 22	Peter Tuplin & Michael Robinson	G-BCRX	WD292	WD292	Flyable
DHC-1 Chipmunk 22 (Lycoming)	Shennington Gliding Club	G-BCSA	WP799	-	Flyable
DHC-1 Chipmunk 22	Chipmunk Flyers Ltd	G-BCSL	WG474	-	Flyable
DHC-1 Chipmunk 22	Michael Turner	G-BCXN	WP800	WP800/2	Flyable
DHC-1 Chipmunk 22	G-BCYM Group	G-BCYM	WK577	WK577	Flyable
DHC-1 Chipmunk 22	Michael Goff	G-BFAW	WP848	WP848	Flyable
DHC-1 Chipmunk 22	Mark Curtis	G-BFAX	WG422	WG422/16	Flyable
DHC-1 Chipmunk 22	Noel O'Neill	G-BFDC	WG475	-	Flyable
DHC-1 Chipmunk 22	Shuttleworth Trust	G-BNZC	WP905	'671 RCAF'	Flyable
DHC-1 Chipmunk 22	Kenneth & Phyllis Tomsett (Portugal)	G-BPAL	WG350	WG350	Flyable
DHC-1 Chipmunk 22	John Simms	G-BTWF	WK549	WK549	Flyable
DHC-1 Chipmunk 22A	TX Fying Group	G-BVTX	WP809	WP809/78	Flyable
DHC-1 Chipmunk 22	Edward Clare	G-BWHI	WK624	WK624	Flyable
DHC-1 Chipmunk 22	Noel O'Neill	G-BWJY	WG469	WG469/72	Flyable
DHC-1 Chipmunk 22	407th Flying Group	G-BWMX	WG407	WG407/67	Flyable
DHC-1 Chipmunk 22	WD390 Group	G-BWNK	WD390	WD390/68	Flyable
DHC-1 Chipmunk 22	Steven Monk & Joanna Willis	G-BWNT	WP901	WP901/B	Flyable
DHC-1 Chipmunk 22	Rob de Man (Netherlands)	G-BWTG	WB671	WB671/910	Flyable
DHC-1 Chipmunk 22	Skycraft Services Ltd	G-BWTO	WP984	WP984/H	Flyable
DHC-1 Chipmunk 22	Terence Henderson	G-BWUN	WD310	WD310/B	Flyable
DHC-1 Chipmunk 22	Herbert Aviation Ltd	G-BWUT	WZ879	WZ879/X	Flyable
DHC-1 Chipmunk 22A	Nevil Gardner	G-BWVY	WP896	WP896	Flyable
DHC-1 Chipmunk 22	Didier Campion	G-BWVZ	WK590	WK590/69	Flyable
DHC-1 Chipmunk 22	Wickenby Aviation	G-BXCT	WB697	WB697/95	Flyable
DHC-1 Chipmunk 22	Ardmore Aviation Services Ltd	G-BXCV	WP929	WP929	Flyable
DHC-1 Chipmunk 22	Felthorpe Flying Group Ltd	G-BXDG	WK630	WK630	Flyable

Type	Owner	Reg	Serial	Marks	Status
DHC-1 Chipmunk 22	Royal Aircraft Establishment Aero Club Ltd	G-BXDH	WD331	WD331	Flyable
DHC-1 Chipmunk 22	Andrew Dinnie & David Spicer	G-BXDI	WD373	WD373/12	Flyable
DHC-1 Chipmunk 22	William Lowe, Lionel Edwards & Glen James	G-BXDN	WK609	WK609/93	Flyable
DHC-1 Chipmunk 22	Andrew Robinson & Mark Miller	G-BXEC	WK633	WK633	Flyable
DHC-1 Chipmunk 22	Nigel Marriott	G-BXGL	WZ884	-	Flyable
DHC-1 Chipmunk 22	Chipmunk GBXGM Group	G-BXGM	WP928	WP928/D	Flyable
DHC-1 Chipmunk 22	Timothy Orchard	G-BXGO	WB654	WB654/U	Flyable
DHC-1 Chipmunk 22	Eaglescott Chipmunk Group	G-BXGP	WZ882	WZ882/K	Flyable
DHC-1 Chipmunk 22	The Real Flying Company Ltd	G-BXGX	WK586	WK586	Flyable
DHC-1 Chipmunk 22	Steven & Helen Roberts	G-BXHA	WP925	WP925/C	Flyable
DHC-1 Chipmunk 22	Hotel Fox Syndicate	G-BXHF	WP930	WP930/J	Flyable
DHC-1 Chipmunk 22	Dales Aviation	G-BXIA	WB615	WB615/E	Flyable
DHC-1 Chipmunk 22	Alan Ashcroft & Peter Joshua	G-BXIM	WK512	WK512/A	Flyable
DHC-1 Chipmunk 22	Ian & Michael Higgins	G-BYHL	WG308	WG308/8	Flyable
DHC-1 Chipmunk 22	Propshop Ltd	G-BYSJ	WB569	WB569	Flyable
DHC-1 Chipmunk 22	The Real Flying Company Ltd	G-BZGA	WK585	WK585	Flyable
DHC-1 Chipmunk 22	Christopher Rees	G-CBJG	1373 Portuguese AF	1373 Portuguese AF	Flyable
DHC-1 Chipmunk 22	Andrew Darby	G-CERD	1317 Portuguese AF	'WK640'	Flyable
DHC-1 Chipmunk 22	G-CGAO Flying Group	G-CGAO	1350 Portuguese AF	1350 Portuguese AF	Flyable
DHC-1 Chipmunk 22	Jose da Silva Costa (Portugal)	G-CHPI	1324 Portuguese AF	1324 Portuguese AF	Flyable
DHC-1 Chipmunk 22	Skyblue Aero Services Ltd	G-CIGE	WK634	WK634/902	Flyable
DHC-1 Chipmunk 22	Peter Walley	G-CPMK	WZ847	WZ847/F	Flyable
DHC-1 Chipmunk 22	Eureka Aviation BVBA (Belgium)	G-DHCC	WG321	WG321/G	Flyable
DHC-1 Chipmunk 22	Peter Meyrick	G-DHPM	1365 Portuguese AF	1365 Portuguese AF	Flyable
DHC-1 Chipmunk 22	Astrojet Ltd	G-HAPY	WP803	WP803	Flyable
DHC-1 Chipmunk 22	Airborne Classics Ltd	G-HDAE	1304 Portuguese AF	'WP964'	Flyable
DHC-1 Chipmunk 22	Paula Jacobs	G-HFRH	WK635	WK635	Flyable
DHC-1 Chipmunk 22	Ian Whitaker-Bethel	G-ITWB	1358 Portuguese AF	-	Flyable
DHC-1 Chipmunk 22	Christopher Adams	G-MAJR	WP805	WP805	Flyable
DHC-1 Chipmunk 22	Connect Properties Ltd	G-PVET	WB565	WB565/X	Flyable
DHC-1 Chipmunk 22	Advanced Flight Training Ltd	G-UANO	1367 Portuguese AF	1367 Portuguese AF	Flyable
DHC-1 Chipmunk 22	Martin Phillips	G-ULAS	WK517	WK517	Flyable
DHC-1 Chipmunk 22	Army Historic Aircraft Flight	-	WD325	WD325	Flyable
DHC-1 Chipmunk 22	RAF Battle of Britain Memorial Flight	-	WG486	WG486/G	Flyable
DHC-1 Chipmunk 22	RAF Battle of Britain Memorial Flight	-	WK518	WK518/C	Flyable
DHC-1 Chipmunk 22	RN Historic Flight	-	WK608	WK608/906	Flyable
DHC-1 Chipmunk 22A	Roger Brookhouse	G-BAPB	WB549	-	Restoration
DHC-1 Chipmunk 22	Double Oscar Chipmunk Group	G-BCOO	WB760	-	Restoration
DHC-1 Chipmunk 22	Neil & Andrew Barton	G-CMNK	WB721	-	Restoration
DHC-1 Chipmunk 22	BG Chipmunks Inc	N458BG	WG458	WG458	Restoration
DHC-1 Chipmunk 22 (Lycoming)	The RAF Gliding & Soaring Assoc	G-AOUO	WB730	-	Stored
DHC-1 Chipmunk 22A	Martin Harvey	G-ARMF	WG322	-	Stored
DHC-1 Chipmunk 22	Peter Wood	G-BBMR	WB763	-	Stored
DHC-1 Chipmunk 22 (Lycoming)	RAF Gliding & Soaring Assoc	G-BCKN	WP811	-	Stored
DHC-1 Chipmunk 22A (Lycoming)	Portsmouth Naval Gliding Club	G-BVZZ	WP795	WP795/901	Stored
DHC-1 Chipmunk 22A	Andrew Darby	G-BWUV	WK640	WK640	Stored
DHC-1 Chipmunk 22	Declan Curtis	G-BXDA	WP860	WP860/6	Stored
DHC-1 Chipmunk 22	Nigel Skinner	G-BXNN	WP983	WP983/B	Stored
DHC-1 Chipmunk 22	Gordon Briggs	G-BZGB	WZ872	WZ872/E	Stored
DHC-1 Chipmunk 22	Devonair Executive Business Transport Ltd	G-CHPY	WB652	-	Stored

Chipmunk G-AKDN is one of the few non-military Chipmunks still flying. It is the oldest DHC-1 in existence and was the 11th off the production line in 1946. Steve Bridgewater

The Battle of Britain Memorial Flight operates a pair of Chipmunks. WK518 wears an authentic 1970s-era 'DayGlo' scheme while WG486 wears a contemporary black training scheme similar to the RAF Tucano and Hawk fleet. Jamie Ewan

Peter McMillan's Chipmunk, G-AOSK, wears its original markings at WB726. It was retired by the RAF in 1961 and has been in civilian hands ever since. *Steve Bridgewater*

Edward Moore's Chipmunk G-APPM aloft from Sywell in 2006 with Matthew Boddington at the controls. The aircraft flew with the RAF as WB711 until 1958. *Steve Bridgewater*

de Havilland DHC-2 Beaver

Although it was designed as a civilian aircraft for passenger and cargo operations the Beaver's short take-off and landing characteristics made it attractive to the military and 970 joined the US Army alone. The British Army also operated 42 examples and they served in all corners of the Empire.

▶ Beaver G-DHCZ is operated by the Aircraft Restoration Company/Propshop Ltd at Duxford in a stylish civilian scheme. The aircraft began life as XP772 and was delivered to the Army Air Corps in 1960.
Steve Bridgewater

DHC-2 Beaver	Propshop Ltd	G-DHCZ	XP722	-	Flyable
DHC-2 Beaver	Historic Aircraft Flight Trust/ Army Air Corps	G-CICP	XP820	XP820	Flyable
DHC-2 Beaver (U-6A)	Thomas Harris	G-EVMK	53-3718	-	Restoration
DHC-2 Beaver	Seaflite Ltd	G-BVER	XV268	XV268	Stored

Dornier Do.27

The Dornier Do.27 was a German single-engine STOL utility aircraft that could seat up to six. The prototype first flew in 1955 and the type was the first mass-produced aeroplane in post-war Germany.

| Do.27A-1 | Matthew Wood | G-BMFG | 3460 Portguese AF | - | Flyable |
| Do.27A-4 | Invicta Aviation Ltd | G-DOTS | 57+63 | - | Stored |

Focke Wulf/Piaggio FWP.149D

The all-metal, low-wing P.149 was developed as a four/five-seat touring variant of the earlier P.148. The prototype first flew in June 1953 but only a few were sold until the German Air Force selected the aircraft for a training and utility role. Piaggio delivered 72 aircraft to Germany and another 190 were built in Germany by Focke-Wulf as the FWP.149D.

FWP.149D	Private Owner	D-EARY	90+43 German AF	-	Flyable
FWP.149D	Private Owner	D-EHJL	90+32 German AF	-	Flyable
FWP.149D	Private Owner	D-EOAJ	90+18 German AF	-	Flyable

Fokker S.11 Instructor

One of the first activities undertaken by Fokker after World War Two was the design of a new military aircraft for initial pilot training. The resulting S-11 Instructor flew on December 18, 1947 and large numbers were sold to the Royal Netherlands Air Force as well as the Brazilian Air Force, Bolivian Air Force, Israeli Air Force, Italian Air Force and Paraguayan Air Force.

| S.11 Instructor | Carl Tyers. Malcolm & Stephen Isbister | G-BEPV | 6274 | 174/K Royal Netherlands Navy | Flyable |
| S.11 Instructor | Fokker Syndicate | G-BIYU | E-15 | E-15 RNIAF | Flyable |

120 | WARBIRD DIRECTORY

Helio H-295 Courier

The Courier was designed in the late 1940s as an extremely short take-off and landing aircraft suitable for civilian and military uses. The type was used extensively by US forces and the CIA during the Vietnam War.

▶ David Hanss' Courier is marked to represent a USAF example operated during the Vietnam War.
Steve Bridgewater

H-295 Courier	David Hanss	G-BAGT	-	'66-374/EO'	Flyable

Max Houlste MH.1521 Broussard

Often referred to as the 'French Beaver' the twin-finned Broussard first flew in 1952 and was powered by a 450hp P&W Wasp radial engine giving it excellent STOL performance. The type has always been popular with private owners.

MH 1521 Broussard	Keith Perkins/Aero Legends	G-CBGL	19 French AF	'3303 Portuguese AF'	Flyable
MH 1521 Broussard	Robert Fleming	G-CIGH	255 French AF	255/5-ML French AF	Flyable
MH 1521 Broussard	Bremont Watches	G-HOUR	149 French AF	-	Flyable
MH 1521 Broussard	Eggesford Heritage Flight	G-YYYY	208 French AF	208/IR French AF	Flyable
MH 1521 Broussard	Private Owner	F-GKRO	154 French AF	154/315-SM French AF	Flyable

Left: Keith Perkins' Broussard flew with the French Air Force as '19' but has been restored to depict a Portgguese Air Force example. **Right:** The English brothers' Broussard wears the logos of their Bremont Watch company. The aircraft is seen here wearing the French civil registration F-BXCP but it has since gained the appropriate UK registration G-HOUR.

Mitchell-Proctor Kittiwake

The Kittiwake was a single-seat, single engine sport aircraft designed for amateur building. Only four examples of the all-metal machine were ever completed including one produced by Royal Navy apprentices to operate as a glider tug. The aircraft remains in storage but has not flown for some time.

Kittiwake	Hayden Price	G-BBRN	XW784	XW784	Stored

Morane-Saulnier Alcyon

The Morane-Saulnier MS.370 Alcyon (Kingfisher) was a three-seat basic trainer designed in France in the late 1940s. A total of 40 were delivered to the French Navy, 145 to the French Air Force and 15 to the Cambodian Air Force. The type replaced the Stampe SV.4 in French service and many of the French examples were later fitted with machine guns. Some were even converted for counter-insurgency operations for use in Algeria.

The Alcyon Flying Group's G-MSAL is the only example of the type currently flying in the UK, although G-SHOW was a very common airshow performer during the 1980s. *Jamie Ewan*

MS.733 Alcyon	Alcyon Flying Group	G-MSAL	143 French Navy	143 French Navy	Flyable
MS.733 Alcyon	Francis Forster & Peter Cartwright	G-SHOW	125 French Navy	-	Restoration

Nanchang CJ-6A

Although the Chinese Nanchang CJ-6 is often mistaken for a version of the Russian Yak-18 it is very different (the CJ-5 was actually based on the Yak-18). The CJ-6 features an aluminium semi-monocoque fuselage, the airframe is flush-riveted throughout and the wing features a modified Clark airfoil design with pronounced dihedral. The first flight of the CJ-6 took place on August 27, 1958 but soon the aircraft needed more power and a 260hp locally manufactured version of the Soviet AI-14P radial (the Housai HS-6) replaced the original 'flat-four' engine. In 1965 the HS-6 engine was upgraded to 285hp and aircraft fitted with that powerplant are designated the CJ-6A. A total production run of more than 3,000 aircraft supplied have been supplied to China as well as Albania, Bangladesh, Cambodia, North Korea, Sri Lanka and Tanzania.

The Nanchang CJ6A Group's White Waltham-based aircraft (G-BVVG) wears the markings of the Chinese People's Liberation Army Air Force (PLAAF).

CJ6A	Nanchang CJ6A Group	G-BVVG	2751210	'1219/68' (Chinese AF)	Flyable
CJ6A	Robert Davy, James Swallow & Peter Lloyd	G-BXZB	2632019	'CT190' (Sri Lankan AF)	Flyable
CJ6A	Bruno Blanchard (France)	G-CGFS	1532008	'CT190' (Sri Lankan AF)	Flyable
CJ6A	Martin Harvey	G-CGHB	1532009	'61387' (Chinese AF)	Flyable
CJ6A	James Ware & Matthew Elmes	G-CJSA	3151215	-	Flyable

Nord NC.856

The Nord NC.856 was a light aircraft developed in France in the late 1940s for use by French aeroclubs, but which also saw military use as an airborne observation post.

| NC.856A | Rikki McLain | G-CGWR | 54 French Army | 54 French Army | Restoration |
| NC.856 | Ronald & Jennifer Cooper | G-CDWE | 01 French Air Force | 'N856 French AF' | Stored |

Nord N.1203 Norécrin II

The Norécrin was a French three (later four)-seat cabin monoplane designed to meet a French Ministry of Transport sponsored design competition. Later versions were delivered to the French Air Force equipped with machine guns and rockets.

| N.1203 Norécrin II | Private Owner | OO-AJK | 261 French Army | - | Stored |

Nord N.3202

The Nord 3202 was developed in the 1950s to meet a French Army requirement for a two-seat basic trainer to replace the Stampe SV.4. Altogether, 101 examples were built.

▶ Alistair Milne's Nord N.3202 G-BIZK has been a UK resident since 1985. It was previously based with Anthony Hodgeson in North Wales but has been with the current owner since 1990.

| N.3202-B1 | Alistair Milne | G-BIZK | 78 French AF | 78 French AF | Flyable |

North American T-28 Trojan

With the departure of Radial Revelations T-28B N14113 to France in early 2017 there is now just one example of the big American trainer based in the UK. The Fennec version was the counter-insurgency ground attack variant sold to the French.

| T-28A Fennec | Groupe Fennec | G-TROY | 51-7692 | 517692/TL-692 |

T-28A G-TROY rolled off the former Consolidated-Vultee Aircraft production line at Downey, California in early 1953 and was delivered to the USAF Training Command. It had been retired by 1958 and in 1962 it was delivered to the USAF's 'Military Aid Assistance Program' where it was made available for sale to friendly air arms. It was acquired by the French, brought back to flying status and flown to Norfolk Naval Air Station, Virginia and from there it was embarked onto a French aircraft carrier as deck cargo for the Atlantic crossing to St. Nazaire. In France it became Fennec No 142 and part of the Armée de l'Air Light Aircraft Ground Support Squadron that flew operational missions in the counter insurgency role in Algeria. For the 2017 airshow season G-TROY has reverted to its original USAF markings as TL-692.

Percival Pembroke

The Pembroke was a military development of the Percival Prince civil transport. It had a longer wing to give extra lift at higher laden weights and the prototype flew on November 21, 1952. Production was complete in early 1958 by which time 128 had been delivered. The type replaced the Avro Anson in RAF service. The Royal Navy used the type as the Sea Prince.

▶ Since it retired from the RAF Pembroke WV740 has been owned by ACM Sir John Allison, Martin Willing and Andrew Dixon. In 2012 it was sold to Mark Stott and is now based at St Athan. Steve Bridgewater

Pembroke C.1	Mark Stott	G-BNPH	WV740	WV740	Flyable
Pembroke C.1	Private Owner	G-BNPU	XL929	-	Stored
Pembroke C.1P	Air Atlantique Ltd	G-BXES	XL954	XL954	Flyable
Sea Prince	Mark Stott	G-BRFC	WP321	-	Stored

Percival Prentice

The Percival Prentice was designed as a basic trainer for the RAF in the early post-war period. The all-metal aeroplane could accommodate an instructor and two students within its capacious cockpit and the type has proved popular with pleasure flyers in recent years.

▶ Prentice G-APJB/VR259 plied her trade with Air Atlantique for almost 20 years but in 2015 she was sold to Aero Legends and departed for Headcorn. She joins the organisation's very active pleasure flying fleet.
Steve Bridgewater

Prentice T.1	Neil Butler	G-AOKL	VS610	-	Stored
Prentice T.1	Neil Butler	G-AOLU	VS356	-	Stored
Prentice T.1	Keith Perkins/Aero Legends	G-APJB	VR259	VR259	Flyable
Prentice T.1	Susan Saggers	G-APPL	VR189	-	Flyable

Percival Provost

The low-wing Percival P.56 Provost basic trainer was developed in the 1950s as a replacement for the RAF's Percival Prentice. The Provost has the distinction of being the last piston-engine basic trainer aircraft to be operated by the RAF and more than 450 were produced. The type used to be a common warbird but today they are a rare sight.

Provost T.1	John Bradshaw	G-AWPH	WV240	-	Flyable
Provost T.1	Alan House	G-AWRY	XF836	-	Stored
Provost T.1	Alan House	G-BKFW	XF597	XF597	Stored
Provost T.1	Paul Childs	G-BZRF	WV499	-	Restoration
Provost T.1	Shuttleworth Trust	G-KAPW	XF603	XF603	Flyable
Provost T.1	Yeopro Group	G-MOOS	XF690	XF690	Flyable
Provost T.51	Andrew & Karen Edie	G-BLIW	IAC.177	'WV514 C-N'	Stored

Left: Kennet Aviation restored XF603 as G-KAPW in 1997 and painted the aeroplane in the camouflage applied to examples exported to Malaysia. In 2001 the aircraft was transferred to the Shuttleworth Collection but continues to operate in the same scheme. **Right:** Another Kennett Aviation Provost restoration was XF690/G-MOOS. The aircraft now flies regularly from RNAS Yeovilton under the control of the Yeopro Group syndicate.

Ryan L-17 Navion

The Ryan (originally North American) Navion was a single-engined, unpressurised, four-seat aircraft envisioned as a machine that would perfectly match the expected post-war boom in civilian aviation. However, it was with the military that the Navion really found its niche with US forces using it as the L-17 liaison and training aircraft.

| L-17C Navion | Private Owner | N4956C | - | '60344 USAAF' | Flyable |
| L-17C Navion | Eames Aviation | N8968H | - | 'USAF' | Flyable |

Scottish Aviation Bulldog

Beagle Aircraft developed the Bulldog as a military training version of its popular Beagle Pup light aircraft. The prototype flew on May 19, 1969 at Shoreham Airport and an order for 78 was received from Sweden just as Beagle ran out of money and ceased trading. The rights to the aircraft were taken over by Scottish Aviation Ltd and a total of 320 were eventually made – including 130 for the RAF. The RAF sold off its Bulldogs in 2001 and today the type is one of the most popular warbirds in the UK.

Left: The oldest Bulldog still flying is G-ASAL, which was used as the company demonstrator by Scottish Aviation.
Right: Old Sarum-based G-BCUV was the last of seven Bulldogs built for the Ghanaian Air Force as G-112 but has been painted to represent 'XX704'. The 'real' XX704 resides in California where it flies as N706BD. Both Steve Bridgewater

124 | WARBIRD DIRECTORY

Two ex-Hong Kong Auxiliary Air Force are based in the UK. The former HKG-5 is now G-BULL and HKG-6 flies as G-BPCL. Both Steve Bridgewater

Bulldog	Pioneer Flying Company Ltd	G-ASAL	-	-	Flyable
Bulldog	Thomas Harris	G-AZHX	Fv61126 SwAF	'XX625/45'	Flyable
Bulldog	Cranfield University	G-BCUO	G-106 Ghana AF	-	Flyable
Bulldog	Falcon Group	G-BCUS	G-109 Ghana AF	-	Flyable
Bulldog	Flew LLP	G-BCUV	G-112 Ghana AF	'XX704'	Flyable
Bulldog	David Bonsall	G-BDOG	-	-	Flyable
Bulldog	Airplan Flight Equipment	G-BHXA	OD-1 Botswana Defence Force	-	Flyable
Bulldog	David Curties	G-BHZT	OD-6 Botswana Defence Force	-	Flyable
Bulldog	121 Group	G-BPCL	HKG-6 Royal HKAAF	HKG-6 Royal HKAAF	Flyable
Bulldog	Bulldog Aeros Ltd	G-BULL	HKG-5 Royal HKAAF	HKG-5 Royal HKAAF	Flyable
Bulldog	David Rae	G-BZDP	XX551	XX551/E	Flyable
Bulldog	Risk Logical Ltd	G-BZFN	XX667	XX667/16	Flyable
Bulldog	Mad Dog Flying Group	G-BZMD	XX554	XX554/09	Flyable
Bulldog	XX698 Bulldog Group	G-BZME	XX698	XX698/9	Flyable
Bulldog	Michael Hingley	G-BZMH	XX692	XX692	Flyable
Bulldog	Ian Anderson	G-BZML	XX693	XX693/07	Flyable
Bulldog	David Critchley	G-BZON	XX528	XX528/D	Flyable
Bulldog	Colin Wright	G-BZXZ	XX629	XX629	Flyable
Bulldog	Mid America (UK) Ltd	G-CBAB	XX543	XX543/U	Flyable
Bulldog	Adam Reynolds	G-CBAN	XX668	XX668/I	Flyable
Bulldog	Bulldog Flyers Ltd	G-CBBC	XX515	XX515/B	Flyable
Bulldog	Andrew Cunningham	G-CBBL	XX550	XX550/Z	Flyable
Bulldog	David Keene	G-CBBS	XX694	XX694/E	Flyable
Bulldog	Kerr Johnston	G-CBBT	XX695	XX695	Flyable
Bulldog	Stuart Robottom-Scott	G-CBBW	XX619	XX619/T	Flyable
Bulldog	Mark Minary	G-CBCB	XX537	XX537/C	Flyable
Bulldog	Donald Wells	G-CBCR	XX702	XX702	Flyable
Bulldog	James Randle	G-CBDK	XX611	XX611/7	Flyable
Bulldog	Francis Sandwell & Andrew Butcher	G-CBEF	XX621	XX621/H	Flyable
Bulldog	James Lewis	G-CBEH	XX521	XX521/H	Flyable
Bulldog	Bernard Robinson	G-CBEK	XX700	XX700/17	Flyable
Bulldog	Robert Nisbet & Andrew Dix	G-CBFP	XX636	XX636/Y	Flyable
Bulldog	John & Simon Huggins	G-CBFU	XX628	XX628/9	Flyable
Bulldog	Bulldog GX Group	G-CBGX	XX622	XX622/B	Flyable
Bulldog	The Red Dog Group	G-CBID	XX549	XX549/6	Flyable
Bulldog	William Mott	G-CDVV	XX626	XX626/ W-02	Flyable
Bulldog	Stephen Wood	G-DAWG	XW522	XX522/06	Flyable
Bulldog	Ian Whiting	G-DISA	420 Jordanian AF	-	Flyable
Bulldog	Paul Sengupta	G-DOGG	XX638	XX638	Flyable
Bulldog	Edwalton Aviation Ltd	G-EDAV	XX534	XX534/B	Flyable
Bulldog	Derek Sharp	G-GGRR	XX614	XX614/1	Flyable
Bulldog	Horizons Europe Ltd	G-GRRR	G-105 Ghana AF	-	Flyable
Bulldog	Derek Wright	G-JWCM	OD-2 Botswana Defence Force	-	Flyable
Bulldog	Simon Tilling	G-KDOG	XX624	XX624/E	Flyable
Bulldog	Michael Cowan	G-KKKK	XX513	XX513/10	Flyable
Bulldog	Power Aerobatics Ltd	G-RAIG	Fv61037 SwAF	-	Flyable
Bulldog	Power Aerobatics Ltd	G-RNRS	Fv61026 SwAF	-	Flyable
Bulldog	Michael Miles	G-SIJW	XX630	XX630/5	Flyable
Bulldog	Geoffrey Taylor	G-TDOG	XX538	XX538/O	Flyable
Bulldog	Marc van Den Broeck (Belgium)	G-UDOG	XX518	XX518/S	Flyable
Bulldog	Kryten Systems Ltd	G-ULHI	Fv61038 SwAF	-	Flyable
Bulldog	Alexander Bole	G-WINI	XX546	XX546/03	Flyable
Bulldog	Robert Skinner	G-BZEP	XX561	XX561/7	Restoration
Bulldog	Andrew Robinson & Mark Miller	G-BZPS	XX568	-	Restoration
Bulldog	White Knuckle Air Ltd	G-BHZR	OD-4 Botswana Defence Force	-	Stored
Bulldog	Kieran Thompson	G-BZXS	XX631	XX631/W	Stored
Bulldog	DeltaAero Ltd (Spain)	G-DDOG	XX524	XX524/05	Stored

Scottish Aviation Twin Pioneer

The Scottish Aviation Twin Pioneer was a 1950s-era STOL transport aircraft designed for both civil and military operators. It could operate from an area just 99ft x 912ft (30m x 275m) and was used extensively by the RAF.

Twin Pioneer	Air Atlantique Ltd	G-APRS	XT610	-	Stored
Twin Pioneer	Air Atlantique Ltd	G-AZHJ	-	-	Stored

Left: Although it still shows on official records as belonging to Air Atlantique the UK's only potentially airworthy Twin Pioneer has been sold to Christy Keene in Weston near Dublin. G-APRS has not flown for some years due to concerns over the fatigue life of the wing attachment points and now Mr Keene has acquired 'RS and a second airframe (G-AZHJ) that Air Atlantique had in storage.

SIAI-Marchetti SF.260

The SF.260 was designed by Italian aircraft designer Stelio Frati and marketed as a military trainer and civilian aerobatic/touring aircraft. Armed military versions proved to be popular with smaller air forces but most of the examples in the UK have no military provenance and fly in civilian paint schemes – apart from these three.

▶ Neil Whatling's ex-Italian Air Force SF.260AM wears its former military markings and is seen here visiting RAF Waddington. Steve Bridgewater

Geoffrey Boot uses his SF.260W for air racing and has had the aircraft painted in the markings of the Burkina Faso Air Force.

SF.260	Neil Whatling	G-ITAF	MM54-532	70-42 (Italian AF)	Flyable
SF.260	Geoffrey Boot	G-NRRA	-	BF8431 Burkina Faso AF	Flyable
SF.260	Private Owner	N405FD	-	'206 USAF'	Flyable

Slingsby T-67 Firefly

Although the Yorkshire-designed and built Slingsby T-67 was used to provide basic training for the UK armed forces from 1995 to 2010 the aircraft were privately owned so do not fall under this book's remit of being 'ex-military. However, a pair of former Royal Hong Kong Auxiliary Air Force examples tick the right boxes.

▶ **Ex-Royal Hong Kong Auxiliary Air Force T-67M-200 Firely HKG-11 continues to honour its former operator, despite now flying 6,000 miles from its old home.**

| T67M-200 | Jean-Francois Jansen & Alain Huygens (Belgium) | G-BXKW | HKG-12 RHKAAF | HKG-12 RHKAAF | Flyable |
| T67M-200 | James Clowes | G-BYRY | HKG-11 RHKAAF | HKG-11 RHKAAF | Flyable |

Soko J-20 P-2 Kraguj

The Kraguj (Sparrowhawk) is light, single-piston-engined, single-seat, low-wing attack aircraft, capable of performing close air support, counter insurgency (COIN), and reconnaissance missions. It was manufactured in the former Yugoslavia and first flew in 1962. Several used to fly regularly in the UK but now there is just one air airworthy example.

Kraguj G-BSXD is now the sole airworthy example in the UK. It served with the Yugoslavian Air Force as 146. Steve Bridgewater

P-2 Kraguj	Simon Johnston	G-BSXD	30146	146 Yugoslavian AF	Flyable
P-2 Kraguj	Simon Johnston	G-RADA	30140	-	Stored
P-2 Kraguj	Paul Avery	G-SOKO	30149	149 Yugoslavian AF	Stored
P-2 Kraguj	Private Owner	-	TBC	131 Yugoslavian AF	Stored
P-2 Kraguj	Private Owner	-	TBC	139 Yugoslavian AF	Stored
P-2 Kraguj	Private Owner	-	TBC	151 Yugoslavian AF	Stored

Yakovlev Yak-12

The Yak-12 was designed by Yakovlev's team to meet a requirement of the Soviet Air Force of 1944 for a new liaison and utility aircraft to replace the obsolete Polikarpov Po-2 biplane. It was also ideal for civilian use and almost 5,000 have been built.

▶ **Roger Bade's Yak-12M was registered SP-FKD before he placed it on the UK register. It is the only one of its type flying on a 'G' registration.** Steve Bridgewater

| Yak-12M | Roger Bade | G-PKFD | 210999/HA-HUB | - | Flyable |

WARBIRD DIRECTORY | 127

Yakovlev Yak-18

In May 1945 Yakovlev began work on the Yak-18 two-seat primary trainer to replace the Yakovlev UT-2 and Yak-5 in service with the Soviet Air Forces and DOSAAF. The new aircraft was powered by a 160hp Shvetsov M-11 five-cylinder radial engine and featured pneumatically operated retractable main landing gear and a fixed tailwheel. The Yak-18 spawned the later Yak-18A (featuring a nose-wheel and a 300hp engine), Yak-52, single-seat Yak-18PM, Yak-18PS and Yak-50 as well as the four-seat fully aerobatic Yak-18T.

Yak-18A	Will Moore	G-BMJY	627 Egyptian AF	'07' (Soviet AF)	Flyable
Yak-18A	Robert Fleming	G-CEIB	1160403	'03' (Soviet AF)	Flyable
Yak-18T	David Cue	G-CIDC	15-35/HA-YAU	-	Flyable
Yak-18T	Richard Goode	G-CIYM	7201413/HA-YAZ	-	Flyable
Yak-18T	Anthony Leftwich	G-HAHU	12-33/HA-HUE	-	Flyable
Yak-18T	Paul Beardsell	G-PYAK	12-35/HA-YAB	-	Flyable
Yak-18T	Carol Brightwell	G-UYAK	22202023842/HA-JAB	-	Flyable
Yak-18T	Nigel Parsons (Switzerland)	G-VSOZ	10-34/HA-YAN	-	Stored
Yak-18T	Alasdair McRobbie	G-VYAK	01-32/HA-HUA	-	Flyable
Yak-18T	Mark Blokland	G-YAKG	22202034023	-	Stored
Yak-18T	Teshka Aviation Syndicate	G-YAKJ	01-33/HA-HAJ	-	Flyable
Yak-18T	Private Owner	HA-SMD	13-35	-	Flyable
Yak-18T	Private Owner	LY-CCP	22202044623	-	Flyable

The Teshka Aviation Syndicate's Yak-18T four-seater was formerly registered HA-HAJ but has now transferred to the UK register as G-YAKJ. Steve Bridgewater

Rober Fleming's Breighton, Yorkshire-based Yak-18 wears a typical Russian green scheme along with the unit codes 'White 03'. Steve Bridgewater

Yakovlev Yak-50

The desire to win the World Aerobatic Championship in Moscow in 1966 led Yakovlev to create the Yak-18PM single-seater. Just 25 of the tricycle-geared aeroplanes were made but they achieved their goal. For the 1970 championships they came up with the Yak-18PS – which had a tailwheel and a lighter, fabric-covered wing. This time just six were made but, again, they won Gold. In 1976 Yakovlev raised the bar even further with the Yak-50 – not only did it win the World Aerobatic Championship, it also broke the World Speed Record. By the time production had ended 312 Yak-50s had been produced.

G-YAKM, wearing the code 'Red 61', is assigned to the Yakovlevs formation team but also conducts solo displays. Steve Bridgewater

Phil Ansell lands back after another display with the Yak-50 display team The Aerostars. Steve Bridgewater

Yak-50	Airborne Services Ltd	G-BTZB	801810	10 Soviet AF	Flyable
Yak-50	Fox Mike Group	G-BWFM	781208	-	Flyable
Yak-50	Foley Farm Flying Group	G-BWYK	812004	-	Flyable
Yak-50	Phil Ansell	G-CBPM	812101	-	Flyable
Yak-50	Mark Rijkse & Mark Levy	G-GYAK	852905	-	Flyable
Yak-50	Skyfalk AS (Norway)	G-HAMM	832409	-	Flyable
Yak-50	Angie Soper	G-IVAR	791504	-	Flyable
Yak-50	Andrew Patton (USA)	G-JYAK	853001	'93 Soviet AF'	Flyable
Yak-50	Stephen Partridge-Hicks & Ian Austin	G-SKPH	853010	-	Flyable
Yak-50	Martin Gadsby	G-SOCT	842804	'AR-B' (RAF)	Flyable
Yak-50	Jez Hopkinson	G-YAAK	812003	'20 Soviet AF'	Flyable
Yak-50	Brad Kosek (USA)	G-YAKA	822303	-	Flyable
Yak-50	Airborne Services Ltd	G-YAKM	842710	'61 Soviet AF'	Flyable
Yak-50	Jez Hopkinson	G-YAKU	822305	'49 Soviet AF'	Flyable
Yak-50	Airborne Services Ltd	G-YAKZ	853206	'33 Soviet AF'	Flyable
Yak-50	Russian Radials Ltd	G-YKSO	791506	'23 Soviet AF'	Flyable
Yak-50	Paul Whitehead	G-EYAK	801804	-	Stored
Yak-50	Eaglescott Yak 50 Group	G-IIYK	842706	-	Stored
Yak-50	The Assets of the Svetlana Group	G-SVET	822210	-	Stored

Of all the UK-based Yak-50s G-BTZB wears undoubtedly the most accurate representation of an in-service DOSAAF Yak-50. Steve Bridgewater

Yak-50 G-HAMM wears a scheme representative of that carried by a World War Two Russian fighter.
Steve Bridgewater

Stephen Partridge-Hicks taxies G-SKPH in at Little Haugh Hall, Suffolk after a private display.
Steve Bridgewater

Yakovlev Yak-52

A descendant of the Yak-50, the two-seat Yak-52 primary trainer first flew in 1976 and is still being produced in Romania by Aerostar. With the fall of the Berlin Wall in the 1990s the mass-produced Yak-52 round a ready home with western pilots.

▶ Jon Windover departs Old Warden in the G-YOTS Syndicate's Yak-52 at the end of an airshow.
Steve Bridgewater

Plus 7 Minus 5 Ltd's G-YAKH wears a World War Two fighter-esque scheme along with the codes 'White 33.'
Steve Bridgewater

Yak One Ltd's Yak-52 G-YAKI wears an eye-catching non-authentic colour scheme.
Steve Bridgewater

Yak-52	Mark Blackman	G-BVVW	844605	-	Flyable
Yak-52	Andrew Dent	G-BVXK	9111306	'26 DOSAAF'	Flyable
Yak-52	Michael Fitch	G-BWSV	877601	'43 DOSAAF'	Flyable
Yak-52	Russian Radials Ltd	G-BXAK	811508	-	Flyable
Yak-52	Yak Display Group	G-BXJB	877403	-	Flyable
Yak-52	ACG Air-Craft GmbH (Germany)	G-BZJB	811601	-	Flyable
Yak-52	Aerobility	G-CBMD	822710	-	Flyable
Yak-52	Ian Jones	G-CBMI	855907	-	Flyable
Yak-52	Michael Babbage	G-CBOZ	811308	-	Flyable
Yak-52	Max Alpha Aviation GmbH (Germany)	G-CBRW	9111415	'50 DOSAAF'	Flyable
Yak-52	Neil & Andrew Barton	G-CBSL	822013	'67 DOSAAF'	Flyable
Yak-52	Grovinvest SRL (Italy)	G-CBSR	877913	-	Flyable
Yak-52	Etienne Verhellen (Belgium)	G-CBSS	833707	-	Flyable
Yak-52	G-CCJK Group	G-CCJK	9612001	'52 Soviet AF'	Flyable
Yak-52	Jeremy Miles	G-CDJJ	899912	-	Flyable
Yak-52	Robert Harper	G-CJBV	867203	-	Flyable
Yak-52	Cosmos Technology Ltd	G-IUII	9111604	'36 Soviet AF'	Flyable
Yak-52	Fox Alpha Group	G-LYFA	822608	-	Flyable
Yak-52	Ian Gough	G-OUGH	877404	-	Flyable
Yak-52	Chewton Glen Ltd	G-RNAC	888912	'123'	Flyable
Yak-52	Nicholas Stillwell	G-SPUT	9111608	-	Flyable
Yak-52	Simon Ducker	G-TYAK	899907	-	Flyable
Yak-52	Martin Gadsby	G-YAKB	9211517	-	Flyable
Yak-52	Airborne Services Ltd	G-YAKC	867212	'86 Soviet AF'	Flyable
Yak-52	Jez Hopkinson	G-YAKE	877610	10 Soviet AF	Flyable
Yak-52	Yak Attack Ltd	G-YAKF	9111205	-	Flyable
Yak-52	Plus 7 Minus 5 Ltd	G-YAKH	899915	'33 Soviet AF'	Flyable
Yak-52	Yak One Ltd	G-YAKI	866904	'100 Soviet AF'	Flyable
Yak-52	Airborne Services Ltd	G-YAKN	855905	'66 Soviet AF'	Flyable
Yak-52	The X-Fliers Ltd	G-YAKX	9111307	'27 Soviet AF'	Flyable
Yak-52	Tzarina Group	G-YKSZ	9311709	'01 Soviet AF'	Flyable
Yak-52	G-YOTS Group	G-YOTS	9010308	-	Flyable
Yak-52	Repxper Sarl (France)	G-YYAK	878101	-	Flyable
Yak-52	Johan van Rossum (Belgium)	G-ZYAK	877415	-	Flyable
Yak-52	BS Offshore Ltd	G-XYAK	899413	'69 Soviet AF'	Restoration
Yak-52	Ian Parkinson	G-BWVR	878202	'52 Soviet AF'	Stored
Yak-52	Benjamin Nicholson	G-ZBEN	822708	-	Restoration
Yak-52	Jez Hopkinson	G-STNR	8333810	-	Stored
Yak-52	William Marriott	G-YAKY	844109	-	Stored

ROTARY WINGS

In recent years the number of historic helicopters flying in UK skies has blossomed with an interesting and varied range of machines now flying in private hands and/or at airshows across the country.

Aérospatiale Alouette

The French-designed Alouette (Lark) was the first production helicopter to be powered by a gas turbine engine instead of the conventional piston powerplant. The prototype SE.3130 first flew on March 12, 1955 and 1,300 of the resulting Alouette II were constructed between 1956 and 1975. In the military world it was mostly used for observation, photography, air-sea rescue, liaison and training, but it could also carry torpedoes or anti-tank missiles.

SA.318C Alouette II	Private Owner	HA-WKS	2204	-	Flyable
SA.318C Alouette II	Private Owner	HA-WKY	A68 Belgian AF	-	Flyable
SA.318C Alouette II	Private Owner	HA-WKZ	A79 Belgian AF	-	Flyable
SE.3130 Alouette II	Private Owner	F-GXFP	2152 French Army	-	Flyable
SE.3130 Alouette II	Historic Aircraft Flight Trust/ Army Air Corps	G-CICS	XR379	XR379	Flyable
SE.3130 Alouette II	Private Owner	HA-IDL	75+48 German Army	-	Flyable
SE.3130 Alouette II	Private Owner	N297CJ	9212 Portuguese AF	-	Stored
SE.3130 Alouette II	Michael Cuttell	G-BVSD	V54 Swiss AF	V-54 (Swiss AF)	Flyable

Bell UH-1 Iroquois

The Bell UH-1 Iroquois (nicknamed 'Huey') is one of the most iconic helicopters of all time. Developed in the 1950s for the US Army the type served with distinction in Vietnam and was the first turbine-powered helicopter to enter production for the US military. More than 16,000 have been built since. The Iroquois was originally designated HU-1, hence the 'Huey' nickname, which has remained in common use, despite the official redesignation to UH-1 in 1962. The UH-1 first saw service in combat operations during the Vietnam War, with around 7,000 helicopters deployed. The Bell 204 and 205 are versions of the Iroquois developed for the civil market.

Bell	UH-1H Huey	MX Jets Ltd	G-HUEY	AE-413 (Argentine AF)	-	Flyable
Bell	UH-1H Huey	MSS Holdings (UK) Ltd	G-UHIH	72-21509	72-21509/129	Flyable
Bell	UH-1H Huey	Yorkshire Helicopters USA Inc	N911DN	67-17426 (US Army)	-	Flyable
Bell	UH-1H Huey	Bell Asset Management Inc	N250DM	66-16114 (US Army)	-	Stored
Bell	UH-1H Huey	Bell Asset Management Inc	N338CB	66-16118 (US Army)	-	Stored

Left: MX Jets' Huey was built in 1973 and given the serial number 73-21872 but was destined for Argentina and given the military designation AE-413. On the April 14, 1982 it was transported to the Falkland Islands by a C-130 Hercules to play its part in the conflict. After the surrender of the Argentinean forces Sqn Ldr Rob Tierney 'borrowed' the helicopter from a sports field in Stanley and it was used extensively for transportation of personnel and freight around the island and from shore to ship. Later that year it was transported to the UK on the ship *Tor Caledonia* and it was eventually registered G-HUEY and flown in support of the RAF Benevolent Fund. It was subsequently auctioned off and is now based at North Weald and displays regularly in the hands of Mark Fitzgerald. Dr Nia Jones

Right: MSS Holdings' Huey was delivered to the US Army in July 1972 and immediately assigned to the 129 Assault Helicopter Company in Vietnam. During the Vietnam War 72-21509 flew 108 combat sorties and amassed 559 combat hours before it was returned to the US in February 1973. It then flew with various Army National Guard units until it was sent to the Aerospace Maintenance Central in Arizona for storage in 2000. The helicopter arrived in the UK in 2003 and is now resplendent in its original Vietnam-era markings. Steve Bridgewater

Hiller UH-12 Raven

The Hiller OH-23 Raven was a three-place light observation helicopter based on the Hiller UH-12. The Royal Navy's 705 Training Squadron used Hiller HTE-2s for several years from 1953 and later operated Hiller 12E's for many further years as its basic helicopter trainer based at RNAS Culdrose.

▶ Hields Aviation's Hiller UH-12E G-ASAZ is painted to represent Royal Navy HTE-2 'XS165'. G-ASAZ was the helicopter flown in the 1964 Bond movie *Goldfinger* and has appeared in various films and TV series over the years.

UH-12B	Private Owner	N38763	102 Royal Thai Police	-	Flyable
UH-12C	Hiller Group	N62171	-	'62171 USAF'	Flyable
UH-12C	Private Owner	N5315V	-	'779465 USAF'	Flyable
UH-12E	Hields Aviation	G-ASAZ	-	'XS165'	Flyable
UH-12B	Private Owner	N831M	330 Royal Thai Police	-	Stored

Hughes OH-6 Cayuse

The Cayuse (nicknamed 'Loach') was based on the civilian Hughes 369 helicopter and designed to operate with the US Army in the personnel transport, escort and attack missions, casualty evacuation and observation roles.

◀ MSS Holdings' 'Loach' was built in 1969 as 69-16011 and shipped direct to Vietnam where it served in the US Army's 20th Transport Company. On August 17, 1970 the helicopter was on a reconnaissance mission when it came under fire and took eleven hits from small arms and automatic weapons. A hit to the fuel system forced the helicopter to land but fortunately just one member of crew was lightly injured. The 'Loach' was then flown to a maintenance unit underslung from a 'Huey'. It was then deemed beyond economical repair in country and it was shipped back to the USA where it eventually returned to service in 1972. It remained in service with various National Guard duties until August 1992 where it was transferred to the Drug Enforcement Agency (DEA). In 2004 it was finally retired and acquired by MSS Holdings' Phil Connolly. Restoration work began in 2008 and what began as a 6 month long project turned into a 28 month long epic.
Steve Bridgewater

OH-6A Cayuse	MSS Holdings (UK) Ltd	G-OHGA	68-16011	16011	Flyable
OH-6A Cayuse	Private Owner	N239MY	68-17172	-	Flyable

Saro Skeeter

The Saunders-Roe Skeeter was a two-seat training and scout helicopter dating from 1948. Examples were flown in private hands for many years – including XL812 with the Army Air Corps Historic Flight and XL809 (G-BLIX) - but concerns over the ageing rotor blades mean none have flown for some years, although G-BLIX remains on the UK civil register.

Skeeter AOP.12	Kathryn Scholes	G-BLIX	XL809	XL809	Stored

Westland Bell 47 Sioux

The Bell 47 Sioux first flew in December 1945 and the following March it became the first helicopter certified for civilian use. More than 5,600 Bell 47s were produced, including those under license by Agusta in Italy and Westland Aircraft in the UK. Distinctive for its bubble canopy, exposed welded tube tail boom and saddle fuel tanks the Bell 47's two bladed rotor made a 'chop-chop' sound, leading to the now familiar 'chopper' nickname applied to all helicopters. The Sioux was affectionately referred to as the 'clockwork mouse' in the British Army.

Type	Owner	Reg	Serial	Marks	Status
Bell 47G Sioux	Kevin Mayes	G-BFYI	XT167	-	Stored
Bell 47G Sioux	TR Smith (Agricultural Machinery) Ltd	G-BHBE	XT510	-	Stored
Bell 47G Sioux	Leamington Hobby Centre	G-CHOP	XT221	-	Flyable
Bell 47G Sioux	Michael Romeling	G-CIGY	XT191	-	Flyable
Bell 47G Sioux	Anthony Smith	G-MASH	-	'USAF'	Flyable
Bell 47G Sioux	Peter Rogers	G-XTUN	XT223	XT223	Flyable
Bell 47G Sioux	Historic Aircraft Flight Trust/Army Air Corps	G-CICN	XT131	XT131	Flyable
Bell 47G Sioux	Stephen Hutchinson	G-BHNV	XW180	-	Restoration

Left: The Army Air Corps Historic Flight's Bell 47G Sioux was actually built by Agusta SpA at Gallerate in Italy in 1964 and delivered to the British Army the same year as XT131. It was one of the first helicopters to join the force and was ordered as a 'stop-gap' until the Westland-built Siouxs started coming off the Yeovil production line in 1965. It served as a trainer until 1980 when it joined the Historic Flight. XT131 was handed over to the Historic Aircraft Flight Trust on February 1, 2015 and placed on the civilian register as G-CICN. *Steve Bridgewater* **Right:** Whereas many of the ex-Army Siouxs have adopted civilian colour schemes Peter Rogers' G-XTUN still carries its original military markings.

Westland (Aérospatiale) Gazelle

The Aérospatiale Gazelle is a French-designed five-seat helicopter used by the British armed forces for light transport, scouting and light attack duties. It is powered by a single Turbomeca Astazou turbine engine and was the first helicopter to feature a fenestron tail instead of a conventional tail rotor. More than 140 were ordered by the British military and the type entered service with 660 Sqn Army Air Corps in July 1974. The type also served with the RAF, Royal Navy and Commandos and more than 30 are scheduled to remain in service with the Army until 2025. However, many have been retired and sold into private hands as either fast executive transports or fun 'warbirds.'

Type	Owner	Reg	Serial	Marks	Status
Gazelle AH.1	Aerocars Ltd	G-BZYD	XZ329	XZ329/J	Flyable
Gazelle AH.1	CJ Helicopters	G-CDNO	XX432	-	Flyable
Gazelle AH.1	Falcon Aviation Ltd	G-CDNS	XZ321	-	Flyable
Gazelle AH.1	Howard Stott Demolition Ltd	G-HSDL	XW909	-	Flyable
Gazelle AH.1	The Gazelle Squadron Display Team Ltd	G-ZZEL	XW885	-	Flyable
Gazelle AH.1	The Gazelle Squadron Display Team Ltd	G-CGJX	XW892	-	Restoration
Gazelle AH.1	Gazelle Flying Group	G-CIEX	ZB682	-	Stored
Gazelle AH.1	Gazelle Flying Group	G-CIEY	XW851	-	Stored
Gazelle AH.1	Falcon Aviation Ltd	G-FUKM	ZA730	-	Stored
Gazelle HT.2	Skytrace (UK) Ltd	G-SIVJ	ZB649	-	Flyable
Gazelle HT.2	Gregory Demolition	G-BZDV	XW884	-	Flyable
Gazelle HT.2	D Weatherhead Ltd	G-CBGZ	ZB646	-	Flyable
Gazelle HT.2	Flying Scout Ltd	G-CBKD	XW868	-	Flyable
Gazelle HT.2	Falcon Aviation Ltd	G-CBSF	ZB647	-	Stored
Gazelle HT.2	RSE 15119 Ltd	G-CTFS	XW857	-	Flyable
Gazelle HT.2	David Fravigar	G-DFKI	XW907	-	Flyable
Gazelle HT.2	Buckland Newton Hire Ltd	G-IBNH	XW853	-	Flyable
Gazelle HT.2	Paul Whitaker, Sandra Qardan, Andrew Moorhouse	G-ZZLE	XX436	XX436/CU	Flyable
Gazelle HT.2	Steven Atherton	G-CIOW	XX446	-	Restoration
Gazelle HT.3	Karl Theurer (Germany)	G-CBJZ	XZ932	-	Flyable
Gazelle HT.3	John Windmill	G-CBKA	XZ937	-	Flyable
Gazelle HT.3	Alltask Ltd	G-CBSH	XX406	XX406/P	Flyable
Gazelle HT.3	Peter Unwin	G-CBSI	XZ934	XZ934	Flyable
Gazelle HT.3	Falcon Flying Group	G-CBSK	ZB627	ZB627/A	Flyable
Gazelle HT.3	The Gazelle Squadron Display Team Ltd	G-CGJZ	XZ933	XZ933	Flyable
Gazelle HT.3	Andrew Parkes	G-ONNE	XW858	XW858/C	Flyable
Gazelle HT.3	Richard Illingworth	G-RBIL	XW902	-	Flyable
Gazelle HT.3	Eddie Coventry	G-VOIP	ZA802	-	Flyable
Gazelle HT.3	Armstrong Aviation	G-CBZL	ZB629	-	Stored

Left: Gazelle HT.2 G-CTFS began life as XW857 and was delivered to the Royal Navy in September 1973. Today it flies in a stylish executive colour scheme. **Right:** XZ934 was built as a Gazelle HT.3 for the RAF in August 1978 and spent most of its career with 2 FTS at RAF Shawbury until 2002 when it was sold into private hands and registered G-CBSI. In 2014 it was repainted to represent a Gazelle HT.4 operated by 32 (The Royal) Sqn for VIP duties. It is now owned by Peter Unwin and forms part of the Gazelle Squadron Display Team. Steve Bridgewater

◀ Gazelle HT.2 was built for the Royal Navy in 1976 as XX436 and was delivered to RNAS Culdrose where it served for 26 years in a training role with 705 Naval Air Squadron (NAS). In 1978 it was part of The Tri-Service Helicopter Team in the British Helicopter Championships and was also scheduled to take part in that year's World Helicopter Championships in the USSR - but the UK government withdrew their participation on political grounds. The helicopter was retired in 1997 and sold into civil hands in May 2002 as G-ZZLE. It was initially painted in a Royal Marines grey and green camouflage but has recently been re-sprayed into the markings of the 705 NAS 'Sharks' display team. Steve Bridgewater

Westland Scout

The Scout light helicopter served as a land-based general purpose military helicopter with the Army Air Corps. It was operated extensively in conflict zones including Northern Ireland and the Falklands until it was replaced by the Gazelle and Lynx.

Scout AH.1	Christopher Marsden	G-BXRS	XW613	XW613	Flyable
Scout AH.1	Historic Aircraft Flight Trust/ Army Air Corps	G-CIBW	XT626	XT626/Q	Flyable
Scout AH.1	G-CRUM Group	G-CRUM	XV137	XV137	Flyable
Scout AH.1	Orion Enterprises Ltd	G-KAXW	XW612	XW612	Flyable
Scout AH.1	Guy Richardson	G-SCTA	XV126	-	Flyable
Scout AH.1	Graham Hinkley	G-CIMX	XW283	-	Restoration
Scout AH.1	Austen Associates	G-BYKJ	XV121	-	Stored
Scout AH.1	Tim Manna	G-NOTY	XT624	-	Stored
Scout AH.1	Christopher Marsden	G-SASM	XV138	-	Stored
Scout AH.1	Nigel Boston	G-BWHU	XR595	XR595	Stored
Scout AH.1	Saunders-Roe Helicopter Ltd	G-SROE	XP907	XP907	Stored

◀ Scout XT626 served from 1963 until the late 1980s, seeing out service with the Territorial Army at Netheravon. She joined the Army Historic Aircraft Flight on March 30, 1994 and was handed over to the Historic Aircraft Flight Trust on February 1, 2015. The aircraft is now registered with the CAA as a civilian aircraft as G-CIBW.

▶ Tim Manna's Orion Enterprises' operates G-KAXW from Old Warden. The aircraft served as XW612 but has been on the civil register since 1998.

Both photos: Steve Bridgewater

Westland Wasp

The Wasp was the navalised version of the Scout and was designed to meet a Royal Navy requirement for a helicopter small enough to land on the deck of a frigate and carry a useful load of two homing torpedoes. Whereas the Scout had a skidded undercarriage the Wasp had castering wheels to help manoeuvrability on deck. The type also served with the navies of New Zealand, the Netherlands, Malaysia and South Africa.

Wasp HAS.1	Christopher Marsden	G-CBUI	XT420	XT420/606	Flyable
Wasp HAS.1	Graham Hinkley	G-RIMM	NZ3907	'XT435/430'	Flyable
Wasp HAS.1	Terry Martin	G-KAXT	NZ3905	'XT787'	Restoration
Wasp 1B	Christopher Marsden	G-BYCX	92 SAAF	92 SAAF	Stored
Wasp HAS.1	The Real Aeroplane Company Ltd	G-CGGK	XT434	-	Stored
Wasp HAS.1	Tim Manna	G-KANZ	XT782	'NZ3909'	Stored

Left: Terry Martin's ex Royal New Zealand Navy Wasp was restored by Kennet Aviation in the 1990s and painted in a Falklands War-era Royal Navy paint scheme to represent 'XT787'. The aircraft is currently grounded for repairs following a forced landing in the summer of 2016. **Right:** Steve Bridgewater Christopher Marsden's ex-Royal Navy Wasp G-CBUI flies in its original markings as XT420. Steve Bridgewater

Westland Wessex

The Wessex was a British-built turbine-powered development of the piston-powered Sikorsky H-34. The type was initially produced for the Royal Navy and later for the RAF and while the Wessex operated as an anti-submarine and utility helicopter it is perhaps best recognised for its use as a search and rescue helicopter. Three examples are earmarked for restoration in the UK. XT671 is currently at Biggin Hill as G-BRYC and XT761 and XT771 have recently been acquired by Andrew Whitehouse's team with a view to making one of them airwrthy to operate alongside his Whirlwind HAR.10.

Wessex HC.2	Daniel Brem-Wilson	G-BRYC	XT671	-	Restoration
Wessex HU.5	Andrew Whitehouse	-	XT761	-	Restoration
Wessex HU.5	Andrew Whitehouse	-	XT771	-	Restoration

Westland Whirlwind

The Whirlwind was a British licence-built version of the Sikorsky S-55/H-19 Chickasaw and served with the RAF and Royal Navy in anti-submarine and search at rescue roles.

Whirlwind XJ729 served in the search and rescue role with 22 Sqn and has been restored into its famous yellow SAR scheme. It is now a regular attendee and UK airshows.

Whirlwind HAR.10	Andrew Whitehouse	G-BVGE	XJ729	XJ729	Flyable

Wallis WA-116

Perhaps most famous for its role in the 1967 James Bond film *You Only Live Twice* the Wallis WA-116 Agile autogyro was also evaluated by the British Army. XR942, 943 and 944 were all built for the Army and the latter is still registered with the CAA as G-ATTB – although it has not flown for some time.

WA-116	Aerial Media Ltd	G-ATTB	XR944	-	Stored

COLD WAR WARRIORS

The classic jet preservation 'scene' in Britain rose to prominence in the 1990s following the disposal of the RAF's Jet Provost fleet and the post-Glasnost availability of relatively cheap former-Soviet Bloc hardware. The tightening of restrictions, partly as a result of the tragic accident at the 2015 Shoreham Airshow, has stifled the industry in recent times but there are still a variety of interesting Cold War-era aircraft flying in UK skies. This section also includes the myriad of ground-running/taxi-able classic jets maintained by dedicated groups of enthusiasts around the country. The sun hasn't set on the classic jet scene just yet.

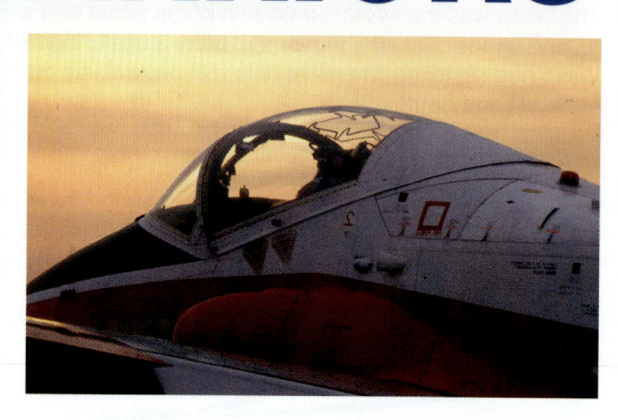

Aero L-29 Delfin

The Delfín ('Dolphin') was the standard jet trainer for the air forces of Warsaw Pact nations in the 1960s. It first flew in 1959 and was Czechoslovakia's first locally designed and built jet aircraft. More than 3,500 were built and the type used to be a very popular jet warbird in the UK. Today just four flyable examples grace the UK register, one of which is based in Hungary.

L-29 Delfin	Mark Grimshaw & Miachael Hall	G-BYCT	395142	-	Flyable
L-29 Delfin	Stephen Norman	G-BZNT	893019	'51 Soviet AF'	Flyable
L-29 Delfin	Komo-Sky KFT (Hungary)	G-DELF	194555	'12 Soviet AF'	Flyable
L-29 Delfin	AMP Aviation Ltd	G-DLFN	294872	-	Flyable
L-29 Delfin	Graham Smith & Mark Boffin	-	66654	'53 Romanian AF'	Ground Runner

Left: L-29 G-DLFN was one of a pair painted black as part of the Red Star Rebels display team. The group performed a very limited number of displays and the aircraft now fly on with new owners. This airframe flew with the Soviet and Estonian Air Forces before joining the Russian civil register as RA-3413K. It later flew on the Estonian register as ES-YLE before arriving in the UK in 1998. Neil Harris **Right:** Graham Smith & Mark Boffin's former Romanian AF L-29 has been returned to its original markings and is maintained in taxi-able condition at Bruntingthorpe, Leicestershire. . Jamie Ewan

Aero L-39 Albatros

The L-39 Albatros was designed during the 1960s as a replacement for the L-29 Delfín. It was the first trainer aircraft to be equipped with a turbofan powerplant and nearly 3,000 were built for air arms around the world. The type was once a common sight in the UK but just one remains on the register now; albeit with an owner based in France.

| L-39 Albatros | Sarl Jet Concept (France) | G-JMGP | 831125 | - | Flyable |

Avro Shackleton

Developed from the Avro Lincoln (itself a development of the Lancaster) the Shackleton was a long-range maritime patrol aircraft. The type soldiered on in the Airborne Early Warning role until 1991.

Shackleton WR963 was one of the last AEW.2 examples retired by the RAF in 1991. It was flown to Coventry Airport where Air Atlantique maintained it with a view to possibly returning it to the sky. In more recent years custodianship has passed to the Shackleton Preservation Trust and a plan has been formulated to make the aircraft airworthy again as G-SKTN. It has also been returned to MR.2 standard and is capable of ground running and taxiing. Steve Bridgewater

| Avro | Shackleton MR.2 | Shackleton Preservation Trust | G-SKTN | WR963 | WR963 | Ground Runner |

Avro Vulcan

Perhaps the most recognisable, iconic and loved aircraft of all time, the Vulcan always draws a crowd. With the retirement of XH558 in 2015 there is no longer a flyable example but three airframes are maintained in ground running condition and are taxiable.

This summer Vulcan XL426 is being moved indoors at its base at London Southend Airport. The jet will relocate to the airport's Hangar 6, initially for five years. The hangar is set to become the Vulcan Restoration Trust's engineering and visitor base. The aircraft has been maintained outdoors since it arrived at the airport in 1986. VRT

Vulcan B.2	Vulcan to the Sky Trust	G-VLCN	XH558	XH558	Ground Runner
Vulcan B.2	Vulcan Restoration Trust	G-VJET	XL426	XL426	Ground Runner
Vulcan B.2	655 Maintenance and Preservation Society	-	XM655	XM655	Ground Runner

Blackburn Buccaneer

The Buccaneer was designed in the 1950s as a carrier-borne attack aircraft that could carry a nuclear bomb or conventional weapons. It entered Royal Naval service in 1962 and following the cancellation of the TSR.2 and F-111K programmes joined the RAF seven years later. In the twilight of their career the RAF aeroplanes saw active service in the first Gulf War but the type was soon retired in 1994. Hawker Hunter Aviation Ltd's G-HHAA is potentially airworthy (should a military contract call for it to be activated) and five others are maintained in ground running condition in the UK.

Buccaneer S.2B	Hawker Hunter Aviation Ltd	G-HHAA	XX885	XX885	Stored
Buccaneer S.2B	The Buccaneer Aviation Group	-	XW544	XW544/0	Ground Runner
Buccaneer S.2B	The Buccaneer Aviation Group	-	XX894	XX894/020	Ground Runner
Buccaneer S.2B	Cold War Jet Collection	-	XX900	XX900	Ground Runner
Buccaneer S.2B	Gatwick Aviation Museum	-	XN923	XN923	Ground Runner
Buccaneer S.2B	Yorkshire Air Museum	-	XN974	XN974	Ground Runner

◀ The Yorkshire Air Museum's XN974 has recently been restored and returned to Royal Navy markings. It is capable of ground running at Elvington. Jamie Ewan

▶ The Buccaneer Aviation Group at Bruntingthorpe maintain two jets in full taxiing condition, including ex-RAF machine XW544. Steve Bridgewater

Hunting Percival/BAC Jet Provost & Strikemaster

The Jet Provost was developed by Hunting Percival and based on the earlier piston-powered Provost T.1. It introduced 'all-jet' training to the RAF and was the force's basic jet trainer aircraft from 1955 to 1993. It was much developed during its lifetime with the British Aircraft Corporation (BAC) producing the final T.5 versions as well as the armed Strikemaster variant. The type remains popular in the UK.

▶ G-AOBU is the oldest surviving potentially airworthy 'JP'. Built as a T.1 in 1955 it is painted as 'XD693' but has not flown for at least a decade. Steve Bridgewater

WARBIRD DIRECTORY | 137

Jet Provost T.1	Tim Manna	G-AOBU	P84/6	'XD693'	Stored
Jet Provost T.3	G-BKOU/2 Ltd	G-BKOU	XN637	XN637	Flyable
Jet Provost T.3	Dave Thomas	-	XN584	XN584/E	Ground Runner
Jet Provost T.3A	Newcastle Jet Provost Group	G-BVEZ	XM479	XM479	Flyable
Jet Provost T.3A	Weald Aviation Services Ltd	G-BVSP	XM370	-	Restoration
Jet Provost T.3A	Aviation Heritage Ltd	G-BWDS	XM424	XM424	Stored
Jet Provost T.3A	Damian Bryan	G-BWOT	XN459	-	Stored
Jet Provost T.3A	Global Aviation Ltd	G-BWSH	XN498	-	Stored
Jet Provost T.3A	Dave Thomas	-	XM365	XM365	Ground Runner
Jet Provost T.3A	Ollie Suckling & Dave Webber	-	XN582	XN582	Ground Runner
Jet Provost T.4	Century Aviation Ltd	G-BXLO	XR673	XR673	Flyable
Jet Provost T.4	Gary Spoors	-	XP672	XP672	Ground Runner
Jet Provost T.52	The Provost Group	G-PROV	XS228	104 South Arabian AF	Flyable
Jet Provost T.5	Dave Thomas	-	XW290	XW290	Ground Runner
Jet Provost T.5	Techair London	G-BWOF	XW291	-	Flyable
Jet Provost T.5	Jeff Bell	G-BWSG	XW324	XW324	Flyable
Jet Provost T.5	Victor Mike Group	G-VIVM	XS230	-	Flyable
Jet Provost T.5A	Global Aviation Ltd	G-BVTC	XW333	XW333	Flyable
Jet Provost T.5A	John Ashcroft	G-BWCS	XW293	-	Restoration
Jet Provost T.5A	C2 Aviation	G-BWEB	XW422	XW422	Stored
Jet Provost T.5A	G-JPVA Ltd	G-BWGF	XW325	XW325	Flyable
Jet Provost T.5A	Mark Grimshaw	G-BWGS	XW310	-	Stored
Jet Provost T.5A	Air Atlantique Ltd	G-JPRO	XW433	XW433	Stored
Jet Provost T.5A	Century Aviation Ltd	G-JPTV	XW354	XW354	Flyable
Strikemaster	High G Jets Ltd	G-FLYY	1112 Saudi AF	-	Restoration
Strikemaster	Stephen Partridge-Hicks	G-MXPH	311 Singapore AF	311 Singapore AF	Flyable
Strikemaster	Mark Petrie	G-RSAF	1120 Saudi AF	'417 Omani AF'	Flyable
Strikemaster	Strikemaster Flying Club	G-SOAF	425 Omani AF	425 Omani A	Flyable
Strikemaster	Private Owner	N21419	1104 Saudi AF	-	Restoration

Left: G-BKOU is now the only Jet Provost T.3 flyable in the UK. Built in 1971, it joined 3 FTS at RAF Leeming. In 1978 aircraft collector Sandy Topen acquired XN637 and it was moved to Duxford by road and restoration was begun by the Vintage Aircraft Team. The jet finally returned to the air as G-BKOU in 1988 and became a regular on the airshow circuit, painted in camouflage and then as a Tactical Weapons Unit JP based at Brawdy. In 1995 XN637 moved to North Weald where it has been based ever since. It is now painted in red/blue/white RAF colour scheme in the care of G-BKOU/2 Ltd. **Right:** Once a familiar aircraft on the airshow circuit the Newcastle Jet Provost Group's JP T.3A XM479/G-BVEZ has recently returned to the skies after a period of storage at St Athan, Wales. Both Steve Bridgwater

Left: Jet Provost T.3A XM424 was built in 1960 and during its RAF career flew with many different units. Perhaps the highlight of its career was being selected as the 1992 RAF Jet Provost display aircraft, for which it received a special colour scheme and was flown by Flt Lt Steve Howard. After retirement in 1993 passed through various hands before gaining a 'Blue Diamonds' scheme reminiscent of that worn by the RAF Hunter display team. In 2008 it was acquired by the Air Atlantic Classic Flight (AACF) at Coventry and was ultimately repainted into a trainer silver/yellow scheme. The aircraft has recently been sold but still appears on the UK register under the care of AACF parent company Aviation Heritage Ltd. **Right:** Jeff Bell's BAC Jet Provost T.5 XW324 was built at Warton in 1970 and flew with 3 FTS at Leeming. In 1973 it formed part of the Gemini Pair display team and although it was never upgraded to T.5A standard it flew on until 1993. In February 1994, XW324 was one of 65 Jet Provosts acquired by Global Aviation at Binbrook airfield and after restoration was sold into private hands as G-BWSG. Both Steve Bridgwater

Lockheed/Canadair T-33

The T-33 Shooting Star was developed in 1948 from the Lockheed P-80 fighter. More than 6,500 of the two-seat trainers were ultimately built including 656 Canadair CT-133 variants built under licence in Canada.

▶ The Norwegian Air Force Historic Squadron's CT-133 NX865SA is normally based in the UK during the summer months. The former RCAF jet is now painted in a scheme based on T-33s operated by the Norwegian Air Force in the 1960s. When Norway co-founded NATO it soon received American aircraft through the Military Aid Program and the nation's proximity to the USSR meant its jets averaged 500–600 interceptions each year during the Cold War. Steve Bridgewater

Canadair	CT-133 Silver Star	Norwegian Air Force Historic Squadron	NX865SA	133559 RCAF	559 RCAF	Flyable

de Havilland DH.106 Comet

Famous as the first commercial jetliner to enter service the Comet also flew with the RAF. Although no example still fly the former XS235 is maintained in taxi-able condition with the Cold War Jet Collection at Bruntingthorpe

DH.106 Comet 4C	Cold War Jet Collection	G-CPDA	XS235	XS235/*Canopus*	Ground Runner

de Havilland DH.110 Sea Vixen

The twin boom Sea Vixen was a carrier-based fleet defence fighter that served from 1959 into the 1970s. It had the distinction of being the first British two-seat combat aircraft to achieve supersonic speed, albeit not in level flight. Although numerous examples survive in museums just two are 'alive.'

▶ In May 2017 Sea Vixen XP924 performed its first display of the season. However, on arrival back at its base it suffered a problem and the pilot was forced to make a skilful belly landing after being unable to lower the undercarriage. The aircraft is now being restored and the charity that supports it is in need of donations to ensure the work is completed.
Steve Bridgewater

Left: XP924 first flew in 1963 and following service with 899 NAS it was retired in August 1971 and sent to the Royal Aircraft Establishment (RAE) at Llanbedr. The aircraft was converted into D.3 Drone configuration featuring a red and yellow paint scheme and flew infrequently until 1996 when it was sold to de Havilland Aviation and registered as G-CVIX. It made its first display in May 2001. **Left:** In May 2003 G-CVIX was painted in the colours of new sponsor Red Bull. The distinctive scheme may not have been authentic but it kept the expensive and complex aircraft in the skies. Both Steve Bridgwater

Sea Vixen FAW.2	Naval Aviation Ltd	G-CVIX	XP924	XP924/134	Restoration
Sea Vixen FAW.2	Cold War Jet Collection	-	XJ494	XJ494/121	Ground Runner

de Havilland DH.100/DH.115 Vampire

Although the prototype first flew in 1943 the Vampire did not see action in World War Two. The first examples of the DH.100 entered service in 1946 and despite its primitive wooden design it proved very successful with both the RAF and the countless air forces which operated it. The two-seat DH.115 Vampire T.11/T.55 also saw extensive service in the UK and with export operators. Today most airworthy survivors are ex-Swiss Air Force examples that were retired as late as the 1990s.

▶ The two ex-Swiss AF Vampires operated by the Norwegian Air Force Historic Squadron are based in the UK throughout the summer months. The single-seat FB.52 (LN-DHY) served the Swiss as J-1196 but is now marked as PX-K of the Royal Norwegian AF. The two-seat T.55 flew as U-1230 with the Swiss AF but now carries the Norwegian AF codes PX-M. Steve Bridgewater

Vampire FB.52	Norwegian Air Force Historic Squadron	LN-DHY	J-1196 Swiss AF	'PX-K' (RNoAF)	Flyable
Vampire T.11	Vampire Preservation Group	G-VTII	WZ507	WZ507/74	Flyable
Vampire T.11	de Havilland Aviation Ltd	G-OBLN	XE956	XE956	Stored
Vampire T.55	Norwegian Air Force Historic Squadron	LN-DHZ	U-1230 Swiss AF	'PX-M' (RNoAF)	Flyable
Vampire T.55	Aviation Heritage Ltd	G-HATD	U-1229	U-1229	Stored

Left: The accolade for being the first British jet to be restored in the UK and flown in civilian hands falls to de Havilland Vampire T.11 WZ507. This ex-RAF Vampire was retired in 1969 and placed on static display at the Solway Aviation Society at Carlisle airport but in 1980 it was registered G-VTII and returned to airworthy condition by volunteers at Carlisle. She later passed through various hands and is still airworthy with the Vampire Preservation Group today, although she is currently for sale. Jamie Ewan **Right:** The Air Atlantique Classic Flight/Aviation Heritage Ltd purchased former Swiss Air Force Vampire T.55 U-1299 in 2013. It had been flying in France as F-AZGU and wears a pseudo-Swiss AF colour scheme. It has not flown since it arrived at Coventry at the end of its ferry flight from France. Steve Bridgewater

de Havilland DH.112 Venom

In 1948 de Havilland proposed a development of the Vampire with a thinner wing (with a swept leading edge) and a more powerful engine. The resulting Venom flew a year later and 1,431 would ultimately be built for the RAF and other air arms.

▶ The two Venoms operated by Aviation Heritage Ltd/Air Atlantique Classic Flight's have not flown since the entire collection was put up for sale in 2015. It is believed the two flyable aircraft are destined for a new home in the USA with the World Heritage Air Museum in Detroit, Michigan but it is not known if the spares-ships that are currently in storage will follow suit. G-DHVM – seen here – began life as J-1542 with the Swiss Air Force but flies as 'WR470' of 208 Sqn.

Steve Bridgewater

Venom FB.50	Aviation Heritage Ltd	G-DHVM	J-1542	'WR470'	Stored
Venom FB.50	Aviation Heritage Ltd	G-VENM	J-1614	'WK436'	Stored
Venom FB.50	Aviation Heritage Ltd	-	J-1629	-	Stored
Venom FB.50	Aviation Heritage Ltd	-	J-1649	-	Stored

English Electric Canberra

The Canberra was developed during the late 1940s as a jet powered replacement for the Mosquito fast-bomber. The type entered RAF service in 1951 and the last one was not retired until 2006. There are two potentially flyable Canberras in the UK (both in storage as of summer 2017) and one ground runner at Bruntingthorpe.

Canberra B(I)8/B.6 Mod	Canberra WT333 Operating Team	G-BVXC	WT333	WT333	Ground Runner
Canberra B.2/6	Vulcan to the Sky Trust	G-CTTS	WK163	WK163	Stored
Canberra PR.9	Kemble Airfield Estates Ltd	G-OMHD	XH134	XH134	Stored

Left: Canberra B(I)8/B.6 Mod WT333 is maintained in ground running condition at Bruntingthorpe and regularly demonstrates its smoky cartridge start system. Jamie Ewan **Right:** When the Midair Squadron ceased trading its Canberra PR.9 (XH134) was put up for sale. It failed to meet the reserve and is now owned by the airport at which it resides. Both Steve Bridgewater

English Electric Lightning

The Lightning was the only all-British Mach 2 fighter aircraft and used by the RAF, Kuwaiti Air Force and the Royal Saudi Air Force. Although it was the RAF's primary interceptor for more than two decades it was never required to fire a shot in anger. The Lightning is not permitted to fly in civilian hands in the UK but four examples are kept 'live' as ground runners.

The Lightning Preservation Group's Lightning F.6 XR728 powers down the runway in 'full burner' during an open day at Bruntingthorpe. Jamie Ewan

Lightning F.6 XS904 poses outside the Lightning Preservation Group's 'Q Sheds' at Bruntingthorpe. Jamie Ewan

◀ The Gatwick Aviation Museum's ex-Saudi Lightning F.53 recent returned to ground running condition following a lengthy restoration programme. Richard Hall

▶ Russell Carpenter's Lightning T.5 XS458 is the only two-seater maintained in ground running condition in the UK. It is seen here taxiing in after a run down the runway at its home at Cranfield. Steve Bridgewater

Lightning F.6	Lightning Preservation Group	-	XR728	XR728/JS	Ground Runner
Lightning F.6	Lightning Preservation Group	-	XS904	XS904/BQ	Ground Runner
Lightning F.53	Gatwick Aviation Museum	-	ZF579	53-671 RSAF	Ground Runner
Lightning T.5	Russell Carpenter	-	XS458	XS458	Ground Runner

Fairey Gannet

The carrier-borne Fairey Gannet was originally developed to meet the Navy's requirement for an anti-submarine aircraft but it was later adapted for electronic countermeasures and airborne early warning (AEW) duties. An example of the AEW variant is being returned to the air at the former RAF St Athan.

| Gannet AEW.3 | Mark Stott | G-KAEW | XL500 | XL500 | Restoration |

Folland Gnat

Perhaps most famous as the mount of the Red Arrows the Folland Gnat T.1 jet trainer was developed in the 1950s. The T.1 only flew with the RAF but the single-seat F.1 variant was sold to Finland, Yugoslavia and India.

Left: The Heritage Aircraft Trust's single-seat ex-Indian AF Gnat F.1 is making rapid progress and will return to the skies in an eye catching IAF 'Tiger' scheme. It has been registered G-SLYR in tribute to the 'Sabre Slayer' nickname given to the Gnat in Indian service. **Right:** Gnat XS102/G-MOUR was originally restored in the 1990s for Pink Floyd guitarist Dave Gilmour and is now owned by the Heritage Aircraft Trust. The aircraft wears the markings of the Yellowjacks – the forerunner of the Red Arrows. Both Steve Bridgewater

Gnat F.1	Heritage Aircraft Ltd	G-SLYR	IE296	IE296	Restoration
Gnat T.1	Heritage Aircraft Ltd	G-MOUR	XS102	'XR992'	Flyable
Gnat T.1	DS Aviation (UK) Ltd	G-NATY	XR537	XR537	Flyable
Gnat T.1	Heritage Aircraft Ltd	G-RORI	XR538	XR538	Flyable
Gnat T.1	Chris Hudson	G-BVPP	XP534	'XR993'	Ground Runner
Gnat T.1	Red Gnat Ltd	G-FRCE	XS104	XS104	Stored
Gnat T.1	Heritage Aircraft Ltd	-	XR541	'PF179'	Stored
Gnat T.1	Heritage Aircraft Ltd	N513X	XP513	-	Stored

Gloster Meteor

The Gloster Meteor was the first British jet fighter and the only Allied jet aircraft to conduct combat operations during World War Two. In the summer of 2017 there were just five potentially flyable Meteors in the world and two of the UK examples are expected to depart for a new home in the USA imminently.

Meteor NF.11	Aviation Heritage Ltd	G-LOSM	WM167	WM167	Flyable
Meteor T.7	Aviation Heritage Ltd	G-BWMF	WA591	WA591	Flyable
Meteor T.7 (Mod)	Martin Baker Aircraft Company Ltd	G-JSMA	WL419	WL419	Flyable
Meteor T.7 (Mod)	Martin Baker Aircraft Company Ltd	G-JWMA	WA638	WA638	Flyable

As well as being the only surviving Night Fighter Meteor left in airworthy condition WM167 was one of the first privately owned jet fighters to operate in the UK. Built by Armstrong Whitworth as a NF.11 variant in 1952 it flew with 228 OCU at RAF Leeming. In 1961 it was converted to TT.20 target towing configuration and was declared surplus in 1975. Purchased by well-known collector Doug Arnold for his Warbirds of Great Britain collection she was ferried to Blackbushe by the late-Neil Williams and converted back into NF.11 Night Fighter configuration (as G-LOSM) before entering storage. In 1984 G-LOSM was sold to Mike Carlton's Hunter One collection at Bournemouth and following Mike's death in 1986 it transferred to the Jet Heritage Collection. G-LOSM was acquired by Air Atlantique in March 2004 and since then has taken part in a number of important flights – including carrying the ashes of jet-engine designer Sir Frank Whittle. In early 2017 WM167 was sold to the World Heritage Air Museum in Detroit but remained on the UK register at the time of publishing.

Air Atlantique Archives

◀ Built in 1949 Gloster Meteor T.7 WA591 is now the oldest airworthy British jet aircraft. This two-seat trainer variant flew with 203 Advanced Flying School at RAF Driffield (the colours it wears today) and after passing through various units – and being damaged on several occasions – was retired in 1965. WA591 subsequently found itself on the gate at RAF Woodvale, Cheshire and was rescued in 1995 by Meteor Flight – a group of enthusiasts formed by Colin Rhodes. Restoration work began in earnest at Yatesbury and was progressing well until Colin was tragically killed in a freak accident on August 8, 1997. Restoration continued and in 2007 Air Atlantique's Classic Flight agreed to help fund a fulltime engineer to speed up the progress. The aircraft moved to Kemble at the end of 2008 and flew again in June 2011. In early 2017 WM167 was sold to the World Heritage Air Museum in Detroit, Michigan but remained on the UK register as these words were written in June.

Steve Bridgewater

Handley Page Victor

The Victor was developed as a nuclear bomber as part of Britain's V-Force. In 1968, the type was retired from the nuclear mission following the discovery of fatigue cracks and the Victors were re-tasked as reconnaissance aircraft and tankers. The Victor was the last of the V-bombers to be retired, the final K.2 tanker version being withdrawn in October 1993. Although no examples have flown in private hands two are maintained as ground runners.

| Victor K.2 | Andre Tempest | - | XL231 | XL231 | Ground Runner |
| Victor K.2 | Cold War Jet Collection | - | XM715 | XM715 | Ground Runner |

Andre Tempest's Victor K.2 XL231 was built as a bomber in 1961 and later converted to tanker configuration. She served with 55 Sqn during Operation *Granby* (the first Gulf War) and was was finally retired on October 15, 1993. Her last flight was on November 25 of that year when she was delivered to the Yorkshire Air Museum's site at Elvington. She still wears her Granby nose art and the name *Lusty Lindy*. Jamie Ewan

Victor XM715 was produced as a B.2 and served with 100, 139 and 543 Sqns as well as 232 OCU before being converted to K.2 standard for 55 Sqn. In 1993 XM715 was retired and flown to Bruntingthorpe to form part of the Cold War Jet Collection. She regularly undertakes fast taxi runs and retains her Operation *Granby* colour scheme and *Teasin' Tina* nose art.
Jamie Ewan

Hawker Hunter

The swept wing, transonic Hunter was developed for the RAF in 1951 and replaced the Meteor and Venom from 1954 onwards. Successively improved variants were produced and the type was also exported to 21 overseas air forces. The Hunter has long been a popular aircraft with civilian owners but since the tragic accident at the 2015 Shoreham Airshow civilian operated examples of the type have been grounded by the Civil Aviation Authority. With the accident report now published it is hoped the Hunter can soon return to the skies.

◀ One of the most colourful Hunters registered in the UK is the Stichting Dutch Hawker Hunter Foundation's G-BWGL. Built as XF357 for the RAF it is now marked as 'N-321' of the Royal Netherlands Air Force.
Steve Bridgewater

WARBIRD DIRECTORY | 143

Type	Operator	Civil Reg	Serial	Marks	Status
Hunter F.58A	Hawker Hunter Aviation Ltd	-	ZZ190	ZZ190	Flyable
Hunter F.58A	Hawker Hunter Aviation Ltd	-	ZZ191	ZZ191	Flyable
Hunter F.58A	Hawker Hunter Aviation Ltd	-	ZZ194	ZZ194	Flyable
Hunter F.58A	Hawker Hunter Aviation Ltd	G-CJWL	J-4110	J-4110	Stored
Hunter F.58A	Hawker Hunter Aviation Ltd	G-HHAC	J-4021	J-4021	Stored
Hunter F.58A	Heritage Aviation Developments Ltd	G-PSST	J-4104	-	Stored
Hunter F.6A	Stichting Dutch Hawker Hunter Foundation	G-KAXF	XF515	'N-294'	Stored
Hunter GA.11	Hawker Hunter Aviation Ltd	G-GAII	XE685	XE685	Stored
Hunter PR.11	Horizon Aircraft Engineering Ltd	G-PRII	WT723	WT723	Stored
Hunter T.7	Hawker Hunter Aviation Ltd	-	XF995	XF995	Flyable
Hunter T.7	Mark Stott	G-BVGH	XL573	XL573	Stored
Hunter T.7	Hawker Hunter Aviation Ltd	G-HPUX	XL587	XL587	Stored
Hunter T.7A	G-FFOX Group	G-FFOX	WV318	WV318	Stored
Hunter T.8B	Canfield Hunter Ltd	G-BZSE	WV322	WV322	Stored
Hunter T.8C	Stichting Dutch Hawker Hunter Foundation	G-BWGL	XF357	'N-231'	Stored
Hunter T.8C	Hawker Hunter Aviation Ltd	G-CGHU	XF994	XF994	Stored
Hunter T.8M	George Begg	G-BWFT	XL602	XL602	Stored
Hunter GA.11	Dave Thomas	-	WT806	WT806	Ground Runner
Hunter T.7	Geoffrey Pool	-	XL565	XL565/Y	Ground Runner

Restored by Delta Jets in the 1990s as G-FFOX 'Firefox', Hunter T.7A WV318 is now operated by the G-FFOX Group and currently located in Sweden. Once the ban on the type flying is lifted the plan is to return the aircraft to the UK. *Steve Bridgewater*

Canfield Hunter Ltd's ex-Fleet Air Arm Hunter T.8C WV322/G-BZSE is painted in an 'Admiral's Barge' scheme but has yet to fly following a lengthy rebuild at North Weald. *Darren Harbar*

◀ Heritage Aviation Developments Ltd's distinctive multi-coloured Hunter F.58A G-PSST (standing for Personal Super Sonic Transport) is a crowd favourite at airshows and its reappearance is eagerly awaited. *Steve Bridgewater*

▼ The only Hunters permitted to fly in UK airspace at this time are those operated on the military register by Hawker Hunter Aviation Ltd on defence contracts. These consist of single-seat F.58s ZZ190 (ex-J4066/G-BXNZ), ZZ191 (ex-J4058/G-BWFS) and ZZ194 (ex-J-4021/G-HHAC) as well as two-seat T.7 XF995. ZZ191 is seen here departing on another sortie. *Steve Bridgewater*

Hawker Sea Hawk

The Sea Hawk was Hawker's first jet and following the type's acceptance in the Royal Navy a number were also produced for the export market, notably with the Dutch, West German and Indian Navies. The last operational Sea Hawks, operated by the Indian Navy, were retired in 1983. The Royal Navy Historic Flight Sea Hawk (WV908) has been placed into storage at RAF Shawbury due to a lack of funds.

Sea Hawk FGA.6	RN Historic Flight	-	WV908	WV908	Stored

Hawker Siddeley Harrier

The world's first true V/STOL fighter has always had a place in the public's heart and while there is not yet a privately owned flyable Harrier in the UK two examples are maintained in ground running condition.

▶ Harrier GR.3 XZ130 has been restored to full ground running condition by Jet Art Aviation in Selby, Yorkshire. The aircraft is for sale and could easily be made airworthy. Jet Art Aviation

Harrier GR.3	Jet Art Aviation	-	XZ130	XZ130	Ground Runner
Harrier GR.3	Privately Owned	-	XV808	XV808	Ground Runner

Hawker Siddeley Nimrod MR.2

The Nimrod was a maritime patrol aircraft developed as an extensive modification of the de Havilland Comet airliner. The type was retired in 2011 and although none are maintained in airworthy condition three are kept in ground running condition in the UK.

Nimrod MR.2	Cold War Jet Collection	-	XV226	XV226	Ground Runner
Nimrod MR.2	AIRBASE Coventry	-	XV232	XV232	Ground Runner
Nimrod MR.2	Yorkshire Air Museum	-	XV250	XV250	Ground Runner

Mikoyan Gurevitch MiG-15/17

The MiG-15 was one of the first successful jet fighters to incorporate swept wings to achieve high transonic speeds. In combat over Korea, it outclassed straight-winged jet day fighters, which were largely relegated to ground-attack roles. When refined into the more advanced MiG-17, the basic design would again surprise the West when it proved effective against supersonic fighters such Phantom II in the Vietnam War.

The Norwegian Air Force Historic Squadron's MiG-15UTI (actually a Polish-built SBLim-2) N104CJ is based at Duxford for the 2017 airshow season. The aircraft wears the markings of a jet flown by Yuri Gagarin before he became a cosmonaut. Steve Bridgewater

David Miles MiG-17 (a Polish-built Lim-5) was imported into the UK in the 1990s by the Old Flying Machine Company. It has passed through several hands but has yet to fly in private ownership. Steve Bridgewater

MiG-15UTI (PZL Mielec SBLim-2)	Norwegian Air Force Historic Squadron	N104CJ	104 Polish AF	'18' (Soviet AF)	Flyable
MiG-17F (PZL Mielec Lim-5)	David Miles	G-MIGG	1211 Polish AF	'1211' (North Vietnamese AF)	Restoration

North American (Rockwell) OV-10 Bronco

The Bronco is an American-designed turboprop light attack and observation aircraft developed in the 1960s specifically for counter-insurgency (COIN) combat. Two are UK registered to Belgian owners but one spends much of the airshow season in Britain.

OV-10B Bronco	Invicta Aviation Ltd	G-BZGL	99+26	99+26	Flyable
OV-10B Bronco	Invicta Aviation Ltd	G-ONAA	99+18	99+18	Flyable

The Bronco Demo Team/Invicta Aviation Ltd operate a pair of OV-10Bs. G-BZGL flew again in 2015 and is now at the company's base in Wevelgem, Belgium for further renovation whereas the current display aircraft is G-ONAA (illustrated). The aeroplane had previously been on static display at the International Aviation Museum Manfred Pflumm in Schwenningen-am-Neckar, Germany since 1991. *Steve Bridgewater*

Panavia Tornado GR.1

First flown in 1974 the Panavia Tornado has served the RAF for more than 35 years and is expected to continue operating until 2019. One example (the former Boscombe Down 'Raspberry Ripple' GR.1T) is being restored to full ground running condition at Bruntingthorpe.

| Panavia | Tornado GR.1T | Tornado ZA326 Preservation Group | - | ZA326 | ZA326 | Ground Runner |

PZL Mielec TS-11 Iskra

The Iskra (Spark) was designed in response to a Polish Air Force requirement for a jet trainer. Work started in 1957 and the first prototype (powered by an imported British Armstrong Siddeley Viper 8) flew in February 1960. More than 400 would ultimately be built and the type remains in service in Poland. Elsewhere it has become a popular warbird, but no example has yet to fly in the UK.

▶ TS-11 Iskra G-ISKA was built for the Polish Air Force as 1018 in 1978. It is now owned by the Cold War Jet Collection at Bruntingthorpe and regularly performs high speed taxi displays at the airfield open days. *Jamie Ewan*

| PZL Mielec | TS-11 Iskra | Cold War Jet Collection | G-ISKA | 1018 | 1018 | Ground Runner |

SEPECAT Jaguar

The Anglo French SEPECAT Jaguar first flew in 1968 and was introduced into service five years later as an attack aircraft. To date no privately owned Jaguars have taken to the skies but XX145 is being restored to ground running condition at Bruntingthorpe

| Jaguar T.2A | Private Owner | - | XX145 | XX145 | Ground Runner |

Vickers VC10

Designed as an airliner but soon developed into a military transport and then aerial refueller the VC10 was the fastest airliner in the world until Concorde arrived. When the RAF retired its last VC10 tankers in 2013 a number were passed into private ownership and two are maintained in ground running/taxi-able condition.

▶ Ex-RAF Vickers VC10 ZD241 begins a high speed taxi run down the runway at Bruntingthorpe. *Jamie Ewan*

| Vickers | VC10 K4 | Brooklands Museum | - | ZA150 | ZA150 | Ground Runner |
| Vickers | VC10 K4 | GJD Services (Bruntingthorpe) | - | ZD241 | ZD241 | Ground Runner |